T0290327

ANGELS OVER MOSCOW

JULIETTE M. ENGEL, MD

Published by:
Trine Day LLC
PO Box 577
Walterville, OR 97489
1-800-556-2012
www.TrineDay.com
trineday@icloud.com

Library of Congress Control Number: 2021940088

Engel, Juliette M.
ANGELS OVER MOSCOW—1st ed.
p. cm.
Epub (ISBN-13) 978-1-63424-362-9
Print (ISBN-13) 978-1-63424-361-2
1. Ethical issues: prostitution & sex industry -- Russia (Federation). 2. Human trafficking -- Government policy -- Russia (Federation) 3. Human trafficking -- Russia (Federation) 4. Human trafficking -- Former Soviet republics -- Public opinion. 5. SOCIAL SCIENCE -- Prostitution & Sex Trade. I. Title

FIRST EDITION
10 9 8 7 6 5 4 3 2

Printed in the USA
Distribution to the Trade by:
Independent Publishers Group (IPG)
814 North Franklin Street
Chicago, Illinois 60610
312.337.0747
www.ipgbook.com

Publisher's Foreword

... if we don't know the particular origins of children,
how do we tell which was brought by a stork,
which was found in a cabbage patch,
and which was purchased in a store?

maybe that's why people are so different?
some fly in the clouds,
others idle about with their eyes peeled to the ground,
and yet others madly love money...

why are there fewer and fewer children?
maybe because the business of children ...
has not yet achieved mass-market status?
maybe because there are more and more sales of genetically modified
cabbage and children don't linger in gmo cabbages?
or maybe because in our country the storks are oppressed by the
burden of high taxes and they take their business elsewhere?

maybe we don't need children?
and how did you get here?
are you children?
what are you doing here?
and what am I doing here?
what am I all about here?

—Benediktas Januševičius
LITUANUS Foundation, Inc.

This book blew me away. TrineDay published Juliette's first book, *Sparky – Surviving Sex Magick*, which tells of her childhood involvement in a MK-Ultra type mind-control "experiment." Luckily she escaped from that and moved on with her life, burying those experiences deep within. She mentioned to me she was writing another book about her experiences in Russia with sex trafficking, and would TrineDay want to publish? I said yes, but when I received the manuscript and read, my first thoughts were this is an incredible book, and deserves more than my small efforts at righting wrongs and hoping to create a better world for our children.

So I ask you, dear readers, to please tell your friends about this book. We all live on one planet and as President John Fitzgerald Kennedy so eloquently said in his "A Strategy of Peace" speech at American University on June 10, 1963:

> So, let us not be blind to our differences – but let us also direct attention to our common interests and to the means by which those differences can be resolved. And if we cannot end now our differences, at least we can help make the world safe for diversity. For, in the final analysis, our most basic common link is that we all inhabit this small planet. We all breathe the same air. We all cherish our children's future. And we are all mortal.

We need to break through the logjams of nationalism, prejudice, corruption, venality and ignorance, and recognize the truth of President Kennedy's oft quoted words.

For it is from our actions and the grace of God that our world exists. We *can* make this world a better place. This we can do … or not. It is up to us. Let's change the narrative from: "What did you do in the war, Daddy?" to "What did you do in the peace, Daddy?

Please read *Angels Over Moscow* and understand what one person can do to make our world a better place. Read *Angels Over Moscow* and understand that there are folks, who for one reason or another wish to impede natural progress and keep us all enthralled with violence, hate and factional division. Read *Angels Over Moscow* and understand the beauty of people and their determinations to better this world – for everybody not just those who you know, but for everyone, everywhere. We all live on the same beautiful blue ball spinning through space. Lets keep it that way!

TrineDay is honored and humbled to publish Dr. Juliette A Engel's book, *Angels over Moscow*.

We hope, and pray, it gets read!

Onwards to the Utmost of Futures,
Peace,
RA "Kris" Millegan
Publisher
TrineDay
June 10, 2021

I dedicate this book to the lost girls--my angels, sputniks and stars.

TABLE OF CONTENTS

Chapter One

THE SOLACE OF BEARS

Moscow, Russia – December 31, 2009

It's New Year's Eve.

Tonight, there will be feasting and fireworks in Moscow, but not for me. I've just heard the news: Zhenya is dead.

"You little fool!" I want to scream, but my lips won't form the words. "Why didn't you stay in Paris?"

In my mind, Zhenya is full of life, spunky and brave. I press my forehead on the window glass to barely glimpse the gold dome of the Kremlin. Another squall blasts up the Yauza River with snowflakes so thick they erase Red Square. The office dims. Wind muffles the sounds of traffic on the Great Stone Bridge. Trams, buses, and cars are packed with commuters hurrying home with fancy cake boxes and bottles of champagne.

I can't take this in. My heart slows as the snow falls. I am barely breathing, pushing back time to the unknowing moments before receiving the e-mail from Nizhny Novgorod: "Terrible news! Zhenya was killed last night. No details yet." She was threatened, she was warned but she kept on confronting the human traffickers. We'd sent her to safety in Paris. When did she return?

I've also been threatened. Perhaps I should be afraid for my own life, but I can't quit now. We have over one thousand open trafficking cases – women and girls whose lives are in greater danger than mine.

Snowfall darkens my office, and the room closes in. Should I turn on my lamp? No – I prefer shadow. I'll lock myself in this perfect little room with my computer, my Turkmen carpets, and colorful art collection. If I don't move, time will stop.

The phone vibrates – I jump. It's not my land line or regular cell phone, but the unregistered burner phone that I carry in my pocket. Only one person has that number, the "Colonel" from *Glavnoye Razvedyvatel'noye Upravleniye*, Russian Military Intelligence – GRU. I don't know his real name. Since my first visit to Moscow twenty years ago, he has appeared at critical junctures. Twice, he warned me to leave Russia, telling me my life was in danger. I left, knowing that I would come back. This time I'm not merely flotsam caught in another violent shift in Russian history. These new threats to me are personal. I've gotten too close to dangerous people. The Colonel said long ago that one day he'd direct me to leave for good. Is this the day?

The phone blinks and plays "Come Home, Bill Bailey." I switch on the lamp and answer. "*Ya slushayu*," I say – I'm listening.

"*Pyatnadtsat chasov, na ulitsa*," is all the Colonel says before hanging up – three o'clock, outside.

I have less than five minutes to dress for the blizzard and make my way down to the street. "Don't be afraid," I say aloud to my racing heart. I pause to gaze at my treasures from two decades in Russia – birch boxes from Krimsky Val, lacquer boxes from Palekh and Fedoskino, folk art from Nizhny Novgorod, my certificates and publications in Cyrillic. The office walls are decorated with children's paintings, gifts from schools and orphanages. It's the smallest room in this old tower apartment – our headquarters . I chose it for the stone balcony overlooking Red Square. In better weather, I can see St. Basil's. Today, I see snow.

Time speeds up. I am in motion again. People unseen are making decisions beyond my control, forcing me out of this safe place. I resist the urge to look for photographs of Zhenya taken last summer. They're here on my desk somewhere. I reach to turn off my lamp, but decide against it. The computer stays switched on, too, with my briefcase open on the chair like an anchor. "I'll be right back," I promise the room and close the door behind me.

The Angel Coalition rescue team is meeting in the conference room next door where we run a help line that answers a thousand calls a month from trafficking victims in Russia, Europe, America, and Asia, and then initiate rescues by working with police in each country. We've been overwhelmed with victims since convincing the Moscow headquarters of the Federal Bureau of Detectives to raid child brothels along the notorious Yaroslavl Road.

Everyone is busy. The oblong table is covered with photographs of Central Asian children rescued last night. No one notices me in the doorway. Should I tell the Angels about Zhenya? I can't – the news is too raw, a bloody gash in my heart. If I make a sound, I'll burst into tears. I need to see the Colonel first. Maybe this is all a mistake.

I stop by the main office to tell Vlad that I'll be out for a while. He nods. He's on the phone. Murat and Alex are head down, working at their computers. They don't look up. In the entry, I pull on snow boots, slide into my long fur coat and don gloves, scarf, and hat. I lift the latch on the heavy steel door and slip outside.

The eighteenth-floor landing is the warmest part of this old Stalin sky-scraper – the *Vysotka*. It was once a luxury residence for the Communist Party elite. Generations of cigarette smoke and fermented garbage sting my eyes. My glasses steam. The ancient elevator pings, bounces twice, and creaks open. By the time it rattles down to street level, I'm a few minutes late.

I hurry through the vaulted stone lobby beneath cathedral ceilings adorned with Soviet era mosaics. A smiling Joseph Stalin stands with arms akimbo beneath sunny skies. Muscular workers, farmers, soldiers, and athletes smile down on me, or gaze off into the bright future of the USSR.

A white-haired concierge guards the front door. A row of grannies – *babushkas* – sits on a long bench watching the passersby. We nod without smiling. These old ladies can read minds. They know everything that happens in this famous building. I enter the superheated airlock between the lobby and Russian winter. The huge wood-and-glass door requires all my weight to push open before the blizzard is full in my face.

Ice crystals burn my cheeks and freeze my eyelashes. I can barely see the curb. A long, black shadow of a car is parked there, its motor running. The Colonel's Mercedes? The last time I saw him, he was in the back of a silver Volga. The Colonel's bodyguard gets out of the passenger seat and nods at me. He was introduced long ago as Ivan Ivanovich Ivanov – a joke of a name like John Doe. Through the years, I've spotted Ivan giving me a little nod or widening his eyes in the Russian gesture that means, "I'm watching you." He has been my shadow at events in Moscow since I first arrived.

He inclines his head to the back and opens the car door. I slide onto the seat next to the man I call the Colonel. With his thick glasses, white hair and goatee, he looks like he belongs on a bucket of fried chicken. "*Strazvytye, Kolonel,*" I say – hello, Colonel. He never gets the joke but indulges me.

The Colonel offers me his silver flask with the first Sputnik and the year 1957 engraved on it, our ritual. As usual, I decline. "Are you sure, Angelo-va?" He calls me by *my* nickname – "Angel girl." My name, Engel, means angel in Russian. "It's Armenian Cognac." He waggles the flask, then takes a swig. "You might need it today." His face is barely visible under the brim of his black fur hat. He must be well into his eighties.

I unbutton my collar and loosen my scarf. The car's heater is blasting hot air and I'm sweating. I shed my hat and gloves. The Colonel taps the glass partition. The driver nods, the doors lock, and the Mercedes inches into a traffic jam on Yauza Street. "Where are we going?" I ask.

"To the airport. You're booked on the next flight to Seattle. It's time for you to go home."

"What?" I balk. I'd expected a warning – not an evacuation order. My cheeks burn. "I can't go now. I've got more work than I can handle. The brothel raids are going so well on Yaroslavl Road. … "

"Too well." He opens a brown envelope and hands me an 8" x 10" color print. "I'm sorry. I hoped to spare you this unpleasantness, but you're not listening."

At first, I can't make sense of the jumble of forms and colors. I wipe my glasses and hold the picture to the light from the window. A red car protrudes from a ditch. The trunk is open. "Is this Zhenya's car, the old *Zhiguli*?" I make out a hand … and a head – her head. I gag, dizzy, lowering my head to my knees. "My God! What did they do to her?"

"Thugs shot her and cut her into pieces." The Colonel takes the photograph from my trembling hands, but I grab it back. There's something else – another hand and an Astrakhan shawl.

"Oh no," I gasp. "Is that white hair? Is that Baba Maria?"

"They killed the grandmother, too." I let go and he puts the photograph away.

"Who did it?" I demand, choking back tears. "Tell me! I know that you know."

"Albanians? Chechens? Ukrainians? What does it matter? You've made powerful people angry. Now go home before we find you looking like your friends." The Colonel takes another swig from his flask and eyes me through thick lenses. I'm slathered in sweat, suffocating in the heat, heartbroken and furious. "Are you unwell?" he inquires.

"This is my fault. I thought Zhenya was at university in France. I really pushed her to go." I flush with guilt, wiping tears from my face. There is a hole in my heart. I can't breathe. "When did she come back to Russia?"

"A week ago."

"She was so angry when I put her on the flight – like I was sending her into exile instead of law school. We were arguing." I stare at the floor recalling her stinging accusation that I didn't care enough about trafficking victims. I'd been angry, too. "She never contacted me from Paris. I should have known something was wrong."

"You mustn't think in terms of blame, but in terms of survival – your survival. They killed her to warn you off. What more do you need to make you leave?"

"I need air." I push the switch to open a window, but the controls are unresponsive. I wipe condensation from the glass and see the Vysotka looming over us. We've barely gone a hundred feet in the gridlock. I'm suffocating. "Will you please open a window?"

Zhenya at university. This is how I remember her.

"Of course not." He fluffs his scarf and shivers. "Drafts."

"I've got to get back to work." I pull on the door handle. The latch doesn't budge. Ivan Ivanovich glances over his shoulder, making sure that I see his finger on the control switch. I fight down panic, knowing that these aren't the men I should fear. My logical mind tells me to do as they say, but my body is in full rebellion. My heart pumps in my throat. Every instinct tells me to run. "Let me out!" I rattle the handle. "I live here. Moscow is my home."

"I know where you live," says the Colonel. "Everyone knows, and that's a problem."

He's right. I've tried to live quietly, but my rambling old apartment a few blocks downriver on Goncharnaya Embankment is a busy safe house for trafficking victims and a halfway house for orphanage graduates. I love the way I live, surrounded at my long kitchen table by an assemblage of characters who have become *rodnoi* – my extended family.

"You have taken big risks," he says. "You've shown great courage in a difficult country. There was bound to be a day of reckoning." He's right. For a long time, I have pushed the limits of what is allowable for human rights organizations in the former USSR. The Angel Coalition has skirted the edge of legality in everything we've done. We've been protected by powerful people like the Colonel. A rescue network like ours can only operate with the personal support of highly placed officials in government and law enforcement. It has taken years to build. The Colonel continues: "I'm retiring. I can't protect you any longer."

"*Kholodna*," remarks Ivan Ivanovich with a shiver – cold. He cranks up the heat, reminding me that I've spent more of my twenty years in Russia sweating than shivering.

I recall the sweltering summer of 1998 when I traveled from village to village on a bus with my video player, calling town meetings and talking to hundreds of people about human trafficking, or the next year bringing together groups from across the USSR. We met in secret, traveling on an overheated night train from Moscow to Ukraine with the conference funds, $20,000 in cash, strapped to my waist. That was the birth of the Angel Coalition. As trafficking victims were rescued in increasing numbers, our work became widely known.

Now we are up against the elites – the billionaire princes of organized crime who live in luxury high-rise condos on the mid-river island of Moscow City, the City of Gold. What did I think would happen? I cover my face and moan. "I can't let them destroy my life's work. I can't let them win."

He reads my thoughts. "You cannot fight the gangsters in Moscow City. Go home and joust windmills from the safety of Seattle."

"If I leave, the Angel Coalition will be demoralized. Our network will fall apart. Who will rescue the victims?" The Colonel ignores me. I am arguing with air. "I've got to transfer power of attorney, sign bank documents, inform our funders and our partners ... " I grow silent, reminded of another lost girl. "And what if Angela calls? Who will answer?"

"No word from that little redhead of yours, eh?"

I shake my head. "Not yet, but she will call. I need more time."

"There is no time," he says. The car jolts forward, picking up speed. The Vysotka disappears behind us when we turn onto the Ring Road. Russia is closing behind me. Fury overrides my fear. I will not go quietly.

We stop at a traffic light. The kiosks fronting Taganskaya Metro Station are decorated with tinsel and holiday lights. Shoppers wait in lines to purchase flowers, sausages, vodka, and bootlegged DVDs. We've nearly reached the main road to the airport. The men from GRU relax a bit. Ivan Ivanovich takes his hand off the master control to light a cigarette.

I seize my chance to unlock the door and leap out. I jump the ridge of snow on the curb and join the crowd of Muscovites squeezing through the narrow doors of the Metro station. I use my electronic card to pass through the turnstile and step onto a crowded escalator that sweeps me down hundreds of feet into the maze of Metro tunnels. Will Ivan Ivanovich follow and force me back to the car? No – he is the Colonel's bodyguard, not mine, and the Colonel is too old to chase me. I remind myself that they can track my cell phone even in the Metro. I find that a comfort.

I step off the first escalator and cross a mosaicked vestibule to the second one. Crowds grow denser, transported from the center of the city.

The Ring Line trains trace a big circle under Moscow and feed the radial lines to the suburbs like spokes in a wheel. People jostle me in their hurry to get home. Soon gas stoves will be bubbling with borscht and boiled potatoes, steaming up windows across the city in preparation for the grandest fireworks display of the year. My staff will be bringing potluck for a party in our office. From the balcony, they'll have a bird's eye view of the show on Red Square. We have much to celebrate. This has been our most successful year yet – rescuing thousands of victims.

The crowd presses in on all sides smelling of wet wool and garlic; there is no escape from this human tide. Any one of them could be my killer. The flow of commuters pushes me onto the nearest train. I don't resist. Every seat is taken. The Metro car is so packed with Muscovites wearing bulky fur coats and hats that we are held upright like Crayolas in a box. The heat is stifling, the floor wet and gritty with dirt and trodden snow, the air thick with breath and sweat. I can see nothing but the backs of strangers pressed around me. The doors slam. We lurch and the train's familiar whine rises in pitch as it gains speed.

I exhale in relief, strangely comforted by this primordial place. I've become a cub, safe in a den of dark, furry bears. I'll ride the twelve-kilometer circle as many times as it takes to come to grips with what has happened, then answer the question: What do I do now?

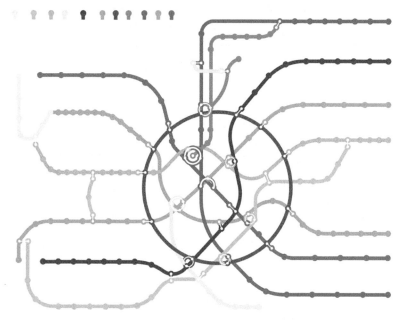

Moscow Metro Map

Chapter Two

INVITATION TO RUSSIA

Seattle, Washington to Moscow, Russia – December 1990

Twenty years earlier, in the time before Russia and long before I met Zhenya, I lived in Seattle with my two children in an old Tudor-style house on top of Queen Anne Hill – Cascade Mountains to the east and Olympics to the west. I had a busy medical practice as Director of Diagnostic Ultrasound at Overlake Hospital and was a Clinical Assistant Professor of Radiology at the University of Washington. My children were growing up fast and, at age forty, I was pondering my future. There were unusual limits to my life and time had become my driver.

For years, I had struggled with sinus tumors – *inverting papillomas*. A few years earlier, surgeons had split my nose open like a book to remove them. They weren't malignant, but they could kill. The team of specialists told me that I wouldn't survive much past forty. All life was finite, they said – mine more than others.

I was afraid to die. I'd barely lived. In a recurring dream, I entered the

At my office in Overlake Hospital, Bellevue, 1989.

Temple of Logic dressed as a bride. I marched slowly across the vast floor of black and white tiles; my arms stacked with white lilies. Clock gears whirred and clicked overhead, marking my passage to the jagged edge where the floor tiles crumbled and gave way to a gaping abyss. I'd wake up sweating, gasping, determined not to fall – determined to stop time.

At home with my son and daughter.

I wanted to know the world before I left it. I had signed up to trek across the Sahara Desert from Mali to Mauritania, certain that the secrets of life lay buried under the African sands. But apparently God had a different plan. It came as a summons, delivered to me at my laboratory in Overlake Hospital by a gold-toothed man who spoke no English. The odd-sized envelope he handed me contained an invitation from the Soviet Peace Committee of the USSR to attend the second Soviet/American Citizens' Diplomacy Summit in Moscow. They wanted me to share my expertise in pre-natal ultrasound with Russian doctors.

For the first time since the Russian Revolution, American professionals were being invited to meet their Russian peers one-on-one, without government interference. The expectation was that personal relationships would strengthen the prospect for global peace – an intriguing idea. Our generation had grown up under the specter of the Cold War. I'd been taught since childhood to fear the USSR. But times were changing. The Berlin Wall had crumbled the year before as the Soviet Union's evil empire collapsed. Now, I'd been beckoned to the dark side of the mirror to build better, safer futures for my children and all children. I accepted.

I knew nothing of Russia except that our family had blood connections. When I was a little girl, my great aunt showed me sepia photographs of her childhood home near Moscow and their country house with gingerbread windows and exuberant gardens. I hadn't seen the pictures for years but I remembered the family, dressed in white, gathered around a table that sagged under a mountain of food. Adults sat ramrod straight on stiff-backed chairs. Children stood beside their parents, squinting into the sunlight. A white-haired granny peeked around a giant samovar at the end of the table. At the edge of the image, a little girl danced in a blur, a ghost with long braids wearing a sailor dress. "That's me," my great aunt would point and say. "I'm the one that got away." No one else in that branch of the family survived the Russian Revolution.

Was I traveling to Moscow because of her sorrow? Childhood memories of Cossack music with rumbling cannons and clattering hoof beats played on my grandfather's phonograph filled my dreams, replacing the dreaded Temple of Logic with warriors on horseback, fearless with raised swords riding into battle. The prospect of seeing the place that had evoked such fear in my family was an irresistible temptation.

The conference was in two weeks – barely time to prepare. I had to arrange coverage for my practice and for my children to stay on nearby Mercer Island with my ex-husband. I bought a heavy purple wool coat at Nordstrom's, the only color they had left, and packed as best I could for January in Moscow. I dug out an old Russian phrase book, a gift from my Uncle Wally from his World War II days in the OSS. He'd been a cryptologist on the international team that decoded the German Enigma machine at Bletchley Park. I was determined to study it on the long flight.

In January 1990, I flew to Ireland to join one hundred and fifty other Americans traveling to Moscow with the Center for Soviet/American Dialogue – professionals from media, entertainment, politics, science, and technology. They seemed as excited to be breaching the mysteries of the USSR as I was.

In Shannon, we boarded an Aeroflot charter and flew through the Iron Curtain into the buffeting winds of the turbulent east. Our Ilyushin jet rattled and shook. Carry-on luggage fell from overhead bins. The fuselage overheated, steaming up the windows and burning my ankle. Dinner was a cold chicken wing with a piece of beet, warm Pepsi, and half a slice of Russian black bread. We made friends onboard by sharing the snacks we'd brought. I passed around a king-size bag of Skittles purchased at Costco.

While others dozed, I studied Uncle Wally's Russian phrase book. It contained sentences like, "Do you have any stone crushing equipment?" and "No, I don't have three children." By the time we approached Moscow, I could count to ten and say, "Boris, would you like some hotdogs, please?"

I fell asleep, waking with a start when the Ilyushin bounced on the runway and settled into a smooth, slow deceleration. I wiped condensation from the window and stared into darkness broken only by flashing runway lights. We deplaned onto the snowy tarmac, bundled in our coats and hats, leaning against the freezing wind. Other planes were unloading, and we were funneled into a long queue of shivering travelers seeking shelter in the terminal.

Once inside, we were escorted by armed guards into a holding area. The American summit organizers met us there, looking harried. They told us to find our passports and visas, which were scattered on two tables, pick out our suitcases from several piles, and proceed through Customs. Our Russian hosts from the Soviet Peace Committee should be waiting in the Arrivals Hall with signs in English.

I was the first of our group to find my passport, visa, and suitcase. I headed into the maze that led to Passport Control. Once through, I realized that no other Americans were behind me. I tried to stop but was propelled forward by a tide of diminutive Asian passengers a foot shorter than me. Scowling armed guards directed me on. The Customs agent barely looked in my suitcase before waving me toward a glass wall that separated Customs from the Arrivals Hall.

On the other side, the waiting Russians looked like bears – huge and fierce in their black fur coats and hats with flaps like wooly ears. They grimaced, pressing their faces to the glass and squinting. Someone saw me and pointed – no, that couldn't be right. What was I thinking? No one knew me here. The flock of Asians fluttered around me and through the sliding exit door like a host of sparrows.

I stopped short of the door, clutching the Russian phrase book with my passport and documents. It didn't contain the phrase I wanted, which was, "I want to go home." I tried again to turn back, but the way was barred. I was stuffing my papers into my open purse when the glass doors slid wide. I was pushed from behind, dislodging my huge bag of Skittles and sending a cloud of brightly colored candies flying ahead of me like pixies.

They bounced and skittered across the floor. The Russian bears looked at one another – then at me. Everyone went on the hunt for Skittles. They gathered them up in soggy, dirty handfuls and brought them to me. I gave up trying to get them into the torn bag and let them dump the muddy candy into my purse.

One of them took my suitcase, another linked my arm in his. Before I could object, I was escorted to an airport café, seated at a table, handed a warm, sticky bottle of orange Fanta and surrounded by bears. I smiled. No one smiled back – they nodded and blinked.

"Are you from the Peace Committee?" I asked. "Does anyone speak English?" I was exhausted, hungry, and jetlagged, but curious.

"No English," was the answer. Tattered phrase books were pulled from pockets and I searched my purse for my own. The overheated air was thick with cigarette smoke, steamy with the smell of wet wool, boiled cabbage, and moth balls. I sweated in the rickety chair, half in and half out of my purple coat. Every time I tried to take it off, a Russian would push it back up my arms, shivering and tsk-tsking like a mother hen.

My companions' phrase books were no better than mine, but I eventually understood that these men and women were doctors inviting me to visit their hospitals and clinics. I was eager to accept but couldn't comprehend why we had to discuss this at the airport.

At a lull in conversation, one of the doctors finally smiled, showing metal teeth. He pulled a well-worn plastic wallet out of his pocket to show me a picture of his family. Others did the same and the table was soon covered with photographs of unsmiling parents and children.

I took out my wallet to share pictures of my children and home in Seattle. A young man with curly blond hair grabbed it and circulated it among a growing crowd of onlookers. He pulled out my passport, driver's license, and credit cards, passing them around for examination. Apparently, no one had ever seen a credit card or driver's license. They were fascinated by the American passport with my smiling photo. After much discussion, everything was returned and I put it away, counting the credit cards – all there.

I kept an eye on the glass doors, but no Americans appeared. Why were they taking so long? They had to come out the same way I did, surely? I sighed and surrendered to the steamy heat while the scruffy Russians competed to sit next to me. Someone gave me a chocolate bar and I opened a fresh bag of Skittles. They passed it around, each taking one, nibbling it, and commenting. I sensed their kindness and accepted their company. Eventually, I even managed to take off my coat.

Two hours later, the Americans appeared, traversing the glass wall with trepidation on their faces. They were accompanied by a jovial group of English-speaking Russians who looked much better fed than the ones at my table. These had to be our hosts, the Soviet Peace Committee. Spotting me, one of the American organizers, Carol Hiltner, waved. "Juliette, there you are. We thought you were lost." I waved back. I hadn't been lost; I'd been found – adopted by a sleuth of bears.

I stood up to gather my belongings, tucking the doctors' business cards into my sticky purse. I thought my new friends would follow me when I walked over to rejoin my group, but they remained standing around the cafe table, staring at the floor. Just then a handsome older man with blue eyes and a broad smile hurried toward me, brushing snow from his coat.

"I apologize for my tardiness, Dr. Engel, and please forgive my poor English." He grasped my hand and kissed it. "I am Dr. Yuri Puchkov, Director of International Programs for the All-Union Center for Maternal and Infant Care. Welcome to Moscow." He handed me a business card printed in Russian and English. "One moment please." He turned to speak with the Russian doctors and then with the Peace Committee representatives, who were hovering nearby, no longer jovial.

I could see my Americans exiting the terminal and boarding buses. I was afraid of being separated, but Dr. Puchkov held my forearm. I took his nonverbal signal, standing silently through twenty minutes of heated negotiations between the Peace Committee, the doctors, and Dr. Puchkov. I didn't know what they were saying, except that my name was repeated on all sides. The Russian doctors wouldn't speak directly to the Peace Committee or look them in the eyes. The Peace Committee glared at the doctors and at me. Dr. Puchkov spoke directly with both groups and eventually a settlement must have been reached. The doctors turned without a word and left.

Dr. Puchkov beamed at me. "Everything is arranged. I will be at your hotel by 8 o'clock tomorrow morning with a car." He released my arm and a smiling Peace Committee agent who introduced himself as Sasha took my suitcase and signaled for me to join the others on the bus.

It was a cranky, jet-lagged group of Americans that finally arrived at the rear entrance of the Hotel Cosmos at about 10 P.M. We entered through the basement and were handed our keys and hotel passes. I ditched my suitcase in the room and joined the hungry group milling about in the lobby, intent on finding dinner. We followed a well-dressed group of Russians into the dining room/discotheque where we were seated in red leatherette booths and handed huge menus in Russian and English that boasted such items as "escaping embryos" and "fermented reptile in a bag." There followed a ritual of pointing to each item as the waitress shook her head no: "*nyet.*"

Finally, I used my one Russian phrase: "Boris, would you like some hotdogs, please?" The waitress eyed me, grunted, and we were served plates of boiled hotdogs, canned peas, and black bread. I was hungry enough to eat the Soviet mystery meat, washing it down with green beer served in warm bottles without labels. Dinner was followed by shots of Rasputin Vodka and vanilla ice cream.

A group of us took to the dance floor beneath a spangled mirror ball. Seeing us, the band came to life with a lively disco tune that sounded like "Staying Alive" only in a minor key. Russians from adjoining tables joined us. Men in polyester suits twirled me skillfully until my feet barely touched the ground and I was dizzy with laughter.

We were invited to have birthday cake with a man named Boris and his family. I applied my one Russian phrase, but Boris declined.

Chapter Three

MEETING THE COLONEL

Moscow, Russia – December 1990

I awoke before daybreak, scratching my arm. My ankles were itching, too. I switched on the bedside lamp and saw that the sheets stopped eight inches short of the top and bottom of the mattress. My ankles and the arm that I'd flung over my head had been ravaged by bedbugs. I treated the bites with Neosporin and hurried down to breakfast. The hotel buffet was in the same discotheque as the previous night and featured hotdogs floating in a tub of greasy water. In the harsh light, they looked like bloated fingers. I ate a piece of black bread spread with butter and sour cream.

Dr. Puchkov was waiting in the lobby when I came back down with my hat and coat. "Call me Yuri," he said, helping me into the heavy coat. It was still dark when we left the hotel. One look and I understood why the buses had taken us around to the back. The front entrance was blocked off on each end of the sloping, circular driveway by dozens of cars parked haphazardly at wooden barricades. From their open trunks, men and women were selling food.

"They've got better stuff to eat out here than in the hotel," I remarked, peering into trunks filled with meat, produce, beer, and jars of caviar. One small car was crammed full of avocados, another with peaches.

"Black marketeers," Yuri scoffed. "My advice is to stay away from them." He guided me past men with thick necks and black leather jackets who paced the drive waving wads of cash and shouting, "*Ne doroga. Pas cher.* Not expensive."

"Don't use those hooligans to exchange your money either," he warned. "Only use the state exchanges." Yuri stopped to exchange a wad of rubles for dollars. "At least don't get caught," he winked mischievously, showing dimples. Further on, he bought bottles of homemade beer and tucked them into a checkered shuttle bag. He stopped again to purchase fruit. "Instructions from my wife," he chuckled. "I must never return home empty-handed." The vendor cut into a peach and offered me a slice. "Take it," said Yuri. "From Azerbaijan – very tasty."

"Yes, it is," I said, accepting another slice while Yuri purchased a bag full.

Eventually we reached a black Volga with its engine idling. Yuri placed his produce in the trunk and joined me on the backseat. He gave instructions to the driver and the Volga crept out of the congested parking lot and onto a main road.

"Where are we?" I asked.

"This is Yaroslavl Road. It becomes the Leningrad Highway to the north."

I had no idea where we were going but was fascinated by all that I saw. The anemic morning sun reflected on huge, gilded statues in the Park of Economic Achievement and the soaring monument to Cosmonaut Gagarin. The sky was clear; snowbanks sparkled. I couldn't know that this drive along the snowy highway called Yaroslavl Road was a journey far into my future.

Yuri broke the silence: "Did you enjoy our little surprise yesterday?" he asked, grinning broadly. "At the airport?"

"What do you mean?" I frowned, recalling scowling guards with guns waving me forward, my alarm at being separated from the other Americans and hijacked by strangers with metal teeth.

"Our reception party. The good doctors paid a month's salary to Dr. Zhigulskaya's cousin who works in Passport Control to get you through first," he said.

I was shocked, surprised, and relieved all at once. "So those doctors *were* looking at me. I thought I was getting paranoid."

"They were waiting for you. They are some of Moscow's finest obstetricians, pediatricians, and researchers in prenatal ultrasound – your specialty. This was their first opportunity to meet a doctor from the West. I was supposed to be there to translate, but I was detained. Traffic in Moscow can be monstrous." I looked out the window. There wasn't another car on the road. "I do hope your countrymen have recovered from their unpleasant delay – two hours, was it?"

"The Americans are fine," I said. "But those men from the Peace Committee didn't look happy."

"Those KGB types never are, except when there's free food," said Yuri.

"The KGB? I thought that was gone now."

"Of course not. Where would it go?"

"Will the doctors be in trouble?"

"Undoubtedly, but it was worth the risk. Before perestroika, they were not allowed any contact with Western foreigners. Such a meeting between

Russian and American professionals would not be allowed. Even now, our doctors had to intercept you at the airport to invite you in person. They want you to see real Russian hospitals, not just the ones on the government approved list."

"What about the conference? It's supposed to begin in a couple of hours."

"With luck, you'll be too busy visiting our medical facilities. Let's see how far we get before the KGB takes over your schedule, shall we?"

"Where will I be going?" I asked, beginning to realize that the citizens' summit wasn't quite so free of government control.

"Our doctors have prepared some suggestions." He handed me an impossibly long list of hospitals and clinics with strange names like the Center for Deviant Motherhood Number One Named for N. Krupskaya.

I pointed. "What does this mean?"

"Krupskaya? She was the wife of Vladimir Lenin. Deviant motherhood refers to single mothers. It's one of the maternity hospitals for ordinary people. We'll visit as many as we can. As a matter of protocol, we shall begin today with my institution, the All-Union Center for Maternal and Infant Care. It's on the approved list. There you will meet Dr. Baranov, the Minister of Health. Aha, we've arrived."

We stopped in front of a multistory cement complex. Yuri retrieved his parcels from the trunk while the driver helped me out of the car, holding my arm while I found my footing on the icy sidewalk. Some of the doctors from the airport waited in the lobby. They took my coat and helped me into a white lab coat. I followed them into a conference room where a long table was spread with Pepsi, Fanta, tins of shortbread cookies, and boxes of chocolates. Yuri added bottles of beer and indicated a seat for me at the head of the table. The rest of the chairs were already occupied. A crowd of white-coated observers stood in back.

"Are these people all doctors?" I inquired. Many looked Asian or Indian. A row of tall Africans lined the wall.

"At the table, yes. Those standing are medical students from Pyongyang, Hanoi, Angola, Bulgaria, and various Soviet Socialist Republics. They've never seen an American before. You might as well have landed from Mars."

An older doctor with a crown of thick white hair swept into the room. Yuri jumped to attention and everyone stood. "Here is Professor Baranov, our Minister of Health." I extended my hand.

"Charmed to meet you, Dr. Engel," Dr. Baranov said in English, kissing my hand. He settled into the seat beside me.

Yuri bent close to my ear, saying, "Excuse me, please. I will speak Russian now." He introduced me to the group. I knew because. Periodically, he would say, "Clinical Assistant Professor, University of Washington, Department of Radiology." He turned the meeting over to Doctor Baranov, who welcomed me to Moscow on behalf of the Academy of Medical Sciences of the USSR. The health minister then took his leave with another kiss of my hand. For the rest of the morning, I listened to the faculty of the All-Union Center present research papers while Yuri translated. The doctors could read and write in English but had never been allowed to speak it. We could have written each other notes at the airport.

Surprisingly, I wasn't asked to say anything. When they were finished, Yuri guided me on a tour through the research facilities, followed by lunch of borscht, hotdogs, and canned peas in the doctors' cafeteria. The afternoon was spent visiting the Maternity Museum while a schedule of hospital and clinic visits was agreed upon for the following day. Eventually, I was escorted outside to the waiting Volga. It was 4:00 P.M. and the sun was setting.

"Where are the patients?" I asked Yuri in the car.

"This is a teaching and research institution. The patients are in another place. You'll see them tomorrow."

The roads were jammed with trucks and cars, slowing traffic to a crawl. Moscow looked tired, choked by fumes. Many of the streetlights were dark. Strings of lights hung along the buildings and bridges had broken bulbs. Shop windows that looked cheerful in the morning light revealed that the goods on display were nothing but faded cardboard cutouts. Lines of Muscovites waited outside each shop, blowing on their hands and stomping their feet against the cold.

We approached Red Square, bumping through potholes on the main thoroughfare. Yuri gave instructions to the driver, who detoured onto a narrow side road and parked. "We will take a short excursion," he said, helping me from the car and taking my arm. We strolled through light snowfall to the end of the passage. Beyond it, an expanse of moonlit cobbles stretched so far that they bent with the curve of the earth. The buildings around the edge were dark, except at the far end where St. Basil's cathedral, brightly lit, floated above the darkness. "Red Square," he said.

I gasped. "It's beautiful, a magical place."

"With a terrible history. The Peace Committee will bring your group here in a few days, but it's best to see it at night. Otherwise, it looks rather shabby."

"Thank you," I said, squeezing his arm, overwhelmed by the sense of history that surrounded me.

We stepped onto the empty square but were stopped by uniformed guards. "We can't go further in any case," said Yuri, guiding me toward the car. "Too slippery."

I was grateful for the heater in the Volga as we inched onto Tverska-ya Street. The traffic was bumper to bumper, moving slowly enough that I could distinguish the faces of exotic women in furs and spiked-heeled boots who smoked in doorways and strutted in front of luxury hotels. They opened their coats and posed as we passed. "Who are they?" I asked.

"Working girls," said Yuri.

"Prostitutes?"

"By night. By day they are shop keepers, accountants, teachers. Women do what they must in these difficult economic times."

"Some of them are just young girls," I said, nodding toward a group of teenagers talking to a man in a Mercedes.

"Orphans, most likely," said Yuri. "Aha. We have arrived at last."

The Hotel Cosmos black market was several times larger than in the morning. Vehicles of all kinds crowded the barricades and we had to leave the Volga some distance away. Yuri held my arm tightly as we negotiat-ed the crowds. The Russian dress code was apparently head-to-toe black. Eyes were riveted on my purple coat. "Hold your purse with both hands," Yuri warned as we squeezed around the barricades. "You might as well have USA tattooed on your forehead."

We started up the circular drive, pushing through moneychangers and hawkers waving lottery tickets, souvenirs, and wrist watches. Everything imaginable was being sold, including dogs, cats, birds, and snakes.

They were also selling girls. Men in black leather chanted, "Hey mister, want to buy a girl? *Ne doroga. Pas cher.* Not expensive." In the shadows, girls opened their threadbare coats. Underneath, they wore see-through teddies or bras and panties. They looked frightened and were much too thin, like starving children.

"How old are they?" I tried to ask, but Yuri propelled me through the outer door of the hotel into the warm vestibule where ordinary Russians weren't allowed. He had me take out my passport and hotel entry card to show the guard. Yuri flashed his ID and escorted me to the lobby but declined my invitation to stay for dinner.

I assured him that there would be plenty to eat. The Peace Commit-tee was sponsoring a reception and buffet in a room off the lobby. He looked skeptical. "We shall see," he said, making me wonder if I should have bought something in the market. "I'll be here tomorrow at 9 A.M. Sleep well. You'll have a busy day." He started to go but must have read my thoughts. "You must promise not to leave the hotel alone." He waited until I agreed. "Those hooligans will sell anything – even you."

I arrived early to the Peace Committee's buffet dinner, but early was too late. The Russian delegates were crowded three-deep around the tables. I couldn't even see the food. The trays were stripped bare in minutes and the Russians left the hotel without a word. Not a crumb was left.

The dining room/discotheque was closed. Hungry Americans relocated to the lobby bar called Sputnik and decorated like a spaceship. Neon stars flickered on the ceiling. Middle-aged hostesses in metallic miniskirts served vodka shooters and pickles. It must have been avant-garde in 1957. I declined the vodka but took a pickle. I tried to talk some of my despondent countrymen into going to the black market with me. I assured them we'd be safe if we stayed in a group, but there were no takers. I don't think they believed me when I described the riches available just outside the front door. I sat at the bar and ordered a plate of pickles.

"Pardon me, Dr. Engel." Sasha from the Peace Committee slid onto the barstool next to mine. "Our Russian delegates are crude people with little culture. Such gluttons! They ate every morsel. You must be famished."

I was cranky, too. "I thought they were professional people – our counterparts in medicine, art, and science." I said, peevishly.

"Oh, they are. But most of them have never been in a restaurant or a hotel. They have no manners around foreigners." He smirked, looking askance as I bit into a pickle. "That's an appalling waste of a good pickle," he said. "You need some vodka with that."

"I'm not much of a drinker," I said, grimacing at the salty gherkin. I wasn't a big fan of pickles.

"Perhaps you don't know how to do it properly. Let me show you." He signaled to a waitress, who brought over a plate of black bread sliced into wedges, and two shots of vodka. Sasha held the bread to his nose, closed his eyes and inhaled. Then he knocked down a shot of vodka. "Now, I give you the properly applied pickle." He took a big crunchy bite, smiled, and said, "Voila! Now you know the secret of how to drink all night and never get drunk." He pushed the bread toward me. "You try it."

"Okay, just once," I said, more interested in the bread than the vodka. I held it to my nose and opened my mouth to take a bite. Sasha grabbed my hand.

"No, no … just smell it." I did as he'd instructed – smelling the bread, then gulping down the vodka and taking another bite of my pickle. Alcohol flushed through every artery, capillary, and vein in my body, warming my skin from my toes to the roots of my hair.

"Wow," I said, reaching for the plate of bread. "That wasn't so bad."

He grabbed it away before I could eat any. "You'll spoil your dinner."

"What dinner?" I asked.

"Tonight, you're the guest of the Soviet Peace Committee. Do you like Jewish food?"

"I'm hungry enough to eat anything." I sighed. "Even hotdogs."

"The correct saying in Russia is, 'I'm hungry enough to eat *anybody*.'" He laughed. "It's a joke from the war." I thought of the bloated, mystery-meat I'd seen at breakfast. Sasha poured two more shots of vodka, raised his eyebrows, and said, "One for the road?" I declined, so he drank them both. I was about to say that I needed my coat when a blond man appeared with it held open. "May I introduce you to Ivan Ivanovich Ivanov," Sasha beamed. "He'll be your driver from now on. Now, let's go eat." He took the vodka bottle from the bar.

"What about the other Americans? They're hungry too. We shouldn't go without them." The vodka was blurring my vision.

"Bring them." Sasha waved his arms expansively. "We'll feed them all."

"What about the bread and pickles?" I asked, but we were moving to the exit in a phalanx of men from the Peace Committee. I looked around for my countrymen. They had vanished. "Where are the Americans?"

"Don't worry so much. No one's going to go hungry. Now get into the car, please."

We careened through Moscow in a smoke-filled Chaika with Ivan Ivanovich driving and squealing the tires on every turn. The radio played Russian rock-and-roll and Sasha sang along. The world outside sped up, while my brain slowed. I'd just been outmaneuvered for the second time since I'd arrived in this country – first by the doctors and now by the KGB.

"My colleagues will be looking for me," I said, though I doubted the Americans would even notice my absence.

"I'm sure your colleagues are tucking into a nice dinner." He looked at his watch. "Right about now. Compliments of your friendly hosts, the Soviet Peace Committee. Everyone – including you – will go to bed tonight with pants full of pleasure."

"Pants full of pleasure? What does that mean?"

"It's American slang, of course. It means that all the foreign guests will be happy and that makes us happy." He smiled, showing perfect teeth and crinkly laugh lines. Everything about him seemed friendly and non-threatening. Yet the doctors at the airport had feared him. Should I be afraid?

I watched him chain-smoking and chugging vodka from the bottle. He was a good-looking man about my age with black hair and an oriental cast to his eyes. He carried at least thirty pounds more weight on him than any of the doctors. I remembered Yuri's admonition about not leaving the hotel on my own. At least I wasn't alone. I sat sidewise on my seat, glancing through the rear window in hope that the other Americans were coming. In the dance of headlights that followed, I couldn't tell. After twenty minutes driving, we pulled into a parking lot. "Where are we?" I asked.

"Prospekt Mira. This is our Peace Committee headquarters."

"Are we eating here?"

"Not unless you want more hotdogs," he chuckled. "Do you?" I shook my head no. "I didn't think so. We're here to pick up my boss. Here he is now – your good friend Igor." A huge man opened the door, nodded to me, and sat in the passenger seat. I recognized him. He'd been with the American group at the airport. Near the city center, we picked up two more beefy men.

Squashed in the middle of the backseat, I couldn't see through the windows. What had I gotten myself into? Did they mean me harm? I didn't think so, but what could they want with me? They passed around a vodka bottle and chattered in Russian. Eventually, we slowed, and Ivan Ivanovich backed the Chaika into a row of cars with their motors idling. "Where are we?" I asked again.

"Paveletskaya Square. We're having dinner at Mount Carmel Jewish Restaurant. Someone wants to meet you," said Sasha, helping me from the car. He guided me down a short flight of icy steps into a narrow, low-ceilinged entryway that smelled of damp stone and garlic. Ahead, I heard laughter and music. I smelled cigars – and food. Sasha knocked on a red door that was pulled open by an armed guard, who saluted us. We entered an arched brick cellar the size of my living room, crammed with long wooden tables covered with food. The tables were lined with benches occupied by men in black suits. On one wall, a four-foot, blue neon menorah flickered through the smoky haze.

Sasha and Igor traversed the room with me in tow, back-slapping and kissing men who swilled vodka and feasted on Middle Eastern appetizers. I was seated in the middle of a long wooden bench with my back pressed against the brick wall. I was the only woman in the room. Sasha slid in beside me. "Who are these people?" I asked.

He looked incredulous. "Don't you recognize your hosts from the Soviet Peace Committee? Here is your friend Pyotor, Pavel, Oleg, and Igor, of course ... what does it matter? Stop worrying and enjoy your dinner."

The neon menorah buzzed hypnotically. I'd barely noticed the man seated on the other side of me until he said in English, "Good evening, Dr. Engel. Welcome to my favorite restaurant. I hope you brought your appetite."

I startled and looked up. "Hello," I replied, taking in the older man with thick-lensed, clear plastic glasses. His wavy, white hair and goatee made me think of Colonel Sanders. He held a copy of the curriculum vitae that I'd submitted to the conference organizers in Seattle. I saw handwritten notes on it and was about to ask, "Why do you have that?" but Sasha clapped his hands, and our table was heaped with meat salads, fish salads, egg, garlic and cheese salad, beet salad, cabbage salad, sliced cheese, deviled eggs, baskets of black bread, and dishes of caviar.

The Colonel opened the first of a dozen bottles of Priviet Vodka lined up on the center of the table. "Just a few drops," he said, filling my shot glass to the brim. Sasha was busy piling my plate with salads. A skinny violinist with wild white hair and his obese accompanist launched into an overwrought rendition of "The Godfather." The crowd cheered, the roar of their voices rising in pitch as music and vodka fumes saturated the room. When I couldn't eat any more, platters of gefilte fish appeared, followed by trays of steak and potatoes that steamed the air. I was soaked in sweat. The Russians were unfazed by the heat.

There was no water or soft drinks on the table – just vodka. I lost track of how much I was drinking. The Colonel lit a cigar and studied my CV, flipping the pages. Above the racket, I could distinguish his soft voice. "I understand you met Dr. Shuev and Dr. Lapukhin and their cohorts at Sheremetyevo Airport," he said, as if the words were written there. "They invited you to their maternity hospitals. Would you like to go?"

"Yes, I would," I answered.

"Foreigners are only allowed to visit hospitals from our approved list. Do you think I should make an exception for you? Why should I do that?"

The heat, the smoke, and the alcohol were making my head pound. I needed to concentrate but could barely focus my eyes. "Can I have some water, please?" I asked. He snapped his fingers at a waiter, issuing a directive. That gave me time to think. "I am here as a physician," I said. "I have no political agenda, only a medical one. I believe in citizen diplomacy and I've come to start a dialogue with Russian medical professionals. I'm sure it will improve healthcare delivery for both our countries."

He looked skeptical. "For us, one would hope so. For you? Not so much, I think." A waiter brought a green bottle and snapped off the lid. The colonel poured me a glass of fizzy water. It looked refreshing. I took a big swallow and nearly spit. It was warm and tasted like seashells.

"Borjomi Water from Georgia," he said. "The finest mineral water in the world." He poured some for himself and drank it. "Very healthy. Full of vitamins."

"It's nice," I said. "I can taste the calcium." I sipped a little more to be polite. It was like drinking salty tears. I fought back the desire to cry. The Colonel was looking at me, but I couldn't read his eyes through the thick lenses.

"I'm going to grant your request with the condition that you visit Hospital 70 in Novogereevo first. Your friend Dr. Lapukhin is the head of the birth house there. It is on your doctors' list, so they shouldn't object. Do you agree?"

"Yes, of course."

"Then it's settled." The Colonel stood up to leave. The room fell silent. Half of the men rose and formed a phalanx that escorted him through the door.

"Time to go," said Sasha.

Chapter Four

THE RED-HEADED GIRL

Moscow, Russia – December 1990

Back in my hotel room, I wrapped myself in my coat and slept on top of the covers to escape the legion of bedbugs. The next morning, I put on hiking shoes, hoping for better traction on the ice. Yuri was waiting in the lobby. He didn't look happy. "I hear you went to dinner with some gentlemen from the Peace Committee." His glare alarmed me.

"I don't quite know how that happened," I replied, blushing. "I had one vodka with Sasha and before I knew it, I'd been swooped into a car and we were driving through Moscow."

"The KGB are very good at that sort of thing – professionals, you might say."

"Was I in danger?"

"Not at all. You were perfectly safe. I hope you enjoyed your dinner."

"Yes, I did. It was a strange little place called Mount Carmel – Jewish food. Very tasty."

"So I am told," he said. "And you met a very important man."

"You must mean the Colonel."

"Colonel?" he scoffed. "Hardly a lowly colonel."

"It's just my nickname for him. He never told me his name, none of them did – just first names. Who is he?" Yuri rattled off a long string of titles that I couldn't understand. I heard the word "general." "What is his name?" I asked, rummaging in my purse for a pen. "I'd like to write it down."

"Just call him 'Colonel.' I'm sure he won't mind."

"Is he from the KGB?"

"Much higher – your stout friends from the Peace Committee are KGB. Their job is to charm foreigners like you and make life for Russians like us miserable." He helped me into my coat. "I understand that you have agreed to change our itinerary."

"The Colonel requested that I go to Hospital 70 first. Is that a problem?"

"Not at all." Yuri forced a smile. He guided me to the bank of elevators instead of the front door. "Today we'll leave the back way. There will be bloody heads in the market this morning – police with batons, I've been told. I hope your Americans are all in the hotel."

"Why did the Colonel request that I visit Hospital 70?" I asked in the elevator.

"For personal reasons, I expect. His daughter died in childbirth there, leaving his infant grandson mentally crippled after a traumatic birth. It was tragic, very sad. But not an uncommon story."

The Volga idled near the basement loading bay. I was surprised to see that the new driver was Ivan Ivanovich Ivanov. He nodded to me and blinked. Yuri ignored him, dozing for most of the drive through miles of identical concrete apartment blocks. He came alive when the Volga pulled to the curb and Ivan Ivanovich announced, "Novogereevo."

"Aha! The best pickles in Moscow," Yuri proclaimed, leaving the car and extending his hand to help me out. "Excuse me one moment. I will tell our driver to meet us on the other side in five minutes."

The market swarmed with shoppers, commuters, and merchants undeterred by the sheet of ice covering the ground. Peddlers stood next to folding tables stacked with jars of pickled fruit and cucumbers, hand-knit hats, gloves, salamis, baseball caps, and Barbie dolls. More fortunate salespeople worked in little kiosks selling vodka, cognac, beer, and flowers through tiny windows. Behind the market loomed a huge, cylindrical building decorated with dancing pigs and carrots.

My first Russian hat.

"What's that?" I asked.

"That's the state grocery store," Yuri said, loading his checkered bag. "Inside you can buy bread for three kopeks and a liter of milk for five kopeks. You can buy hotdogs, canned peas and sometimes eggs, but that's all. The real business is in the black markets like this one." He held up a jar of green cucumbers. "Novogereevo is famous for its lightly salted pickles – *mala solney*." Once he'd paid, he led me to a dilapidated truck. Two dark-skinned boys with curly black hair huddled under a tarp, selling beer. Yuri snorted. "Chechens!" He loaded several cans into his bag. "You're looking at Russia's new class of millionaires. They're probably selling piss in these cans."

"Why do you buy it?"

25

"It's the best piss in Moscow," he laughed. The car met us, and we drove to Hospital 70, a sprawling campus of shabby cement buildings on a fenced, wooded area the size of a city block. At the entry gate, one of the doctors from the airport joined us in the car. He shook hands with Yuri and nodded at me. Yuri said, "You've met Dr. Lapukhin, head of Obstetrics and Gynecology."

Dr. Lapukhin had blue eyes, curly blond hair, and an impish smile. He was the one who had taken my wallet and passed it around. "Welcome to our hospital," he said. "Surgery is in that building, x-ray in that one, pediatrics over here," he explained while Yuri translated.

The car stopped and waited for an old man on a gurney to be pushed across the road. "You take patients outside?" I asked. "In this weather?"

"We tried to build tunnels between buildings, but gave it up," said Lapukhin. "This was a cemetery – a very old one belonging to the Gallitzin family. No matter how deep we dug, there were always more bones. Now the hospital is haunted."

"Haunted?" I said, incredulous. "By ghosts?" Was he teasing me?

"People in the Novogereevo region sleep with lead sheets under their mattresses to keep angry ghosts out of their dreams," said Lapukhin. "It is a serious problem. That's why the city opened a Center for Exorcism here."

A door burst open with a clatter. A line of ladies wearing tall white hats and aprons over heavy coats rolled carts with steaming metal vats down a ramp and across the drive. A woman with a clipboard checked the carts and sent them off to the various buildings. I smelled boiled cabbage. "That must be the kitchen," said Yuri, sniffing. "What are they serving?"

"Same as every day." Lapukhin rolled his eyes. "*Shchi* and *kasha* – cabbage soup and boiled buckwheat."

We approached a smaller building with a stack of what appeared to be six-foot long candy boxes covered in bright satin with ruffles and plastic flowers. "What are those?" I asked.

"That's the morgue," said Lapukhin.

"And the chocolate boxes?"

"Those are coffins. The hospital uses them for a final church service here. Then the families must take the bodies and make their own arrangements."

"Church? I thought that Russians are atheists."

"Not at all," said Lapukhin. He pointed to a wrought-iron gate set back from the drive. "Look over there." Through the bars, I made out the red brick ruin of an onion dome rising crookedly from a crumbling church. "Can you see what's on the ground? That's the 16th Century Gallitzin bell. It's quite famous. It was buried by local people in 1920 before the KGB could destroy it. By next spring, it will hang in a new tower. It will ring on Easter."

Dr. Lapukhin and the Gallitzin bells.

"The Communists made our little church into a dog kennel. Religion was forbidden for seventy years, but now perestroika has changed all that and Bishop Alexander has come to restore our church." He pointed to an old wooden trailer. "That's where he lives." A wisp of smoke curled from the round metal chimney. "Neighborhood folks come every day to help him with reconstruction.

"We're rebuilding our churches all over Russia," said Yuri. "Our synagogues and mosques as well. Atheism was forced, but never accepted. The human soul hungers for God."

We arrived at a dilapidated building on the far edge of the campus. Dr. Lapukhin gestured and said, "Welcome to our birth house." It was gray concrete with rust stains running down the walls. It seemed to be tilting. We parked in front of a blue wooden door that he opened with a key. I was ushered into the stifling heat of a dim hallway with peeling wallpaper, water-stained walls, worn linoleum, and plates of chicken bones on the floor. I caught a whiff of cat pee.

"What are those doing here?" I asked, pointing to the bones.

"Feeds the cats," said Yuri.

"Cats?" I looked incredulous.

"Cats keep away rats. I assume it is the same in America."

We entered another hall where an elderly lady sat at a wooden desk in a white coat and a tall hat. She looked like a baker. "Is this the main entrance?" I asked. "Where are your wheelchairs and stretchers?"

"No need," said Yuri. "Russian women are strong."

Lapukhin explained that a woman in labor was expected to walk into the facility on her own. First, she was stripped and hosed down. Then her pubis was shaved and painted with gentian violet antiseptic.

27

I was shown into a pre-labor room where pregnant women in robes and slippers sat on chairs or paced the room. Some moaned, but most were eerily silent. "Why are they so quiet?" I asked.

"Shame," said Lapukhin.

"They don't want to make nurses angry," Yuri added. "Bad politics."

The birth house had no elevators. We had to climb four flights of stairs to reach the labor rooms. We passed women in gowns, staggering up the worn, uneven steps. "The top floor is best for sanitation," Yuri explained.

In the labor room, a dozen women lay on stretchers. Several turned to stare at us, their faces contorted in pain. Some moaned and some wept. The nurses ignored them and didn't seem to be following triage protocols to determine which woman should be taken to the delivery based on the stage of her labor. Yuri explained: "Everyone is equal here. It is first come, first served."

"What do you do if a child is crowning?" I asked with growing concern. "That woman should be delivered first."

Yuri consulted with the nurses. "They tie her legs together to slow the labor."

"What if the woman who's next in line isn't ready to deliver?"

"They will demonstrate for you," said Yuri. I watched in horror as a nurse climbed up on a table and pushed down on a woman's abdomen with her foot. The woman screamed in agony.

"Stop! That's terrible," I said. "And it's dangerous."

The woman continued to wail. A second nursed rubbed at the base of the noisemaker's nose until she quieted.

"How cruel," I exclaimed. "It's such a painful thing to do."

"The nasal spine is the only thing that hurts worse than labor. It keeps them quiet," said Yuri.

"What about anesthesia? Where are the drugs?" I asked. Yuri shrugged and shook his head. The woman started to cry again, and the nurses screamed at her. "What are they saying?"

"They say, 'This is your fault. You're the one who had sex, not me. Shut up.'"

I was stunned. This was birth by terror – and it didn't end in the labor room. Yuri helped me don a heavy, blood-spattered rubber apron. We followed a stretcher into a delivery room where doctors were delivering babies on three tables at a time. The overheated room reeked of iodine, and the stench of blood and afterbirth was worse than anything I had experienced in my years of medical practice. I felt dizzy. I thought I might vomit. The heat made it worse. Yuri sensed my distress and helped me out of the filthy apron. "Follow me, please," he said, guiding me into a dark corridor. "You may rest here with the mothers."

I leaned against the wall until my eyes adjusted to the dim light. On one side of the hall, the mothers who had just delivered lay on stretchers, unattended. Their naked infants were lined up in bassinets on the other side. Both mothers and infants were still battered and bloody from birth. A tabby cat walked down the aisle between them and rubbed against my ankles.

I'd had enough. "What the hell is this?" I exclaimed. "This is terrible! That woman's vagina is torn. She needs a repair to stop the bleeding. This baby needs to be cleaned and warmed up immediately. And get that damn cat out of here!"

"Please, please," Yuri pleaded. "You'll make the doctors angry." Yuri explained that there would be no vaginal repairs for the mothers and no resuscitation of the infants until two hours had passed. "It is a time of reflection."

One of the infants was in trouble. The edge of her blanket had fallen over her face, blocking her nose. She wasn't moving. I reached out to pull it off. "Stop." Yuri held my arm. "This is in God's hands."

"Baloney," I said, shaking him off. I scooped up the baby and wiped her face and nose with a clean tissue from my pocket. Her skin felt cool and her lips were dusky blue. I wrapped her in my soft cashmere scarf and bounced her in my arms, compressing her chest. "Come on, little girl." I patted and rubbed her back with her head tilted forward. "You can make it. You can grow up and be beautiful. Come on!" The infant jerked and sputtered. She gave a hearty cough and spit out a plug of mucus. Her lips turned pink, her mouth formed a perfect O, and she bellowed like an opera star. "That's my girl. That's my little angel."

The mother was weeping across the hall. "*Moya dochka* … " She extended her arms.

"She's asking for her daughter," said Yuri. I placed the newborn on her chest.

"*Kak ona zavoot?*" she asked, kissing her daughter's cheek.

"She wants you to name her," said Yuri, wiping away a tear.

The child's black curly hair reminded me of a flamenco dancer. "Conchita," I said on impulse.

"Chita … " said the mother. "*Krasivaya* Chita."

"No, madame," Yuri corrected her. "It's beau-ti-ful Con-chita."

"Boo-ti-ful Chita," the mother beamed.

"Chita it is," I said.

The tour moved on to the ultrasound laboratory, where I demonstrated our procedures on their aged equipment. On the way back, I pushed open the door to the corridor where the mothers and babies had been left alone. Something had changed. Every baby was now in its mother's arms. "This looks more like God's will to me," I said. The nurses had thought so, too – they were smiling. The bassinets were empty, except for one – a bawling infant with a shock of bright red hair.

"Where is this girl's mother?"

Yuri asked the nurses, then explained, "She's gone home."

"Without her baby?"

"The parents don't want this child. She'll be sent to a baby house in the country."

"Why? She's a beautiful, healthy child." I looked from face to face. Yuri and Lapukhin exchanged glances. Eyebrows were raised. "What is it," I asked.

"She has red hair."

"So what?" More looks flashed between the Russian staff.

"It's unlucky to have red hair," said Yuri.

"Lots of people have red hair," I exclaimed. "It's perfectly normal."

"Maybe in Ireland or Norway," said Lapukhin. "Not in Russia. As they say, 'There never was a saint with red hair.'"

A nurse leaned close and spoke to him. He said, "They want to name her Angela – after you. Do you give your permission?"

"Of course."

"That's settled," said Yuri. "It's time for lunch."

I wanted an explanation of this whole red-haired superstition. I wanted to know what other reasons were accepted for abandoning children, but the staff was going on lunch break. Yuri had stopped translating.

I shared a quick meal of kasha and tea with the doctors. We said goodbye when Yuri spotted our Volga in front of the birth house. In the car with Dr. Lapukhin, I sensed his anticipation. Should I tell him the truth and say that I was horrified by what I saw? That he had shown me a third world nightmare where women were tortured in childbirth and normal babies abandoned for having red hair? I searched for words that would be honest yet diplomatic. There weren't any.

I was still mulling when we drove past a small building that had been refurbished with a coat of yellow paint. It looked new compared to the rest of the hospital complex. A Yin/Yang symbol was painted above the door.

"What is that?" I wondered aloud.

"This is the new Shamanic Medicine Center. It has replaced the Center for Exorcism," said Lapukhin.

"You mean the Center for Witchcraft," Yuri chuckled.

"Shhh." Lapukhin put his fingers to his lips and winked. I was about to ask what he meant when the door swung open and a kitchen helper pushed her cart through. A tall blond man in a white lab coat held it open for her. He nodded in my direction, startling me with his laser blue eyes.

"That's the famous Dr. Sergey Popov," said Lapukhin. "Our main specialist in spiritual medicine."

"So he's the Siberian shaman that's been in all the newspapers," Yuri said. "I've heard that he's quite successful at treating hopeless cases."

"And their ghosts," Lapukhin added. "Here we are – the administration building. We must say our good-byes now."

We stopped at the gate. Lapukhin kissed my hand and left the car. Ivan Ivanovich drove the Volga into traffic. Yuri dozed, and I stared out the window, trying to make sense of the sights, smells, misery of the women, the cruelty of the staff, the miracle of little Chita and the tragedy of red-haired Angela. It all merged into an indigestible muddle.

I tapped Yuri on the shoulder and woke him: "Will little Angela be adopted?"

"That depends," he said, eyes closed.

"On what?"

"On whether she has relatives."

"They will take her?"

"No, she'll go to an orphanage."

"I don't understand." Yuri had started to snore. After a while, I dozed, too, fatigued by the onslaught of Kafkaesque misery.

I was startled twenty minutes later when Yuri announced our arrival at the women's clinic where his cousin, Tanya, was chief gynecologist. She greeted us in the lobby. "Welcome to the Kolomenskoe Abortion House," she beamed.

"Abortion?" Stunned, I turned to Yuri, "I thought we were visiting birth houses."

"This is on your list," he said defensively. "It was approved by you yesterday."

Tanya was undeterred. "Abortion is offered without cost as a benefit to women in the USSR, no matter their age or position in society," she said with Yuri translating. "It is our best method of birth control."

I was surprised. "What about other contraceptives like IUDs and diaphragms? Why not distribute free condoms? Wouldn't that be cheaper and less traumatic?" I asked.

Tanya shook her head. "No such products are available," said Tanya. "We have birth control pills for men, but they won't use them."

"Why not?"

"Our eyes turn red," said Yuri. "They're not popular."

Tanya handed me what looked like the finger of a rubber kitchen glove. "Russian condom," she said.

"Those are not popular either," Yuri said, his cheeks glowing pink.

We followed Tanya into the waiting room. A line of women stood along the wall, some no more than teenagers, some gray-haired grandmothers. They winced at the cries of anguish from the procedure room. A tattered sofa and chairs were occupied by the prostrate women who'd already had their abortions. Blood soaked through the upholstery and pooled on the linoleum. The smell of rotten meat permeated the cloying, overheated air.

Yuri blanched and announced that he would wait for me in the car. "My cousin speaks perfect English," he lied.

I was ushered into the procedure room where abortions were being performed on twelve women at a time by three gynecologists. Doctors did not change their gloves as they moved from patient to patient in bloody rubber aprons. There was no anesthetic. Nurses would rub the base of the nose of any woman who cried out in pain. "A Soviet woman can have an abortion whenever she wants it," said Tanya cheerfully. "Most have eleven abortions in life."

"That's terrible," I exclaimed. "How do the women feel about it?"

"They suffer great sickness of spirit," she admitted. I thought about all those sorrowful little ghost patients for Sergey Popov in his Center for Exorcism. He must be a busy man.

When I rejoined Yuri in the car, he informed me that the rest of my hospital visits had been cancelled by the Peace Committee. I was disappointed, but also relieved. I needed time to recover. Everything was shocking and happening too fast. We drove to Hotel Cosmos and I joined the other American delegates in the Great Hall of the Soviet Union. Lakota Sioux were pounding drums and dancing on stage with Siberian Yakuts who sounded remarkably similar. I relaxed in the plush seat and dozed to the rhythm of their chants. Someone touched my shoulder. It was Sasha from the Peace Committee.

"Excuse me, Dr. Engel," he said loudly. Annoyance rippled through the auditorium. "Step outside with me, if you would be so kind." In the lobby cafe, he bought me an espresso and explained that the Peace Committee had graciously arranged a special program for me. From now on, he would escort me to the Academy of Medical Sciences, the Cancer Research Center, and other approved institutions. We would start immediately with the Museum of Soviet Medical History.

"Now?" I asked.

He pointed to a black Zil limousine that idled near the front door, undisturbed by the black marketeers. For the next several days I was regaled with tours designed for foreign dignitaries. Sasha was an excellent translator and attentive host. I sat politely and tried to stay awake while Communist Party functionaries gave long speeches about the wonders of Soviet health care.

My mind was far away. I began to appreciate why the Russian doctors had risked so much to show me the reality of the Soviet system. They had brought me to a real birth house to do exactly what I'd done. By my simple, defiant act of moving baby Chita to her mother's arms, I had given them permission to change things – to provide the compassionate care that was already in their hearts to give. I had seen the relief on their faces. I began to visualize how to introduce gentler, kinder techniques that would help both patients and staff recover from the trauma they had suffered. And what about little Angela? Were there orphanages filled with red-haired children? I had to know.

On the day of the final plenary, I sat with the rest of the delegates in the Great Hall. Soviet officials delivered closing platitudes full of good will and bonhomie for the future. I glanced at the strangers around me and realized that I'd barely spoken to another American. My days had been filled with Russians. I had dozens of Cyrillic business cards in my purse. I'd been interviewed for Russian TV.

My countrymen looked tired, but I was energized. I felt inexplicably at home in this strange city. The others might leave Russia behind and return to their American lives, but I had a premonition that a door had opened, and I'd been propelled to an alternate universe. Was it my life's purpose to reduce infant morbidity in this strange land? If so, how?

I shivered, sensing a presence. I turned and met the gaze of a blond man who had taken the seat next to me. He looked familiar.

"Dr. Sergey Popov," he said, holding out his hand.

I shook it. "Yes, of course, from the Shamanic Medicine Center."

He wrapped my hand in both of his, surprising me with the heat of his grasp. "Don't be afraid," he whispered in English, holding my gaze with the intensity of his eyes. "You have a sickness in your third eye. You will need me soon." He kissed my hand and left me holding his business card with the yin/yang symbol above his name.

What did he mean – sickness in my third eye? Was he talking about my sinus tumors? Had they returned? How could he know? I started to tremble.

Chapter Five

THE THIRD EYE

Seattle, 1991

I returned to Seattle and Russia came with me. I would close my eyes and see a jumble of black markets, Red Square, food lines, abortions, candy-box coffins, wailing red-headed babies, and bottles of warm beer. I couldn't sort them. Within that strange mix was the magnetic tug of connections I'd made to the people, both spiritual and energetic. I'd recall the heft of little Chita coming to life in my hands and my joy at seeing the newborns moved across the hall to their mothers' arms. I would blink and stare into the thick lenses that obscured the Colonel's eyes, sensing his plea for me to return. I'd blink again, tumbling back to the immeasurable suffering of women in a country where childbirth was butchery and birth control an assault on a woman's soul.

Jetlagged by the eleven-hour time difference, I would awaken before dawn and prowl my lovely old house, looking in on my children. I watched them asleep, safe and warm in their beds, and wished the same for baby Angela. I wrote to Yuri asking what had happened to her and if there was anything I could do. I offered to find her an adoptive family in America, maybe a family of red-heads – we had plenty of them. He wrote back to say that he'd make inquiries. He enclosed an article translated from *Soviet Women's World* indicating that one third of infants born in Russia were abandoned at birth for reasons of poverty, single-motherhood, and a list of "defects" that included six toes, mixed race, cleft palate, birth marks, or abnormal hair. The fact that most of them had living relatives meant that they were unavailable for foreign adoption and condemned to grow up in state institutions. He wrote again to say that Angela had been sent to Baby House Number Six in Yaroslavl, an industrial city north of Moscow, where she had a grandmother.

By the end of 1990, I considered selling my medical practice. I reasoned that I could use the funds to work on reforming maternal and infant health care in the USSR. I could only travel on weeks when my ex-husband had the children in his home, but I could do a great deal from

Seattle. The suffering I'd seen was too great to turn my back on, and the solution to many of the problems required nothing more than common sense – the basis of good medical practice. I began by starting a nonprofit, nongovernmental organization – an NGO.

"What shall we call our new NGO?" I asked a group of friends gathered in my living room. We had come together to form a board of directors. Most of them were doctors with overseas experience, or businesspeople from Seattle-based companies like Microsoft and Boeing who were old Russia hands.

"How about MiraMed," suggested Carol Hiltner from Center for Soviet/American Dialogue.

"I like it," said Roy Farrell of Doctors without Borders. "*Mir* is the Russian word for *peace*. It also means *world* and *wholeness*."

"And *med* for *medicine* in both languages," said Kyle Johnson our attorney.

We voted and MiraMed had its name. "Now we need to raise money," said Dale Jarvis, our accountant. "Are you ready to make public appearances, give news interviews, and meet with government officials?"

"Sure," I said, with some trepidation. I'd been on a few Seattle TV programs and thought I sounded like Minnie Mouse.

"I'll set up interviews with KOMO and KING 5 for starters," said Kathy White, our journalist.

"Uh huh ... sure," I agreed. "I don't know how good I'll be."

"Speak from your heart like you did to each of us. Tell the stories of Chita and Angela. Seattle will get behind you."

"I know Jill Dougherty at CNN," said Ari Cohen, our big picture guy. "I'm sure I can convince her to send someone undercover with you to the birth house."

After they left, descending the two steep flights of stairs to the street in a noisy group, I sat in my porch swing and gazed at the lights of Seattle. What had I gotten myself into? It started to rain, and I went inside to phone Bella Abzug, former congresswoman from New York. We'd met years before at the United Nations during the Commission on the Status of Women. She was strong, brave, and kind. I considered her my mentor.

"I'm going to sell my medical practice," I blurted. "I'll use the money to launch a nonprofit NGO to reform childbirth in the USSR."

"That sounds like a great idea," she said. "Why do you sound hesitant?"

"I'll have to do fundraising."

"So? What are you worried about?"

"The board wants me to do media and public speaking. What if I'm no good at it?"

"Get over yourself," she scolded with a cackle. "You'll be fine. Women get in their own way by trying to make sure everything's perfect before moving forward. Men just push ahead, make a big mess, and worry about consequences later – if ever."

"I can give it a try for a few years," I acknowledged. "I have a good offer with a clause that I can buy the practice back in three years if this doesn't work out. My ex and I have joint custody so I can travel when our children are with him." There was a long pause on the line. "Are you still there?"

"I'm just recalling the day when I decided to do civil rights work. I argued my first big case in Mississippi. It launched my political career, but I miscarried my baby."

"Are you saying that it wasn't worth it?"

"I'm saying that there are always consequences that we don't bargain for. If you want to do something safe, run for Congress."

Over the next year, I recruited doctors, nurses, and psychologists from across America by contacting professional associations and asking for volunteers. The response was heartwarming. We jointly prepared the first program of childbirth education for hospital staff and prenatal education for mothers in Russia using materials from American maternity centers and teaching institutions. In 1992, they joined me in Seattle for an orientation session before flying to Moscow. Medical companies in the Seattle area had generously contributed sterilizers and other small but necessary items for the delivery rooms. Lufthansa German Airlines had agreed to fly us and our equipment gratis.

In addition to the classes we'd be offering at Yuri's All-Union Center of Maternal and Infant Health, we planned to conduct focus groups with Russian women in their homes, something that had never been done in the USSR. The results of the focus groups would provide data we needed to write grants. We'd been invited to submit proposals for US government funding programs through USAID – the US Agency for International Development – and the State Department.

Dr. Lapukhin and Dr. Shuev posted announcements of the focus groups in pediatric clinics around Moscow. The signup sheets for volunteers were filled within a day. Like women everywhere, Russian women were eager to talk. Kitchen tea parties were scheduled in apartments across the city. I imagined women all over Moscow waiting in lines to buy sugar and flour so they could bake *pechenye* (cookies) to serve with tea.

I was sound asleep in my home when the phone rang at 4 A.M. "Am I speaking with Dr. Engel, please?" A voice boomed over the crackly line.

"Yes?" I fumbled for my bedside lamp and glasses. "Who is this?"

"Why, this is your old friend Sasha from the Soviet Peace Committee."

"It's four in the morning," I grumbled. "Oh yeah – time zones."

"Quite. It's just after lunchtime in Moscow. I've called you with excellent news from my boss."

I sat up in bed, still chasing sleep. "Who?"

"Surely you remember dear Igor. He has decided to provide you with conference rooms at our headquarters at Prospekt Mir. You will use our transportation and interpreters – a most generous offer."

I was silent, uncertain how to handle this. The KGB interfering with our interviews and intimidating women defeated our purpose. At the same time, we couldn't proceed without their blessing. Having learned that Russians were very superstitious, however, I had an idea. It was widely believed that speaking or even thinking about childbirth would make a man impotent.

"Thank you," I said cheerfully. "Your help is most welcome with these intimate female discussions of all aspects of the birth process. We gratefully accept your support in these delicate obstetrical matters. You can translate our graphic illustrations of birth pathology."

Sasha fell silent, the cogs in his brain spinning as he thought of a way to get out of this. "I will call you again with details." He hung up and didn't call back, but I knew the KGB would do their job one way or another.

In the meantime, we went ahead with our plans and finished packing medical supplies for our flight the following night.

Our mood was one of anticipation when we gathered for dinner at the Costas Opa Greek restaurant on the Seattle Ship Canal. I had just been seated and ordered souvlaki when lightning split my skull. I stood up and collapsed.

I was rushed to Overlake Hospital and admitted. Doctors who were my friends and colleagues hovered over me speaking in hushed tones. I knew it was bad. The sinus tumors had returned and were obstructing an artery behind my left eye. I had a fever. The surgeons started intravenous steroids and I was scheduled for emergency surgery the following morning.

That night I was visited by a series of specialists – surgeons, anesthesiologists, otolaryngologists, ophthalmologists. They floated into my room like grim prophets from the Temple of Logic to tell me that if I survived the surgery, I would be blind in one or both eyes and have no sense of smell. The surgeons needed to remove the rest of the bones in my nose to get to the tumors. I would require a metal prosthesis to replace my nose.

They droned on and on, but I stopped listening. I closed my eyes against the pain and dreamed of flying. White feathered wings lifted me into the night sky where the agony of living dropped away. I felt nothing but the pull of the planets. Thunder rumbled. Was it the voice of God? Lightning fractured the sky with electric streaks. A blue flash struck my forehead and I fell in a tangle of wings and legs. The earth was rising fast. Feathers tore, snagging on branches in my free-fall – each jolt releasing voices that shrieked: "Women don't fly." "Girls can't be doctors." "You're a fool for trying to change the world."

A legion of baby ghosts from the Kolomenskoe Abortion House burst into the air and lit the sky like sparklers. "You didn't save us," they wailed. "You're out of time."

I woke up shouting, "No! I'm not!" I was alone in my hospital room, tangled in sweaty sheets, heart pounding, and eyes wide. I had sweated away my fever. My IV chirped, my heart monitor beeped – normal hospital sounds. The steroids had worked for now and the headache was gone. I sat up, taking in gulps of air, wondering what I should do.

I knew that I'd find no refuge in Overlake Hospital – the Temple of Logic with its machines. I'd read my medical records and evaluated my own x-rays and CT scans. Too much bone had been removed from my face already. Any attempt to scrape away more would expose my brain. I would hemorrhage and die. I knew it with every atom in my being. The medical profession could do nothing to save me. To stay would be to surrender.

I pulled out my IV, climbed from the bed, and drew back the window curtain to stare at my image in the dark glass. Forms materialized behind my reflection – a courtroom, an old one from my childhood, black and white like Perry Mason on television. A ceiling fan clicked overhead, throwing shadows across the crowded gallery. Men and women sat and sweated in the heat, murmuring "Bubba, bubba, bubba … "

The bailiff, prosecutor, and defense attorney were all me. I was the defendant, too, standing slump-shouldered before the judge. My trial was near its end and I was losing. The jurors sagged in their seats, fanning themselves in boredom. The verdict would be swift, the sentence merciless. They wanted my story to end so they could go home. The prosecutor stood and shouted, "Cut her open! Get it over with!"

The defense attorney stood and said, "No defense."

I stared at the floor. A crimson stain flowed from my feet, spreading over the black and white tiles of the Temple of Logic.

"Just a minute," said the judge who was also me. "Doesn't the defendant have anything to say?" She leaned forward until we were nose-to-nose. Thunder rumbled and lightning streaked behind her head. "You are only guilty if you surrender, you stupid cow," she said. "Defend yourself or die a coward's death!"

The courtroom walls dissolved. I was once again dressed as a bride walking through the Temple of Logic. Clocks ticked on all sides: "You're out of time ... out of time," they chimed. I approached the jagged boundary of the abyss, but wasn't afraid. I ran to the edge, spread my arms and jumped, tumbling in a cloud of white lilies, floating gently into the darkness weightless as a leaf, surrounded by the beating of my human heart.

"I can help you," Sergey Popov had said in Moscow. I recalled the heat in his hands. If Western medicine couldn't save me, maybe shamanic medicine could. Russian doctors and even the government of Moscow believed in his work with spiritual medicine. Yuri had said that he did wonders with the hopeless cases and that was me – an incurable. Was God showing me a new door, cracking it open so that I could see an alternative to certain death? Or was I simply too desperate to think straight? Did my peers know better? I'd never thought they were smarter than me. I weighed my options. There was loss in any choice I made.

"Well?" demanded the judge while the jury stared at me with indifferent eyes. "Bubba, bubba ... " mumbled the gallery.

"I'm going to Russia," I declared.

"So be it!" The judged slammed down her hammer, and the courtroom vanished.

Energy surged through me. I searched the closets and found my clothes. At the nurses' station, I was confronted by the hospital attorney who demanded that I sign a series of forms stating that I was leaving against medical advice. My attending physician arrived in a fluster to tell me that if I refused the surgery, he was washing his hands of me. I could never come back to Overlake for treatment. Their threats had no effect. I left for SeaTac with a bottle of prednisone to keep the swelling of my brain in check.

I met my group in the International Departures Hall. Lufthansa had donated our tickets for this humanitarian mission and seated us in first and business class. The pilot invited me into the cockpit to watch the sun rise over Greenland.

God's touch ignited the glaciers below with the fiery pinks and oranges of dawn.

Chapter Six

BIG BAG OF MONEY

Moscow, Russia--1991

Our group was lodged a short distance from Moscow in a country retreat for Communist Party elites called *Sosni*, or The Pines. It was perched above the Moscow River amid Red Army spoils looted from Hitler's Eagle's Nest in Berchtesgaden. Bronze statues of seated stags brought to the Führer from Syria by Hermann Göring stood on either side of the entry.

We soon discovered that all our room keys were identical – in other words, useless. While some of our group played billiards on Hitler's table or rode bicycles to Stalin's blood-red dacha deep in the woods, I met with the fiery journalist Olga Bedinskaya – one of Russia's leading investigative reporters. She was producing an undercover exposé on birth houses to broadcast on her popular television news program. When I asked her if she was afraid to air the piece, she said, "I can sit on the face of anyone in Moscow and laugh." I understood her to mean that she had so much dirt on important people that they weren't going to interfere.

We had arranged a bus tour of the city for the Americans on our first day, including a walk across Red Square. Our group had just stepped onto the square when the Peace Committee's black Zil limousine pulled up behind me. Sasha jumped out all smiles, kissing my cheeks. "Move along, now," he said to the Americans, hustling me into the car. "Enjoy your tour." My team didn't move. They stood staring in shocked surprise.

Sasha slid in beside me and lit a cigarette. "Personally," he said, "I am happy to let your ladies go all over the city to discuss your female topics in shabby apartments. But our bosses have other ideas. How many teams do you have?"

I had already sent him all of this information, but I said, "Five teams with three interviewers on each. We'll conduct interviews in seventy-five apartments over the next ten days. You're welcome to come and drink tea with the ladies and discuss childbirth. I'm sure they would be glad to share their stories from the birth houses."

His lips puckered into a grimace. "You're joking, of course. Besides, the bosses don't want to waste important personnel listening to women talk. I have come to propose a compromise. Your teams are free to do their interviews if you will come with us." He paused. I waited. "The Peace Committee will organize the rest of your visit. You will be our distinguished guest."

"Where will I go?"

"What does it matter? Factories, government offices, the usual tour for celebrities. You'll do some television and radio, some newspaper interviews. We'll have a press conference at the Peace Committee. You may speak about our joint work in citizen diplomacy."

"That will be fine. Thank you," I said, smiling to hide my disappointment. This compromise was necessary and there was no point in arguing. "What about my private meetings?" I asked, thinking of Sergey Popov. I hadn't had time to contact him before leaving Seattle. I needed to get to the Shamanic Medicine Center.

"You are welcome to meet with whomever you please – at the Peace Committee," said Sasha. "We will provide you with excellent facilities. I will be your personal interpreter. I'm quite good."

"That is most kind of you." I extended my hand. "I agree to your compromise." He kissed it, obviously relieved. "If we're finished here, I'd like to show my friends Red Square." I reached for the door handle. The locks snapped shut. I looked up and saw Ivan Ivanovich wink at me from the driver's seat. He put the Zil in gear and sped across Red Square.

"Wave good-bye to your Americans," said Sasha. "We're going to dinner." I waved out the back window, smiling to convey to my worried colleagues that I wasn't being kidnapped – or was I? Perhaps my meetings with Olga Bedinskaya had pushed things too far.

We drove out of Moscow into the darkening countryside. Sasha was unusually silent. I didn't know if this was some intimidation technique, or if he was angry. It was making me nervous. I rummaged in my purse and brought out a cassette tape of New Age music my daughter had made for me. I passed it to Ivan, asking if he would play it. He popped it into the cassette player. The Beatles sang "Norwegian Wood" and I focused on the familiar music, trying to relax.

Sasha lit his umpteenth cigarette and said, "You are lucky to have such powerful friends." I assumed he meant the colonel.

We drove for over an hour, arriving at a parking lot with black sedans backed into the spaces, their motors idling. Sasha perked up. "Welcome to Slavyanskaya Bazaar," he said, opening my door and offering his hand.

We climbed up rough-hewn wooden stairs to a log building with bright blue gingerbread shutters. A gun-toting Cossack dressed in camouflage opened the steel door. He kissed Sasha on the lips and ushered us into a crowded, smoke-filled restaurant packed with black-suited patrons. Once again, I was the only woman in the room.

Heavyset men were seated at wooden tables piled with food and bottles of wine. Through the racket, I heard "The Godfather" theme, played too fast this time. A black-haired musician in a tuxedo was pounding it out on an upright piano honky-tonk style. The group from the Peace Committee waved us over to a corner table. They were tucking into salted herring chased with shots of vodka. They all spoke in the same oddly accented, eloquent English as Sasha. A distinctive chuckle accented their speech, something picked up from KGB school, perhaps. Sasha's boss Igor was seated across the table, his face lost in the cigar smoke, but every hair on his head backlit by the light from a brisk log fire. Soon the table was heaped with Russian salads, platters of fresh greens and tomatoes, bowls of raw garlic, beef tongue in aspic, and the ever-present cucumbers. When it seemed that nothing else could fit, raised platters of sturgeon, trout, potatoes, piroshky, and cabbage dumplings arrived to form another layer. "Russian village food," said Sasha, dishing mounds of fish and potatoes onto my plate. "Primitive, but nutritious."

Igor poured me a glass of vodka. "A few drops, just a few drops," he kept saying. I was sticking to the Georgian mineral water. Sasha and his chums polished off several bottles of vodka while toasting each other and chowing down. Eventually, Igor signaled with much throat clearing that our meeting was about to begin. He poured me a water glass full of Armenian cognac despite my protest.

"Well," he said, leaning forward on folded arms until his face was close to mine, "I understand that you have a big bag of money."

I nearly choked. I hadn't expected this. I did have a big bag of money. Back at the hotel, closely guarded, I hoped, by the rest of the Americans, was a flight bag containing cash for the hotel, travel, and program costs – exactly $25,000. Cash was the only way we could pay our expenses.

"About $25,000, am I right?" He paused, raising his bushy eyebrows. Then he continued: "If you want to continue working in this country, you should give it to me, now."

I had no intention of giving him the money. If they had taken me out behind the Sosni Hotel and pointed a gun at my head, I would have handed that cash right over. Instead, these KGB guys were shaking me down

43

in a noisy restaurant surrounded by gangsters with a huge armed guard at the door who looked like he was on steroids. I sipped the cognac and considered my options while "The Godfather" played over and over. This was theater, a big show, a friendly shakedown with a chance to charge an extravagant dinner on their expense accounts. They wouldn't hurt me because they were officially responsible for my safety and answered to the colonel. That's what Sasha meant by "powerful friends."

Maybe the prednisone was impairing my judgement, but I went on the offensive. "That money is to save the lives of Russian babies," I said indignantly. "Your babies." I leaned forward and pointed at Igor, who didn't blink. "You know how terrible the situation is in your birth houses. You've read our stories and our interviews. If you're taking money from us, then Russian babies will die – your babies." I pointed again and this time he blinked.

I launched into a graphic description of the situation inside maternity hospitals, filled with words like blood, placenta, vagina, fistula, pus, fetus, strangulation, gangrene, and hemorrhage. I hoped it would disgust him, and it did. Our table grew silent. Good – no one was eating. I was spoiling their dinner. I could feel these men willing me to shut up, but they had opened this box and I had the floor. Several more bottles of vodka and cognac arrived.

After about twenty minutes of my monologue on the terrors of Russian childbirth, one of the men was sobbing. His daughter-in-law had just given birth to a baby – going into the birth house as a healthy young woman and being rolled out on a stretcher as a vegetable. The baby had died, and the family was in shambles, his son threatening suicide. I leaned forward, close enough to smell the garlic on Igor's breath and said, "I can go home and forget about all of you. I can sip mint juleps and lead a good life. I don't have to be here."

Igor grabbed my arm and squeezed it. "No, you must stay," he said. The tension eased. The bag of money was forgotten. We toasted the future success of our projects to save Russian babies. Igor signaled the pianist who thankfully stopped playing "The Godfather" and launched into "Lara's Theme" from "Dr. Zhivago."

"Americans like this song," said Sasha, pulling me onto the dance floor until Igor cut in and twirled me around.

For the next ten days, I was driven around Moscow in the Zil. If I went for a walk, I was followed by the Zil. If I met with the American team, the Zil hovered nearby with the motor running and Sasha at my elbow.

I never entered any of the apartments or participated in a single-one of the seventy-five kitchen meetings that were held. Instead, I went on the KGB's VIP tour of the city.

Smiling factory directors took me through pharmaceutical plants, clothing factories, and watch-making assembly plants, but I was never left alone until it was time to fall into bed, long after the others were asleep. I visited the Air and Space Museum and was photographed for the newspapers laying flowers on the Tomb of the Unknown Soldier at the Kremlin wall.

Sasha, the Zil and my big fur hat.

I did television and news interviews at Peace Committee headquarters on Prospekt Mira, standing in front of the giant dove that is the Peace Committee symbol. I'm sure the producers hoped that Russian viewers would associate me with the KGB and shun our program. It might have had that effect a few years before, but times were changing. The Iron Curtain had lifted. People were wary, but not as terrified as they once had been. They craved contact with the outside world and were fascinated by America and what it represented.

At the end of the focus groups, we sponsored a banquet to honor the women who had shared their kitchens and their stories. We rented a banquet hall at the Hotel Prague and expected about 200 guests including the families. At that time, an event like that in Moscow cost about $500, or two shopping bags full of rubles. We were even able to hire a band.

I arrived at the banquet hall in the Zil, ahead of anyone else, and sat alone at the head of a long, u-shaped table piled with Russian salads, smoked fish, and bread. I alternated between worrying that no one would come and that too many people would come. The people from the focus groups were working-class Russians who had never been to a restaurant or hotel. Maybe they would be intimidated by the Peace Committee presence and stay away.

The band arrived to set up at a quarter to eight. At eight o'clock, they launched into a set of popular Russian rock songs and the guests arrived

– all of them. They must have been waiting in the street outside the hotel because they came in a single group, followed shortly by the Peace Committee. People found places at the tables and looked about suspiciously. No one smiled or spoke. The bottles of wine on every table were emptied within minutes, but no one was talking.

I gave Sasha $100 and asked him to order two dozen bottles of vodka. At $4 a bottle, it was top of the line. The vodka disappeared and the party warmed up a little. I ordered another 24 bottles and the party turned into a smashing success. At first, only our American doctors and nurses were willing to dance. But a lively Georgian wedding party was underway in the next room and they didn't have a band so they trickled into our banquet hall to show off their Caucasian dances. Not to be outdone, the Russians were soon jumping around like Cossacks.

At one point when we were slow dancing, Sasha whispered in my ear; "You know, I am just like agent 007 – a Russian James Bond, licensed to kill."

"That's good to know," I said. Was he joking?

At 1:45 a.m. the band packed up. At 2 a.m. the lights went out and we went our various ways – my American colleagues in taxis to Sosni while I was transported to the same place in the Zil.

On our final day in Moscow, we were scheduled to give a press conference live on national television to share the findings of our focus groups. It was set up in the Peace Committee Friendship Hall, where they'd held press conferences since the 1930s. I was hung over and frustrated. With Sasha in the black Zil hovering like a vulture, I hadn't been able to meet with Sergey Popov or even call him. I'd barely seen Yuri. He'd warned me that my calls from Sosni were monitored and that might cause problems for the Shamanic Center. He suggested inviting Dr. Popov to the press conference with the other doctors from Hospital 70. I agreed that was the best plan and hoped he would come. I tried not to think about what would happen when the prednisone pills stopped working. I only had a few left.

I arrived early and noticed that the press table was being set up so that the TV cameras would film us against the Peace Committee dove. Before anyone else arrived, I had the cameramen move their equipment around so that they faced a section of the table backed by an exhibition of children's paintings. My group filed in and took their places in front of the cameras, the technicians set up the microphones, and when the Peace Committee hurried in at the last minute, it was too late to change. We were about to go live.

To my chagrin, Igor made a show of clearing a place next to me at the press table, tapping his microphone and rattling a sheaf of papers. Taking over press conferences was a way the KGB controlled media. I was scheduled to speak first. I introduced our project and our American team and was followed by the head gynecologist of the All-Union Maternal and Infant Health Care Center, Dr. Shuev.

While he was speaking about our new program of childbirth education available in Russian, I noticed how the microphones were plugged directly into the table and attached to a connector with the wires hanging underneath. Dr. Lapukhin came next, sharing the preliminary results from the focus groups. He concluded his talk while Igor cleared his throat and put on an obsequious smile. I didn't hesitate. Before he could utter a word, I reached under the table and unplugged him. For several seconds, he tapped on the microphone to no avail. The cameraman was staring at me. He knew what I'd done. My face flushed with guilt. My stomach climbed into my throat. I tried to read his face. I'd just unplugged the KGB. I might be arrested, sent to a *gulag*. I held my breath until he gave me a wink and signaled the next speaker, sending us out over the airwaves without the Peace Committee.

Immediately after the press conference, Russians across eleven time zones from Kaliningrad to Vladivostok watched Olga Bedinskaya's shocking birth house exposé, filmed with hidden cameras. Her report provided Russian men with their first view into the monstrous abuse inflicted on their wives and daughters. Even the Peace Committee men were transfixed by the television set in the lobby.

The other Americans left in taxis to Sheremetyevo Airport for the flight home. I had my suitcase with me ready to load in the Zil, but Ivan Ivanovich was watching the exposé with the others.

Someone touched my hand. Yuri stood beside me with Sergey Popov, who said softly, "Come with me, please, Dr. Engel. I have your ticket to Simferopol. Our flight leaves in one hour."

All I could think to ask was, "Where?"

"We are flying to Crimea in Ukraine and driving to the village of Starye Krem." He signaled for me to come, but my feet were weighted to the floor.

"What about the other Americans?" I asked Yuri. "They'll be waiting for me at Sheremetyevo." My head was a muddle of dancing KGB agents, Zils and unplugged microphones. I felt faint. Nothing was making sense.

"I'll contact them," said Yuri. "Go enjoy a holiday in Crimea with Dr. Popov for a few days. I'm envious."

I stared at Yuri. This was crazy. He was sending me to a place I'd barely heard of with a man I didn't know. Then I thought of the operating table that waited in Seattle and the operation that I knew would kill me. "Why Crimea?" I asked.

Sergey smiled, wrapping me in the warmth of his energy. I felt safe for the first time in two weeks. "My grandmother, Baba Lydia, lives there," he said, taking the handle of my suitcase and rolling it through the door.

"Of course," I said, following him outside.

Chapter Seven

OLD CRIMEA

Crimea, Ukraine--1991

Icouldn't sleep on the flight from Moscow to Simferopol. The gigantic Ilyushin stopped like a bus in every city along the way. People deplaned, fetching bundles and bags from a pile of luggage stacked at the rear. Others boarded, scurrying to find empty seats. In Samara, a family of six came down the aisle with a sheep dog, startling a crate of chickens on the shelf over my head. They started clucking. Feathers dropped onto my clothes.

Sergey seemed oblivious. "I haven't seen Baba Lydia in two years," he said. "I grew up at her house in the desert. There are no trees for a hundred kilometers except in her garden. Her white light energy makes things grow. You'll see."

"The only thing I can remember about Crimea is the Crimean War and Florence Nightingale," I confessed. "It's a desert, you say?"

"It was farmland until the Soviets dynamited the rivers and built a highway. Today only a hundred people live in her village of Starye Krem and they're poor. I want Baba to come work at my clinic, but she isn't fond of Moscow."

"Is that why we're going to Crimea?" I asked, reconsidering my impetuous decision. "To fetch your grandmother?" Exhaustion caught up with me. My head ached and I wanted to cry.

"Don't worry." Sergey lifted my chin and touched my forehead. My sinus burned above the bridge of my nose. "I described your case to Baba Lydia. She said to bring you to Starye Krem without delay."

"What do you know about my case?"

"Your energy is blocked in your third eye and has been for many years. That's the place where your past, present, and future meet. You must be open to the flow of time, or you'll stop functioning."

"You mean that I'll die?"

"As defined by conventional medicine, yes." He placed his other hand on my arm and said: "Show me your fear." The heat drained from my flesh.

The roar of the Ilyushin faded to silence. I sank into the earth, surrounded by the smell of dirt until there was no light. I'd never been so cold. From far away he said, "You needn't be afraid anymore."

"Why?" I shivered, snapping back to the present. "Will Baba Lydia cure me?"

"No," he said. "You will cure yourself."

We deplaned on the windy tarmac in Simferopol. Sergey waved to an old man who stood at the gate: "Here is Uncle Konstantin with his car." I rode the last one hundred kilometers through barren hills, bouncing in the back of Konstantin's tiny, lime-green *Zaparozhets* with his spare canister of gasoline on my lap. At dawn, when Baba Lydia's oasis was finally visible in the distance, it looked like the Garden of Eden.

We drove through a gate and into a courtyard. A tiny woman stood beneath an arbor of wild pink roses. "Seryosha!" she cried, opening her arms to embrace her grandson. He picked her up and swung her effortlessly. "Come in, come in," she said, taking my arm. Her head barely came to my shoulder, but her grip was strong. "Welcome to my home. We've been waiting for you."

Her home was a compound of one- and two-story log houses surrounded by a tall hedge of pink roses. White daisies, blue lobelia, orange calendula, and red salvia lined the walkways. A vegetable garden overflowed with red tomatoes, yellow squash, and shiny green cucumbers with pale stripes. Bees buzzed and butterflies fluttered. Birds sang from apple, pear, and apricot trees. Chickens scratched in the yard.

Baba Lydia guided me to a gazebo where a table was set for breakfast with boiled eggs, sliced ham, and bread with jam. A barefoot girl with a long blond braid poured concentrated tea from a ceramic pot, filling the cup with water from a steaming samovar and handing it to me. I thanked her and sat down. A puppy with outsized paws pounced on my foot and attacked my shoelaces. Others joined us at the table. Some wore dressing gowns and slippers. Baba Lydia poured glasses of amber liquid from a bell jar with pink petals floating in it. "Rose-wine," said Sergey, taking a seat next to me.

"Who are these people?" I asked, smiling at the weathered faces who regarded me intently. "Should I introduce myself?"

"No need," he said. "These are famous healers from the Altai Mountains who have come to consult on your case." The group raised their glasses to me, but didn't drink. "They're waiting for you to drink first. Be careful. It's very strong."

It tasted like sweet pomegranate juice. I was thirsty and emptied the glass. The pressure and fatigue of the past few weeks had left me drained. The rose wine tipped me over the brink. My vision blurred; I couldn't keep my eyes open. Sergey helped me to a cabin where I slid into a feather bed between clean white sheets and surrendered to a rare, perfect sleep, knowing that the dangers of life were locked outside Baba Lydia's hedge of pink roses.

I slept for a day and a night. People came into the room to burn incense and discuss my disease. Some of them entered my dreams, probing into my third eye and marveling at the tangled blockage that resembled the gnarled root of an oak tree. They prodded the knot with their fingers, tugging at roots that went into my brain. Each tug loosed memories of my forgotten childhood. I tried to awaken from the nightmare, but couldn't. Instead, I floated above myself, observing the shamans from the gallery of an operating theater. Under surgical lights, I watched them remove the root from my forehead and expand it to the size of a basketball, its surface smooth and impenetrable. The shamans poked and probed until they found a latch that popped it open. A huge, tormented figure rose up out of the open shell and filled the operating room. She held one hand over her eyes, unwilling to confront the memories that tumbled from her mind and rolled down her gown. She stretched her other arm up to the stars, but couldn't reach them. She was trapped, tethered to the floor.

"What does this mean?" I called to the shamans. "Is that me?"

"You are a prisoner of magic," a shaman said. "It's very strong." They began to chant. My forehead exploded in pain. I retreated deeper into sleep.

Later, Sergey's glowing form appeared inside my sinus. He sat in the lotus position with his palms up, light flickering from his fingers. "Let go of knowledge," he whispered. "Free yourself from everything you believe. You must do this to break the curse that a magician has wedged in your mind."

Sometime during the night, the barefoot girl brought me a bowl of soup. I was enticed awake by its rich aroma. My stomach growled, but my head pounded. I was out of prednisone. The tumors were swelling again. I stared at the soup, too groggy to eat. I awoke at daybreak to a symphony of birdcalls. A cool breeze stirred the lace curtains and I smelled porridge.

The headache was gone, and I was hungry. I finished off the cold soup and found my shoes beside the bed. The puppy had eaten through the laces and shredded the soles. I wrapped myself in a blanket and stepped barefoot into the garden in search of breakfast.

Time slowed in the pale stillness. I heard the rustling of leaves as flowers lifted their faces toward the light. Dew beaded on vegetables, reflected the sun. Blood-red poppies floated like rubies in low-lying mist. A towheaded child tossed scraps to hens that pecked the earth.

Other guests were stirring, walking through the gardens in silence. I followed a path to the gazebo. Sergey sat there in the lotus position – exactly as I'd seen him in my dream. He didn't speak. His eyes were closed, but I heard his thoughts. "The oak tree, *Dub*, is calling you," said his voice in my head. I hadn't noticed an oak tree. I stepped up onto the gazebo to see above the mist. In the middle of the compound stood an ancient oak, the largest I'd ever seen, with a trunk ten feet across and arching leafy branches. "Dub has invited you to go to her." I glanced at Sergey, doubting the voice that sounded like his, but I walked toward the oak, drawn by her beauty and the hum that emanated from her. Layers of light wrapped her in a brilliant cocoon. I entered the energy field of the she-tree and let go of doubt until nothing existed but Dub and me. "Touch her," said Sergey.

I pressed my hands against her bark, but Dub had no substance and neither did I. My life energy slid into her and melded with an ancient spirit who had seen a thousand summers. I felt her phloem and xylem in my veins. Leaves sprouted from my fingers, and warmed in the sun, collecting life from its light. I tried to hum with her but my sinus burned, creating discord in the harmony. My hum became a strangled croaking. I was out of synch, gripped by terror, suddenly afraid of being trapped alive in the wood of the tree. I started to struggle. "Let go of your fear," Sergey's voice said. He was beside me, pressing his thumbs into my forehead, intensifying the pain until it was unbearable. "Breathe in … hold it … " I squirmed, the pressure built, the fire in my brain was horrendous, the hum of the oak amplified into a scream. "Exhale!" Sergey bellowed. "Blow!"

Making salad in Aunt Lydia's garden.

I blew with the force of a typhoon. Demons flew out of my leafy fingers and were scorched by the sun, shrieking and sizzling. They bawled as they burned leaving only the hum and Sergey naked beside me. He was touching my body with his mouth and his hands. I surrendered to the tree and to the shaman, who entered me, expanding my universe until it spread into an endless vacuum of dark matter. I was moaning, ready to explode; "Let go," he shouted; and I released every tangled fiber, every shred of pain in my body and mind until time flowed through me unhindered from the earth to the sky and back again. "It's over," he said.

When I arrived home at SeaTac Airport four days later, I felt like I'd been gone for months instead of days. "Expanded time," the shamans had explained. With no clocks in the compound, time had flowed in its own variable rhythms. The puppy had finished with my shoes. They were now tied to my feet with mismatched twine. My hair had grown over an inch into a shaggy dark thatch, my eyebrows had thickened into a solid line across my forehead. I could feel an exuberant moustache on my lip.

I hadn't seen my face in a mirror since arriving in Starye Krem. Baba Lydia did not allow mirrors – or soap or deodorant. Without enough water for bathing, cleansing meant sweating naked in a heated banya followed by dowsing with a small bucket of cold water. I definitely needed to clean myself up before picking up my children at their father's home.

I waited at the luggage carousel, hoping that I wouldn't encounter anyone I knew. My suitcase was the first to slide onto the luggage conveyor. It had been in good condition when I checked it in Simferopol. Now it was wrapped in clear plastic and spattered with chicken poop and feathers. I grabbed the handle and turned for a quick exit when I heard, "Juliette? Is that you?"

I looked up into the face of my attending physician, the one who had told me not to come back to Overlake two weeks ago. "Hi, Steve," I said, extending my hand and noticing that my fingernails were broken and dirty from digging in the garden. I had mantra bracelets woven from dried herbs on each wrist.

"CT scan on Monday," he said, tapping my forehead. "At Overlake."

I showed up Monday washed, shaved, plucked, and deodorized, ready to accept the verdict and have the surgery. I had let go of fear and was no longer wary of the future. But it wasn't necessary. The tumors were gone.

I expected that my colleagues would be intrigued by my healing – that research could be done, and papers written. Instead, the anomaly was immediately walled off with silence and disinterest.

After a while, I was relieved to leave it that way.

Chapter Eight

CHORT THE DEMON ON MY SHOULDER

Moscow, Russia – Winter 1993

In Russia, a national uproar followed Olga Bedinskaya's television exposé. In response, the Russian government sent Olga with a delegation of doctors, officials and lawmakers to America to witness and report on birthing conditions in the United States. I met up with the group in Washington DC where they were meeting with members of Congress. When the speeches were done, Olga took me aside and introduced me to the director of Roscosmos, the Russian equivalent of NASA. The distraught woman took my hand and dissolved into tears. "You must think that we are monsters – that we don't care for our children." She sobbed. I patted her back sympathetically, hiding my pleasure at her emotional response. If a powerful and influential Soviet leader, a renowned woman scientist, publicly acknowledged the terrible conditions and need for change, then things were bound to improve.

Members of the Russian delegation helped broker an agreement with the Second Medical Institute of Moscow to open a new training facility

Moscow Peace Parade, May 1992. Unknown to me at the time, the building behind me is the Vysotka. Arrow points to my future office on the 18th floor.

called the MiraMed Center for Maternal and Infant Health on the fourth floor of the birth house at Hospital 70. Russian staff salaries were provided by the Moscow Ministry of Health. USAID funded the American side of our training program. Pharmaceutical and medical equipment companies supplied the center as a means of introducing their products to Soviet markets. Throughout 1992, MiraMed volunteers drummed up donations from American hospitals – refurbished anesthesia machines, diagnostic ultrasound machines, and sterilizers. Lufthansa generously provided free shipping.

Just after New Year's Day in 1993 I flew with a group of American doctors and nurses to Moscow to open the newly remodeled and equipped MiraMed Center with an international press conference organized by CNN. The next day, we began training Russian staff to make birth houses medically sound and sensitive to the needs of mothers and infants. We changed policy so the doors of the birth house were unlocked, allowing families to visit for the first time. That resulted in more media exposés when shocked family members photographed the dilapidated facilities in patient care areas and demanded reforms. The city tried to keep the angry fathers from speaking to the media. It didn't work.

The doors were immediately relocked, and families once again forced to send baskets of food and notes of encouragement to the mothers via ropes lowered out of windows and to write messages in the snow. There were no telephones for patients.

The CNN piece resulted in coverage from news networks around the world. *Money Magazine* arranged to send a journalist, Beth Fenner, to do a feature article. Donations flowed in and MiraMed's programs expanded. I was moving fast, flushed with success and soaking up accolades from both sides of the Atlantic.

Sadly, no one had told me about the little Russian demon Chort, who sat on my left shoulder waiting for me to get too full of myself and say something foolishly optimistic. I'd seen Russians spit three times on their left shoulders, but no one explained that they were spitting on Chort, nor did they warn me of the mayhem that tiny demon was capable of unleashing. In 1993, I was oblivious to Chort's curse on success.

We suffered minor setbacks like the pipe that burst, spraying us with superheated steam and shorting out our first anesthesia machine. Steam heating pipes embedded in old cement walls were rusting and exploding all over the city, causing televisions to short-circuit and set apartments on fire. Telltale rust stains ran down the outside of most buildings. Now I understood why Russians hung their carpets on the walls instead of spreading them on the floor.

As a precaution, I pushed the sofa bed of my tiny studio apartment against the only wall covered by carpet and unplugged the Soviet-made television set. The heat from the pipes was stifling. I couldn't turn it off. If I opened the complicated, double-paned windows even an inch, the temperature dropped below freezing. But the rent was $25/week. I could tolerate the heat for that price. No one told me that the former occupant had died at thirty-five of leukemia or that people living on that side of the apartment building commonly died of blood cancers. Nor did anyone mention that the red brick building blocking the skyline was the nuclear cyclotron. Chort was having a good chuckle at my expense.

Yuri rented cheap apartments in the same building for the other American doctors and nurses and the hospital sent a van every morning to drive us to Hospital 70. The winter days were short. The sun didn't rise until about 9:00 A.M. and set again by 4:00 in the afternoon. We ate breakfast of kasha and black bread with the medical staff and lunched in the doctors' room on borscht, black bread, Russian cheese, and tea with jam. Our days were spent in the labor and delivery rooms or conducting classes on the new equipment and instruments. We returned to our apartments at about 6 P.M., where we ate the food we'd brought from the US. When that was gone, we ventured into the black markets or stood in line at the state market, hoping to score a few cans of imported American chicken legs that Muscovites had dubbed "Bush legs." Typically, all we could get was hot dogs and canned peas.

Moscow was not a welcoming place to dine out. The Hotel Prague on Old Arbat Street had an affordable restaurant if you didn't mind smoking waiters who dropped ashes in the food. The Slavyanskaya Bazaar had burned to the ground in an arson fire on New Year's Eve. Trentmos (Trenton-Moscow) Restaurant had done a brisk business with Americans and Europeans until the Fourth of July party, when the Russian partner was sprayed with bullets from an AK 47. Enterprise in Moscow was apt to be deadly.

Sasha from the Peace Committee sometimes invited me for European cuisine at the Casino Royale or Kropotkinskaya 33, and for Italian food at Patio Pizza. I'd give him enough of a report to justify his government expense account. Mostly, he liked telling me about his life in the KGB.

After vodka and cognac one night, he pinched his thumb and first finger together in an exaggerated fashion and said, "I've been this close to Florida. I was stationed in Havana."

"In Cuba? When were you there?"

"1961 to 1963," he said. "I was very young ... and much thinner." He patted his belly.

I froze. 1962 was the year of the Cuban missile crisis. For weeks, every television and radio had been tuned to President Kennedy's dire warnings about Russians in Cuba and the threat of nuclear war. I stared at my food, speechless. I was dining in Moscow with the enemy.

Sasha was unperturbed. He cut into his steak. "Cuba was one big picnic – absolute paradise. It was never cold. Who could imagine – a land with no snow? Lots of good food and everybody was happy. Those hot-blooded Cuban girls ... "

"Wait a minute," I interrupted his monologue. "What about the nuclear warheads?"

He gave me a blank look.

"The nuclear missiles, Sasha. Remember the standoff between Kennedy and Khrushchev? We nearly went to nuclear war."

"Missiles in Cuba? A mere diversion," he said. "We had them on our submarines – polaris class. There was no need for bases in Cuba. If we'd wanted to nuke America, we could have done it from the sea. Besides, I was too busy as an interpreter with the Russian troops at the Bay of Pigs to follow American propaganda. I polished my American accent in the internment camps after your invasion failed."

"I don't understand." I tried to remember the details of the Cuban missile crisis. I was only thirteen at the time and in hospital with a broken arm. "Russian troops?"

"The Americans never had a chance. Russians were waiting on the beach, not Cubans." Sasha raised his arm to order another cognac. I ducked like he was about to slap me. The waiter calmly re-filled my wine glass. "Are we having a crisis of conscience, Angelova?" Sasha smirked. "Does it bother you to be dining with your nation's perceived enemy?"

"Are you my enemy?" I asked, searching his brown eyes, teetering on the edge of a schism between "us and them" – determined not to fall in.

"Of course not," he snorted. "That was long ago. We are all friends now."

"Yes, the future is what matters," I said, relieved and a little drunk. "The future for all of us is our children."

"That's right," he slurred. "And I say hurrah that Americans are building a better birth house. You are free to do what you want. I write reports and you get free dinners. Babies are born. Everybody's happy."

"Why don't you come and visit the center next week?" I invited him, meaning it. "We're making great progress. Come see for yourself. Write a first-hand report. You can take pictures."

Sasha recoiled. "No, thank you." He up-ended his cognac. "You do what you do, and I'll do what I do. Now, forget that ancient history. Eat your steak."

I did forget. I was much too busy at the birth center to think about politics or the long-ago missile crisis – the war that hadn't happened. I'd just discovered that Russian doctors were still encouraging mothers to abandon their babies and using the forced two-hour separation to prevent them from bonding. If newborns were placed in their mothers' arms, not a single mother refused her baby. But if the two-hour "live or let die" rule was in force, one third of the mothers rejected their children. Doctors at the birth house were reluctant to tell me what happened to abandoned babies. I wanted to know what the "baby house" orphanages were like. I wanted to see one.

The journalists with *Soviet* Women's World magazine were more forthcoming than the medical staff. I learned that eight hundred thousand children were growing up in institutions that resembled eighteenth-century poorhouses. They arranged an invitation for me to visit a Moscow orphanage.

"Child House Number Fifty-seven is one of the best ones in Russia," said the editor. "It's a good place for you to start. Baby houses are strictly off limits to foreigners. Talk to the director of Fifty-seven, Tamara Alexeyevna. She has influence with the Department of Social Protection. If you get into a Baby House, we'd love to do an exposé."

On the eve of Russian Christmas in January 1993, Yuri, his wife Irina, and I loaded a box of gifts into the back of their Zhigulli station wagon for the children at Child House Number Fifty-seven.

We drove through the darkened city in light snowfall. The roads were in even worse condition than when I'd first arrived in 1990. But there were positive changes, too. Church bells that had been silenced for seventy years were chiming, calling people to service. *Babushkas* and *dedushkas* – grannies and grandpas – hurried along the streets with grandchildren in tow. Families filed through the ruins of churches lit only by candles. Every week there were more bells and worshippers. When Bishop Alexander rang the Gallitzin bell for Easter Service in the little church at Hospital 70, 15,000 people signed the guest book. The rotted wooden floor collapsed under their weight and church services continued outside in the snow.

At Child House Number Fifty-seven, ninety-three children ages seven to seventeen were dressed up for Christmas dinner – the boys with scrubbed faces and cowlicks, the girls with huge bows in their hair. We gave our box of gifts to the teachers for Father Frost's bag and were escorted to the dining room where rows of tables were set with plates of black bread and bricks of chocolate-flavored lard. Paper decorations were strung from the ceiling. Paper bouquets decked every table.

We took our places with the sixteen- and seventeen-year-olds. The younger children sat at smaller tables, waiting for their dinner of borscht, piroshky stuffed with cabbage and egg, boiled potatoes, and hotdogs. Each course was served from a tin pot carried by one of the children. As the guest of honor, I was given three hotdogs instead of the usual ration of one per person. Fortunately, I had mastered the technique of cutting them in thirds and swallowing each piece whole – the only way I could get them down.

After dinner, we had front row seats in the gymnasium. The children sang, danced, recited poetry and presented me with a crown of paper flowers. Then Father Frost appeared with his flowing white beard and blue robes trimmed in fur. He was followed by the Ice Maiden in a blue gown and headdress embroidered with pearls. She called the name of each child, who came forward to receive a gift from Father Frost's sack and a *praenik*, a holiday honey cake. The teenaged tough guys who heckled the program from the back of the room became children again when their names were called for gifts.

Toys for Christmas at Child House Fifty-seven.)

After the party, we joined the orphanage director for tea. "I compliment you, Tamara Alexeyevna," Yuri said. "This is a fine facility, even in these terrible economic times."

"We do our best," said Tamara, pouring tea and opening a box of Red October chocolates. "These children are the lucky ones. Most orphans are sent to the countryside. They are on the verge of starvation now."

"We never hear about those orphans," said Irina.

"Of course not. Look at how they're kept from view." Tamara pointed to a Ministry of Education map mounted on the wall. "The largest orphanages are in tiny villages along the Volga River. The only way to get to most of them is by boat."

"Can we visit those orphanages?" I asked. "Maybe MiraMed can help."

"It's impossible at the moment – the river is frozen. Wait until summer," she said. "You can take a passenger ship from Moscow to St. Petersburg. Every place you stop will have an orphanage."

"I particularly want to visit Baby House Number Six in Yaroslavl." I told her about little Angela.

"Baby houses are nearly impossible to arrange. They don't want foreigners to see the conditions there," she said. "I'll see what I can do if you promise me – no hidden cameras, at least not the first time."

Yuri and Irina discussed the river cruises on the way home. "I've always wanted to go on one of those ships," said Irina. "I've seen them going up and down the river all my life."

"I'll look into it," said Yuri.

The wind howled and rattled my apartment windows all night. I couldn't sleep thinking about what Tamara Alexeyevna had said about conditions in the baby houses. How was Angela? Was she safe and warm in her bed? I finally got up, wrapped myself in the duvet, and stood at the window. As clouds race across the face of the winter moon, I imagined rows of iron beds with little red heads on white pillows. I recited the children's poem to them: "Good Night Moon, Goodnight stars, Goodnight air, Goodnight noises everywhere… "

When the hospital van arrived at dawn to drive our team to the airport, we were waiting with our luggage stacked in the drive. My colleagues looked tired. They huddled silently in the back of the van. Two weeks of long workdays in difficult conditions with bad food had left them with head colds. I sensed their resentment as they gazed at me askance. I couldn't blame them. From their point of view, they'd been doing the frontline soldiering while I was schmoozing with city officials, and the

Enjoying a farewell dinner of hotdogs and peas.

KGB. I'd had dinners with Sasha at the Casino Royale while they ate hot-dogs and cold peas. It must have seemed glamorous.

Should I tell them about the lunch with the drunken minister who grabbed me and tried to spit vodka into my mouth? I'd managed to get his signature on a contract before he passed out. Or the deputy minister of health who invited me to a party at his flat. When I got there, I was the only guest. I went into the bathroom and pretended to vomit, getting his signature after he called me a taxi. I'd rather be where they were, but as the project grew, I needed to run interference.

At Sheremetyevo Airport, the mood lightened at the prospect of leaving this dark, sad place. We entered the line for Passport Control with our passports and visas in hand. Once through that first hurdle, everyone relaxed a bit. In the line for Customs Inspection, our dignified veneer cracked, and we started joking – laughing shamelessly at the eccentricities of the Russian people. Success stories were shared, and the group grew giddy at the thought of going home.

Of course, that little demon Chort was listening to our careless remarks. We were nearly to the front of the long line when a fracas broke out among the group of North Vietnamese ahead of us. Each one of them carried or dragged a huge, plaid shuttle bag. Customs agents were emptying the bags onto the floor, scattering plastic kitchen utensils, cheap pots and pans, stuffed toys, and other hideous Soviet wares. The women started screaming. A man threw a punch. The airport police were called over to break up the shrieking melee. Guards beat the man with cudgels. Blood was spilt.

Our group froze, mouths open in shock. We tried to look inconspicuous, which was impossible. We were a foot taller than the Vietnamese who hid behind us until the security police grabbed them. They were herded and frog-marched back to the airport lobby. The police threw their shuttle bags after them just as Aeroflot announced the flight to Hanoi. The Vietnamese gathered up their belongings and got back into line.

At that moment, a Customs official looked at me and said: "*Sleduyushchy* – next."

"Come on," I said to the group, but they didn't follow. They were pawing through their bags and checking receipts to show that we weren't carrying any plastic utensils, just some souvenirs. "This has nothing to do with us." I insisted. I was right – no one looked in our luggage. We were waved through to the gate while the ruckus started up again behind us.

"It's their own fault, those bloody Vietnamese," scoffed a well-dressed Russian man in the Lufthansa check-in line. "They buy up Soviet goods on the cheap from state stores and sell them at a big profit in Hanoi."

"Ah, they are capitalists," said someone from our group.

"It shouldn't be allowed." The Russian socialist scowled. "When they're done, there's nothing left for us to buy." The line moved ahead. Our Lufthansa Airbus was boarding.

"I told you they wouldn't bother us." I said to the group, trying to stanch their waning enthusiasm for Russia. I'd been horrified by the violence but kept my face set in a smile. I couldn't afford to lose their support. I wanted them to go home feeling good about what they'd accomplished and ready to recruit other professionals to volunteer. "This is between the Russians and the Vietnamese. It's their fight." I insisted.

The group still looked pretty grim as they found their seats, ordered drinks and slept all the way home.

Chapter Nine

THE INCURABLES

Volga River, Summer 1993

I returned to Moscow for the month of September in 1993 – my longest stretch of time away from my children. My ex-husband had time off and wanted to split the summer. I planned to spend two weeks at the birth house at Hospital 70 and two weeks on a Russian river ship sailing north to St. Petersburg, visiting orphanages along the Volga River.

I settled in the small apartment next to Yuri and Irina's flat and walked to the Kolomenskoe Metro every morning to catch the Green Line Train. A shortcut took me through the grounds of an abandoned sausage factory. Homeless pensioners were sheltering there – more every day as the economy deteriorated. When the ruble tumbled yet again and the price of bread doubled, the city's elderly were forced to stand on street corners hawking the last of their prized possessions to buy food. Old men sold their war medals, women sold their wedding dresses and dancing shoes. Eventually, they sold their apartments and moved into abandoned factories where they begged passersby for kopeks.

The summer of 1993 had been particularly miserable for Muscovites. The weather was hot and rainy nearly every day, the humidity unbearable. By September, I should have seen *dachniks* – summer farmers – selling their prized homegrown tomatoes, cucumbers, and radishes in front of every Metro station. But even onions and potatoes were ruined, and it was too wet for mushrooms.

The oppressive weather was the least of the people's problems, though it lay heavily on their souls. The Soviet Union had splintered into fifteen separate nations and the Russian Federation was in the grips of political and economic struggles that threatened to pull it apart.

The fledgling Russian nation was plunging ahead into uncharted territory. No one was sure what it all meant. Churches were reopening, statues of Lenin and Stalin were torn down across the country until none were left standing. Street signs were removed, and the streets renamed which led to a great deal of confusion. Train stations and entire cities were discarding Soviet era nomenclatures and reverting to pre-revolutionary names.

People clung to normality but that was shifting every day. New laws contradicted old laws though both remained in force. Change was painfully imminent. The old socialist systems were unsustainable, sinking under their bureaucratic weight in a new market economy. Those who couldn't adapt would be left behind, destined to shelter wherever they could.

A constant threat of violence hung in the air as the crime rate rose and police became corrupted by the new class of oligarch millionaires.

"*Shto delat* – What's to be done?" people would say to one another with a shrug. In the privacy of their homes, however, revolution was the topic of discussion. Memories of other turbulent times in their nation's history were shared by those who remembered. Muscovites were arming themselves with black-market weapons, preferring American pistols because they were the easiest to find ammunition for. Mafia groups fought nightly gun battles in central Moscow. A bomb detonated outside KGB headquarters at Lubyanka Square one night setting off every car alarm in a two-kilometer radius.

I kept working. Like my Russian colleagues, hard work seemed the only way to counter the inevitable. Unlike them, however, I had a plane ticket out of the country. I could leave at any time. I missed my children terribly. I'd never been away so long. But returning to Seattle wasn't going to bring us together. They were on a month-long fishing trip in Northern Canada with their father and his new wife. All that awaited me was an empty house on Queen Anne Hill.

I decided that I was less concerned about revolution in Russia than loneliness in Seattle. Besides, I was waitlisted for a cruise up the Volga River to visit orphanages with Yuri and Irina. The cruises had been suspended for most of the rain-soaked summer, but I still hoped for a break in the weather.

We made remarkable progress at the MiraMed Center at Hospital 70 despite the political upheaval and daily thunderstorms. We had funding now from the State Department to partner with Magee Women's Hospital of Pittsburgh and expand the medical training. Three Magee people joined our board and visited Moscow, wisely staying in luxury hotels downtown. They looked prosperous and promised to provide much needed fundraising and prestige to our project. We planned to have our first combined MiraMed-Magee board meeting in Seattle at the beginning of October.

By late September, I was exhausted – everyone was. The Russian doctors were drinking on the job and popping amphetamines to stay awake.

Crime was worse than ever. Moscow was at the breaking point when a miracle happened. The clouds over the city cleared and blue sky shone through. Muscovites felt sun on their faces for the first time in months. I sat on the Puchkovs' tiny balcony and shared the city's collective sigh of relief. Later that day, the cruise line rang. The ships were sailing again. We were booked on the last cruise of the season.

The fine weather held. Yuri, Irina, and I took a taxi to *Retchnoi Vokzal* – Moscow's river station where a fleet of identical cruise ships were docked, each one named for a Communist Party luminary. Ours, the *Dzerzhinsky*, was named after Felix Dzerzhinsky, the ruthless chief of the CHEKA, the post-revolutionary secret police. The ships would soon be renamed after Russian poets.

Yuri and Irina Puchkov

"You are about to see how most Russians live," said Irina as we stood at the rusty deck railing facing a wide expanse of river. "I think you will be shocked."

"Why?"

"There's no electricity in many places, no running water or toilets. We have central heating in Moscow, but country people keep warm with *pechkas* – wood-burning stoves. They sleep on them at night."

"A warm pechka is very comfortable – especially when it's forty below zero outside," said Yuri. "You should try it sometime."

"There are no telephones, no television," Irina mused. "A village might have one radio in the public library. There's no reliable post."

"How do the orphanages know we're coming?"

"We gave letters to conductors on the local trains," said Yuri. "It's our very old, very reliable Russian system."

"Did you hear back from them?"

"Not necessary. I sent the date of our arrival and the name of the ship. A foreign visitor will be the biggest event of their year. They aren't about to miss it."

"What about Baby House No. 6 in Yaroslavl? Are they expecting us? Is Angela there?"

"We'll find out when we get there," said Irina.

"Why don't you get settled in your cabin," said Yuri, squinting at his wristwatch. "Then meet us on the upper deck. The ship casts off in thirty minutes. You'll want to see Moscow from the water."

I unpacked, stashed my suitcase under the bunk, and climbed the metal stairs topside. The *Dzerzhinsky* was old and needed paint, the toilets were communal holes in the deck, the showers were outside with skimpy curtains, but the ship was scrubbed spotless.

Passengers were gathering on deck for departure. I joined them with a growing sense of excitement. I would soon be exploring forbidden territory on a Russian boat. I was thrilled to be leaving the city and breathed in the cool river breeze that smelled like algae instead of diesel.

Departing Moscow River Station

For the Russians, however, there was no joy. Some leaned over the rail, waving sadly at family and friends on shore. Others stood scowling with their arms crossed as if we were leaving for prison instead of a holiday. The Muscovites had carried their sense of doom onto the ship. For them, this cruise represented a few days of respite before their world was plunged into unknown territory. They feared the chaos. They knew that people would die.

I understood their sadness, but the fear was theirs, not mine. Immediately following the cruise, I would finish the last touches at Hospital 70 and head to Sheremetovo Airport for the flight home to my children in Seattle. I would leave the pressure-cooker that was Moscow behind and continue my work in America. I had a board to build, funds to raise, donations to collect.

Yuri and Irina joined me at the rail just as the loudspeaker chimed "bing, bing, bong … " and a cheerful voice announced that: "We are now leaving Moscow and should enjoy excellent weather all the way to St. Petersburg. Dinner will be served at six o'clock."

The moorings were loosed. The smokestack above our heads gave a tooth-rattling blast, the ship's engines revved, and the *Dzerzhinsky* slid over glassy water toward the Moscow-Volga Canal.

"You will see for yourself how quickly civilization fades away," said Yuri. "That's why foreigners haven't been allowed to travel on these ships. They might discover how primitive we are."

I looked around me, listening for languages other than Russian. "Am I the only non-Russian on this ship?"

"Yes, of course. We had to pull some strings for you," said Yuri with a grin. "Your friends high in government helped."

"The Peace Committee?"

"Umm, not so much," said Irina with a sour look. "Now watch the shore and pay attention to our tragic history."

We glided past acres of lumber yards with huge mechanical jaws that slid along overhead tracks, lifting forty-foot logs like pick-up sticks and dropping them onto barges.

The river narrowed and we slipped into a concrete-walled canal – the Moscow-Volga Canal. Sunlight sparkled on the water. Gulls circled in the air but the mood of the passengers on deck grew darker still. An old man with medals and thick glasses was weeping. Soon, most had made their way downstairs to the bar where a folk group was singing sad songs. We were the only ones left at the rail.

"Why is everyone so unhappy?" I wondered. "This feels like a funeral."

"In a way, it is." Yuri sighed. "Political prisoners died by the hundreds building this canal. They were buried in the concrete walls – doctors, writers, artists, professors, politicians, our best people."

"Such a waste of good life," said Irina. "There are far too many unhappy ghosts in this country, too much sadness. It's why Russians don't smile. Why should we smile?"

I learned from Yuri that Stalin had ordered this canal built to connect the Volga and Moscow Rivers to the sea. In the end, it was all for nothing – a complete failure, an ecological disaster. It caused the flooding of dozens of villages, displaced thousands of people.

"Whole villages are under water." Yuri shook his head. "Ultimately, the canal was too shallow for ocean-going ships. Today, goods are still transported on small family-run freighters, the way it's been done forever. This farmland was ruined, lives destroyed, our intelligensia class buried in cement for what? Nothing changed for the better."

I no longer felt like smiling either. I stood in silence until Irina patted my hand and said, "Excuse us please. We must dress for dinner."

They left, but I lingered at the railing, staring into the dark water, wondering whose ghosts were down there looking back at me with mournful eyes. "I'm sorry," I said aloud, then turned to go.

Dinner in the smoky dining room was a hearty, greasy meal of borscht, ground-meat "cutlets," potatoes, and cabbage. The boat reeked of cabbage,

ANGELS OVER MOSCOW: LIFE, DEATH AND HUMAN TRAFFICKING

the open toilets and Russian cigarettes. The mood of the passengers improved with champagne and vodka. Their energy levels rose from morose to nearly frantic by the time the dance band cranked up their speakers in the lounge. Loud music blared most of the day and night. A disco band performed in the bar and a folk ensemble played on deck all night. I had no choice but to join the drunken reverie. We danced and sang, raising toast after toast to better times beneath the full September moon.

After breakfast, I joined the Puchkovs on the sun deck. They were determined to use this time to improve my Russian grammar. Yuri had flashcards and made me conjugate verbs.

"I don't understand it," he grimaced. "We teach you eloquent Russian and you still talk like a *Polshka* – a Polish woman. Not an American, mind you, but a Pole. We are going to teach you to speak like a Muscovite."

Eventually, he gave up and left to play cards, leaving Irina and me free to gossip. Irina was a PhD epidemiologist from the Cancer Research Center. She had Asian eyes and a wild thatch of straight, Mongolian hair that she called "an explosion in a macaroni factory." Irina's ancestors were Decembrists – revolutionaries of noble birth who were exiled to Siberia in 1825 after attempting to assassinate the Tsar. Irina never forgave them for failing. "I wouldn't have missed," she said.

I asked about Sergey Popov. I hadn't seen or heard from him since I'd left him in Simferopol. "Dr. Lapukhin told me that Sergey is living in a secret shaman's compound in the Altai Republic of Siberia. He didn't say why."

"It's never easy to be a spiritual being like him, not in any culture at any time in history," she said. "Even now, it's risky for a shaman to be too public."

"What do you mean?"

"Their powers prove the existence of the supernatural entities beyond the control of Church or State," said Irina. "And they used to practiced sexual orgies and human sacrifice."

"Hmmm," I said, recalling my experience with Sergey and the oak tree.

"Shamans can enter the human soul to heal it, or devour it. They can curse a family line for generations. As Christians, we believe that only God should influence a human soul through Jesus Christ. Any other influence is demonic."

"Is Dr. Popov in trouble because of me?"

"He took you away from the Peace Committee – right out from under the noses of the KGB." Irina laughed. "What do you think?"

"I'm sorry," I said.

"He knew the risks and made his choice. He's very famous, you know. His work with you made him even more famous. The Peace Committee will have to get over it – eventually."

"Will he be all right?"

"He's safe in the heart chakra of the planet. The shamans have had compounds in the Altai Mountains for centuries. Did you meet his grandmother? She's quite famous as well."

"Baba Lydia? Yes, and other shamans." I paused to remember how they had taught me to listen to the counsel of plants and trees, and to channel the healing powers of light. "How was it that they could speak English, when the Russian doctors can't?"

"Those shamans don't speak English." Irina laughed, crinkling her eyes. "Not one word."

"I understood everything they said." I insisted. "Dr. Popov speaks perfect English."

"Does he? Remember that shamans can enter your mind. That's why the Soviets never trusted them. You cannot lie to a shaman. He hears the truth in the language of your soul and that makes him impossible to control."

The loudspeaker chimed "bing, bing, bong … " and announced that we were docking for an excursion into Mishkin, a little town that was once saved by a mouse.

The Russian tourists lined up to go ashore – the men wore khakis and sunglasses, ladies in cool cotton dresses and broad-brimmed straw hats, children in shorts and caps. They seemed a bit more relaxed today.

After they'd departed to visit the local monastery with their walking guide and maps, Yuri pointed to a flat-bed motor cart that waited idling at the end of the wooden pier. An old man and a young woman with bright yellow hair were waving enthusiastically. "There's our transportation to the *Detsky Dom Neizlechimyy*."

"What does neizlechimyy mean?"

"Incurables." Irina winced. "This is the Orphan House of the Incurables."

"It won't be pleasant," said Yuri in a typical understatement.

"I'm Mikhala Dimitrovna, director of Mishkin Orphan House," said the cheerful woman, shaking my hand. She reminded me of Yuri's smiling cousin who ran the ghastly abortion clinic in Moscow. Their exaggerated bonhomie must be something that Russians learned in school. "This is *Dada Losha* – Uncle Losha."

Dada said, "Climb in back and hold on. Our roads don't have potholes, our potholes have roads." We laughed at the popular joke and boarded the cart. I sat cross-legged on the rough planking, holding onto the metal side rails as the cart revved and jerked along a rutted dirt track.

"Welcome to Mishkin," Mikhala shouted as we bounced up a hill and into a forest, going much too fast. We stopped in a clearing above a small river. On the other side, a two-story building resembled a stone schoolhouse, except that it was surrounded by sties and squealing pigs.

"Step out, please," said Mikhala. "There is our orphan house. Unfortunately, our cart cannot go further – the river is too high. We must walk from here." We followed a winding footpath that disappeared into a stream. We crossed it on stepping-stones.

"How do you get your supplies?" Yuri inquired.

"From the Volga, and by cart up the hill. We have some strong boys. They carry it the rest of the way. There is a road in back, but it's blocked. Trees fell and knocked out the power lines. We're waiting for repairs."

"How long?" asked Irina.

"Two years," said Mikhala with a shrug. "*Shto delat* – What to do?"

"Look at the windows," said Irina, pointing. "I think we've been spotted." Small faces were appearing, followed by shouts. A dozen children burst into the courtyard, all wearing identical striped uniforms, their heads shaved except for a fringe of bangs. The rest stayed upstairs, watching through the glass.

"Are these all boys?" I asked.

"Girls and boys," said Mikhala. "We shave their heads in the spring and fall. It's lice in the winter and ring worm in summer."

"What are their ages?"

"We have thirty-five children from seven to seventeen. And then there are the incurables. There are usually about twenty of those."

"Teenaged boys and girls together?" I asked, thinking I'd misunderstood the word "incurable." "Doesn't that lead to problems like pregnancy?"

"Never," she said, looking away.

Irina threw me a withering look and I dropped the topic. Two children approached – one with a plate of bread and the other a bowl of salt, the traditional Russian greeting. "Here are our oldest girls to welcome you as honored guests. Please take some bread and salt. We will have tea and the children will sing for you." I tried to take photographs but Mikhala insisted that I put my camera away. "I'm sorry. Our bosses in Mishkin won't allow it."

We sat outside at a plank table laid with bread and homemade jam. The wind bent the tops of the trees overhead and the brook gurgled through the forest. It was a lovely pastoral setting until the wind shifted and the stink of pig made me gag. The Russians ignored the stench. I held a piece of bread to my nose like a mask and concentrated on the program of music and poetry performed by the children.

After tea, I learned from Mikhala that the state subsidies had been cut back drastically and a day's food ration for a child was now a bowl of boiled buckwheat and a lump of chocolate-flavored lard on black bread. "Growing children need much more than that."

"What about all those pigs that I can smell?" I asked. "Don't the children eat the pork?"

"Sadly not," said Mikhala. "Those pigs are donated to us each year by the church. We raise them to feed our staff. We have no other way to pay the people who work here."

I changed the conversation. "What happens after the children reach seventeen years and they have to leave here. Do they continue their education?" I asked. How could children who had spent their lives in a forest wearing striped uniforms transition into any kind of life in the cities.

"None of these lost souls are qualified for higher education. They cannot pass the exams because their educations are so poor. I am sad to say that ten percent of them commit suicide within the first year. Many others are recruited into lives of crime or prostitution. They don't live much longer." She shrugged again. "*Shto delat?*--What to do?"

"Where do they come from?" I asked, expecting to hear that they were from rural villages.

"Moscow, mostly," said Mikhala. "They are abandoned by their mothers at birth for one reason or another."

"I've seen how doctors encourage women to abandon their babies," I said. "How could they condemn their children to this awful life?"

"It's better than the alternative," said Mikhala defensively. "If you think this is terrible, there are one million children living on the streets of Moscow and St. Petersburg. When they are caught stealing food or begging, they're sent to a prison and you don't want to imagine what happens there. Here they're fed and have a bed to sleep in. We do the best we can to educate them, hoping that conditions in this country will improve before they grow up."

"Can we go inside?" I asked, looking up the faces in the windows.

Mikhala hesitated until Yuri said, "Americans are very generous. If there's anything that you need, they will send it if they can." I was already scheming how to get supplies.

"All right," she said, giving me a desperate look. "Please don't be too shocked." She unlocked the front door and pushed it open. "We do the best we can with what we have." The stench of the pig sties was nothing compared to the reek of urine that burned my throat, making my eyes water. We followed Mikhala inside. "These are the incurables, sent here to be forgotten and die – but they're human beings, children's souls locked in tormented bodies. We read to them and teach them music." Mikhala unlocked room after room of deformed children. Many were strapped to their beds. "It's for their own protection. They bite themselves and bang their heads. There is no one to watch them most of the time."

"I notice that they're separated by diagnosis," said Yuri. "Down syndrome children are in this room, microcephaly in that one, and here we have congenital heart defects – blue babies."

"That makes it easier for the doctors who come to see them."

"How often do they come?"

"Once a year now that the road is blocked."

A loud blast sounded from the ship. "It's time to go," said Irina. "Our next stop is Yaroslavl."

I felt guilty to feel relieved. We crossed the river and piled onto the cart. It started to rain.

Most of the passengers were packed into the bar or stayed in their cabins to avoid the downpour. I found a place on deck sheltered by a lifeboat and sat watching the sky fall. The balalaika band started playing inside. Vodka was poured, voices grew louder, laughter raucous. I didn't want to go in. I suddenly felt like the foreigner that I was. What was I doing in this dystopian world where children were abandoned in institutions like Mishkin – sent there to die unloved?

I started to cry. My chest burned with yearning to hold my own children – to put my nose to their skin and smell their healthy kid scent. I'd been gone twenty-seven days. I ached to hear their voices, settle their silly disputes, drive them to soccer. I wanted to run as far as I could from the desperate eyes of the dying children, imprisoned in rooms that reeked of death. But that was what everyone did. That's why they were exiled to a lonely death where no one could see. What kind of person would I be if I didn't do what I could to help?

We docked in Yaroslavl that evening and were met by the director of Baby House Number Six. She informed us that permission to visit had been denied for health reasons. "Foreigners carry diseases," she said, eyeing me suspiciously. I asked her about Angela.

"The little red-head?" Her face crinkled into a smile. "She's a spirited girl, that one."

"Is it possible to see her?"

"Of course. She's too old for the baby house. She's been transferred to Uglich Orphanage."

"Is Uglich far from here?" I asked.

"We sailed past it this morning," said Yuri. "We'll stop on the return."

"You won't be able to see her until school starts," said the director. "The children are all at summer camp. It's two kilometers out of town."

We did stop in Uglich, but as predicted, the orphanage was deserted. We did a walking tour of the monastery and the Church of St. Dimitri on the Blood, our only touristic endeavors.

Our guide was a tall, skinny young man with near-perfect English named Vlad.

Church of St. Dimitri on the Blood, Uglich   Young Vlad Suprunov

Chapter Ten

COUNTER-REVOLUTION

Moscow, Russia – Fall 1993

After the cruise, Yuri and Irina flew to Siberia to visit relatives. I stayed in their flat with Oskar, the Kerry Blue Terrier. Irina's brother would be driving him to their dacha in the morning. I'd be flying home in a few days and could scarcely wait. My only business remaining was a USAID document that needed to be signed and notarized at Hospital 70.

The scorching fall had stretched on into *baba lyeta* – Indian summer. I had the balcony doors and all the windows open, but the apartment was sweltering. There was no relief from the heat – no window shades, air conditioners, or electric fans. People fanned themselves with newspapers and sweated in their underwear. I left the Puchkovs' green plastic telephone in the sun and it melted. It wasn't much use anyway. International calls had to be booked at the post office on Tverskaya Street and local calls involved a great deal of shouting "Allo, allo? Do you hear me?" with silence on the other end.

"Come, Oskar," I said to the Puchkov's panting dog who stared at me with yearning eyes. "We'll be cooler by the river. Let's go to the park."

He perked up at the word park. I snapped on his leash and let him lead me to the elevator. He simpered as the lift rattled down to the lobby, then pulled me through a copse of birch trees that stretched to the street. I waited while he rooted around and marked his territory. It took longer than usual. Poor Oskar was dehydrated and sluggish. His black fur had been clipped short but absorbed the heat of the sun. He panted at my side until we entered the long, cool pedestrian tunnel under Andropovsky Boulevard and emerged in Kolomenskoe Park.

It was cooler under the tall oaks that lined a path to the childhood home of Peter the Great. The lush park sprawled down a sloping hill to the riverbank. Stone skeletons of once-great churches reached skyward above the trees like bony fingers in prayer.

I let Oskar off his leash to drink from the river. Insects hummed, children laughed, and dogs barked. Women strolled in cotton dresses, flirting with men in shirtsleeves. I sat on the grass and swatted mosquitos and black flies. It never got this hot or buggy in Seattle. Instead, it rained two-hundred and seventy days a year. I guess that kept the air cool and the bug population down.

After half an hour, I called to Oskar, who was socializing with a poodle named Natasha, and snapped on his leash. We climbed the steep bank to the bluff that led into a shady orchard. At the crest of the hill, a black Zil limousine idled on the sidewalk. Ivan Ivanovich leaned against the hood in shirtsleeves and sunglasses, smoking. He saw me and ground out his cigarette, ushering me inside the car.

This could only be bad news. I handed him Oskar's leash as I climbed onto the backseat, across from the Colonel. The upholstery felt cool on my bare skin. The Zil was air-conditioned. The Colonel waggled his Sputnik flask in my direction. "Hair of the dog, Angelova?" he offered, and I declined. He took a swig and said, "You must leave the country immediately."

"Excuse me? Leave the country?"

"That's what I said – today, tomorrow morning at the latest."

"But I'll be leaving in two more days. I have my ticket." I argued, trying to wrap my head around this. "I need to do some things at Hospital 70."

"The hospital is closing as we speak. The Ministry of Health has moved your equipment to their offices in the White House for safekeeping. You must change your ticket and go home." He tapped on the window and Ivan Ivanovich opened the door. "Moscow won't be safe for foreigners."

I got out and took Oskar's leash. "I don't know if I can get my ticket changed that fast." Then I added optimistically, "I'll be okay for two more days, surely."

Ivan Ivanovich frowned and spit three times on his left shoulder. I should have done the same, but I'd underestimated Chort once again. The Zil drove away. It turned onto Andropovsky Boulevard and disappeared in traffic.

I was left standing amidst family picnics, Frisbee games, and soaring kites. An occasional radio was broadcasting news, but most were playing rock music. I studied the faces around me. No one seemed concerned.

Yuri and Irina hadn't mentioned anything ominous before leaving for Siberia. How serious could this be? If I had been able to understand the rapid-fire speech of news anchors, I would have known that Moscow was on the cusp of revolution. The Nationalists in Russian Parliament had polarized against liberal globalist President Boris Yeltsin and the Red Army was undeclared. It could go either way. The parliamentarians had barricaded themselves in the White House with a cache of weapons. The next move was up to the military.

I fed Oskar his dinner and switched on the television news. I couldn't follow the frenetic speech of the anxious Russian newscaster. Reporters were speaking faster than usual and cutting to video footage of gunfire. I couldn't understand where it was or what they were saying. I turned off the television and stood on the balcony. Lights shimmered in the heat along the curve of the Moscow River all the way to the Red Square.

The city looked serene but Russian flags flew over the brightly lit Kremlin and White House. That meant they were busy tonight. I tried calling the US Embassy, but no one answered. I dug out my Lufthansa ticket, passport, and visa. My fears were confirmed. My visa had expired during the river trip. That typically involved paying a small fine at the airport, not a big deal – but the airline might not be willing to issue m a new ticket without a current visa. I put the papers and ticket in my fanny pack and fell asleep on the couch. I'd worry about it tomorrow.

In the morning, the sky was clear. It would be another scorcher. I drank coffee on the balcony. Down in the street something wasn't right. By the end of September, families should be returning from their dachas on the trains, hauling bags of fruit and vegetables for winter. Instead, my neighbors were carrying children and belongings toward Kolomenskoe Metro Station. They were leaving town.

I heard televisions and radios tuned to the news in other apartments. I knocked on my neighbors' door. A frazzled Mrs. Belikov opened it and went back to stuffing clothes and food into shuttle bags. Mr. Belikov was cleaning a revolver on the coffee table.

"Come in, Angelova," he said.

"What's happening?" I asked. "I can't understand what's going on."

"Who can?" He waved his cigarette toward Red Square, then pointed it as his gun. "Does my pistol shock you?"

"I'm from Seattle. Everyone has guns – except me."

"Crazy, crazy," shouted Mrs. Belikov from the bedroom. She poked her head out, "We're going to our dacha in Ferzikov. You should come with us."

"Thanks," I said. "I'm going to change my ticket and fly back to Seattle today." I looked at my watch. The Lufthansa office opened at ten. I could go to Hospital 70, get the papers signed and notarized, and be at the airline office when it opened. From there I'd go straight to Sheremetyevo

Airport and wait for the flight to Frankfurt. If Lufthansa couldn't help me, Aeroflot on Novy Arbat would be my next stop.

"What about Oskar?" asked Mrs. Belikova. "We could take him to the country."

"Irina's brother is coming to get him this morning. He has his own key."

"Well, you better hurry. The boys will walk Oskar" said Mrs. Belikov, hauling shuttle bags and chasing children into the hall while issuing instructions. "Do you need a ride to the Metro?"

"Thanks," I said. "Let me grab my purse."

Tension was palpable on the crowded Metro train. I understood that this was serious from the faces of the Muscovites. They looked confused and angry. When I arrived at Novogereevo and exited the Metro across from Hospital 70, the busy black market had been abandoned. There were no tables stacked with jars of pickles or trucks selling beer. Kiosk windows were shuttered. The state market with the dancing pigs was padlocked.

The main gate to the hospital complex stood open with no guards in sight. Patients were leaving in dressing gowns and slippers, piling into cars and onto buses. I pushed against the human tide to the birth house. The blue door stood open. The birth house had been stripped of everything but some furniture and blackboards. All of our equipment was gone.

I found Dr. Lapukhin in his office, packing. "Everything's going to hell," he said. "Get out of this miserable country as fast as you can."

"I will. But while I'm here, we'd better sign and notarize these papers," I said. "I won't be back until next summer."

"No use. The notary isn't open. I'm going home now and so are you." He guided me through the door and drove me back to the Metro. "Go straight to the airport," he said.

Traveling from Novogereevo to Sheremetyevo Airport meant traversing the city center where the airlines had their offices. I took the Metro to the Lufthansa office on Trubnaya Square, but it was closed. I sat on the steps and waited half an hour, but no one came. I went on to the main office of Aeroflot in Novy Arbat. It was also closed.

I walked down Kalininsky Boulevard, known as "luxury road" because of all the posh foreign shops. The only store open was The Irish House. It was crowded with shoppers brandishing dollars and buying food. I bought a can of Spam and hurried back toward the Arbat Metro, determined to go straight to the airport.

A dull rumble grew into a thunderous roar behind me. Tanks and armored cars rolled down the wide boulevard, speeding toward the Kremlin. I didn't know they could move so fast. Someone screamed. People ran. Shots rang out from the tall apartment building across the street. A tank slowed. The turret rotated and fired. An apartment exploded, showering us with glass and burning debris. People ducked and scattered in every direction, knocking me to the ground. I crawled behind a row of kiosks, cutting my hands on broken glass.

I struggled to my feet and ran toward the Metro. Rounding the corner, I was diverted, swept down a flight of stairs by a crowd sheltering in a cellar. People of all ages sat on the floor of the dank rooms or stood along the walls watching the news on a black and white television. We cowered at the sound of artillery fire on the street. Yeltsin's face filled the screen: "Today, the destiny of Russia and the fate of our children are being decided. The forces of civil war will not succeed."

Was this a civil war? Men around me were armed, passing boxes of ammunition and loading guns. Were these rebels? Is this where I should be? I pushed my way back onto the street. I couldn't see the tanks anymore but felt their rumbling vibrations. They fired sporadically. I started down the steps of Arbat Metro, but was forced back by a crowd shouting, "It's broken. Train's not running. They've stopped the Metro. Get away."

I stepped onto a side street and flagged down a motorist by waving a $20 bill. I offered him $40 to take me to the airport.

"Not possible," he said. "No one can get across town without getting shot. I'm going south."

He agreed to drive me to my flat in Kolomenskoe for $40. I got in. The car sped south through empty streets and away from the airport. The tanks quieted, but the pounding of my heart was deafening. My hands bled from the broken glass. I wiped blood on my jeans.

Oskar was at the flat. I heard the poor dog howling from the street. I let myself into the lobby of our apartment block. My downstairs neighbors, the Melinkovs, were in the foyer. They had boarded over the first-floor windows and were preparing to nail the steel security door shut – I'd just made it. From that point on, tenants would have to climb through a padlocked and barred first-floor window to get in or out. Only the Melinkovs had a key.

"Go to your flat and lock the door," said Granny Melinkova. "Do not turn on your lights or stand in the window." Granny was one of the babushkas who sat on a bench outside the front door every day. She kept a watchful eye on who came and who went. Every day the babas would teach me a new Russian word – always something like "snitch, traitor, rat, firing squad." During the Second World War, she and her five sisters had been partisan fighters in the infamous Ukrainian Women's Brigade. They had terrorized the German invaders and been declared Heroes of the Soviet Union. She might look like a frail little grandma, but she was in her element with a pistol in her hand.

"Electricity is off. The lift is kaput," she said. She gave my arm a squeeze, tsk-tsked at my bloody hands, then shooed me up the dark stairs.

On my landing, I fumbled with the locks to the flat. They were difficult enough to manage when the hall lights were working, and my fingers weren't bleeding. Each of the three locks required different, ill-fitting keys that I could barely see in the dim light.

Boom ... kaboom ... Tank fire echoed through the building, rattling my teeth. My hands shook. Tears of fear and frustration weren't helping, nor was my racing pulse. Kablam ... blam ... blam ... . Flashes of artillery fire lit the hallway. The fighting was half a mile away, but the sound penetrated my body. I slid to the floor with my arms over my ears – it didn't help. With each explosion, my body wanted to run in a thousand different directions. I was paralyzed. I buried my face in my knees and held my breath. Oskar knew I was there. He whimpered at the door.

I floated above my body, staring at the cowering, terrified creature I'd become. "You've been panicked before," I called to myself. "Remember how scared you were the first time you jumped into the ocean in scuba gear – tumbling into cold, dark water and holding your breath, knowing how stupid that was? How did you keep from drowning? Use your brain. Think!"

"Amazing Grace," I said aloud, gulping air. "I sang."

I began to hum, slowly at first, concentrating on the vibration of my voice in my ears, shutting out the artillery. When my breathing calmed a bit and my heart ceased its wild pounding, I raised my voice until it echoed in the stairwell. "Amazing grace, how sweet the sound, that saved a wretch like me. I once was lost, but now I'm found, was blind, but now I see."

"Owww ... wowww ... wowww ... ." Oskar let loose on the high notes.

"Atta boy, Oskar. Good dog!" I shouted. "Let's do another. How about 'Star Spangled Banner'?" I sang as loudly as I could, trying to hit the climax of "the rockets' red glare, the bombs bursting in air" as explosions shook the walls. "It's beautiful!" I declared, pushing to my feet. "Life is good." I matched the keys to the locks and opened the door. Oskar was wide-eyed and quaking. He dashed past me into the hall, peed and pooped in front of the elevator, and rushed back. I locked us inside.

I tried to call the airport, but the lines were dead. There was still no electricity, so I picked glass slivers from my palms and fingers in the fading daylight and wrapped my hands in toilet paper. I fried slabs of Spam on the gas stove and shared them with Oskar. We had a clear view of the Russian White House – brightly lit and encircled by tanks. Gunshots echoed in the streets. There were snipers in our neighborhood. I stayed off the balcony and kept my head below the windowsill.

When the power came back on, Oskar and I sat on the living room floor with the lights off, watching the Red Army bombarding the White House on television. Parliamentary rebels were throwing hand grenades from the upper floors. One hit an armored personnel carrier and the explosion shook our building. Burning men leapt from the truck. I was afraid to look outside. The ensuing explosion rocked the flat.

Suddenly, the news was interrupted. A disheveled reporter came on the air to say that Ostankino Central Television Station was under siege. Armed militia were breaking down the doors and battling with police in the lobby. Explosions sounded and, at 7:15 P.M., Russian State Television went off the air.

"Open the fucking door!" Someone pounded on the security door downstairs. Men shouted, "Rats, come out, you fucking rats!"

"Get lost, you black-arsed vermin," Granny Melnikova shouted back. "Or I'm gonna shoot your hairy balls off and stick um in your ears." Glass shattered. Shots were fired. Oskar vomited and trembled in my arms. I struggled to keep a clear head, controlling my breath by humming. The sound of my voice calmed the dog.

The phone lines came back. I left a message on the Lufthansa machine. I tried Aeroflot, but no one answered. I tried the airport – no answer. The lines went dead again. Were the airlines even flying? I lay on the couch, listening to the kablam ... blam ... blam ... of artillery and pop ... pop of snipers wishing that I was in Seattle, realizing that I might be killed and never see my kids again.

I dozed sporadically in spite of the gunfire and woke at daybreak with my arms around Oskar. We shared the last of the Spam. There was a dial tone, so I tried Lufthansa, Aeroflot, Hospital 70, Dr. Lapukhin at home, the Peace Committee, and the American Embassy. I couldn't reach anyone.

I decided to make a run for the airport. I put on an old house-dress of Irina's so that I'd look more Russian and climbed through the Melnikovs' barred window. My hands were still bleeding. Kolomenskoe Station was deserted. The steps and railings were smeared with darkening blood. I tracked bloody footprints onto the marble floor wondering what had happened there.

I was the only person on the platform when a train arrived overflowing with tired, disheveled Muscovites, some of them injured. We stopped in four more stations where people crowded aboard. At Paveletskaya Station, policemen boarded and emptied the train. Overhead speakers announced that no one could travel from one side of the city to the other. Roads and public transportation were closed. Mortar fire pounded the street above. Plaster dust fell onto my hair. When an empty southbound train appeared, we crowded aboard and sped away.

The Melnikovs helped me back into the apartment and told me that Irina's brother had taken Oskar to the country. I spent the night alone, lying flat on the balcony watching the army shell the White House. The top floors belched flames and the tanks kept firing. Electricity went off in our region. The darkness was filled with explosions and the pounding of guns.

I woke up on the sofa when the television started working again, but instead of news, they were broadcasting old Deanna Durbin movies on one channel and Swan Lake on the other. I lay in a stupor watching Deanna sing and dance in black and white. I kept phoning the airlines to no avail. My hands were infected from the filthy glass. I had a fever. I needed oral antibiotics. I was out of food.

At dawn, the phone rang. Dr. Vladimir Voronov, a surgeon from Hospital 70, was calling to check on me. "The counter-revolutionaries have been arrested and Boris Yeltsin is back in power," he said.

"Why are they still shooting?"

"Paramilitary groups are fighting the Russian Army. It could go on for a while."

"Who are these militants?" I asked.

"Cossacks, Afghan veterans, ex-KGB troops, Azeri mafia, who knows? Probably all of them," he said. "I'm taking my family to our dacha in Uglich. I can pick you up in one hour, if you'd like."

Uglich – maybe I'd find Angela after all. "Yes, I'll come." I told him about my infected hands, and he promised to bring antibiotics.

"Pack one small flight bag and no more," he said. "It's going to be crowded in the ambulance."

Chapter Eleven

Angela in Uglich

Uglich, Russia – Fall 1993

When the Hospital 70 ambulance pulled up, I climbed out the Melnikovs' window and jumped in back. Colleagues from Hospital 70 were crowded on the floor eating apricots and drinking vodka. I squeezed between a surgeon and an ophthalmologist, relieved to be among friends. Vladimir handed me two antibiotic capsules and bottled water. I swallowed them. He bandaged my hands, then shut the curtain dividing the driver from us, cutting off the light. We dashed through the center of Moscow bouncing in darkness with red lights flashing and the siren wailing. Only police cars and ambulances were allowed through the barricades.

Eventually, we slowed, and the sirens were turned off. I hadn't realized how terrified I'd been until I knew for sure that Moscow was behind me. Uglich was still a five-hour drive on country roads. I leaned my head against the bony shoulder of Dr. Grigor Stepanich, the Head of the Department of Surgery, and fell asleep.

"Wake up," said Grigor, nudging my arm. "We're almost there." The curtain was open. I leaned forward to peer through the windshield. Birch forests lined the country lane with the first hints of red and gold in their leaves. We bumped through a pothole, splashing water. "The roads get worse the farther you get from Moscow."

The Voronov dacha was a cozy two-room shack on the bank of the Volga River. I was assigned a sleeping place on top of the cold *pechka* – stove. It wouldn't be lit until the first snowfall. That evening, we sat on logs at the river's edge steaming local perch in an old oil pan with *Traktor* stamped on it. The humid air was thick with mosquitoes and a panoply of blood-sucking insects. We drank vodka, ate juicy red plums from the garden, and swatted bugs. The violence in Moscow seemed a million miles and a century away from this peaceful place.

After dinner, we climbed the bluff above the Volga River to the Uglich Historical Society. We joined the villagers listening to the evening news on the town's only radio. Judging from their worried looks, the news wasn't good. I found the urgent, high-speed speech of the reporters incomprehensible. I gave up and went outside to sit on the library steps. I would ask the others to explain later.

The Historical Society afforded a moonlit view of the town of Uglich. I recognized the Chaika Watch Factory and, beyond that, the shabby domes of the ancient church of St. Dimitri on the Blood. I knew that the orphanage was a short walk from the church and decided to stroll down the hill for look.

I started along the path but was stopped by a skinny young man in a Peace Corps tee shirt. I recognized him. "Hi Vlad," I said. It had only been a week since the cruise ship *Dzerzhinsky* docked in Uglich and Vlad had escorted the Puchkovs and me around town on the only English language tour.

"I don't mean to alarm you," he said in English. "Uglich is a dangerous place at night, a mafia town. No one should go into town after dark, especially a lady."

"Thank you," I said. "Your English is remarkable." He looked pleased. It was a relief not to have to speak Russian. "What do you do during the rest of the year once tourist season is finished?"

"I'm an English teacher at the local institute. I also teach Russian to Peace Corps volunteers." He stubbed out a cigarette. "Let me introduce myself properly. My name is Vladislav Viktorevich Suprunov." We shook hands. "What do you do when you are not a tourist?" he asked.

I told him about the MiraMed Center in Moscow and our research in orphanages. "There's one little girl that I'd especially like to find. She was transferred to the Uglich Orphanage from Yaroslavl Baby House Number Six – a red-head named Angela, about four years old. Maybe you've seen her?"

"There are several red-heads – boys and girls. You'll have to ask the director, Tatyana Safarovna."

"How many children live at the orphanage?"

"About sixty. They are at the *lager* – summer camp. The city has delayed the start of school. It isn't safe in town for the children."

"Can I get to the camp? Is there transport?"

"You can walk," he said, lighting another cigarette and offering me one. "It's just a few kilometers from here – an hour walk, or two hours at most. I can take you tomorrow if you'd like."

The broadcast came to an end. *Swan Lake* began to play. My colleagues assembled on the porch to smoke and share a bottle of local cognac.

Yeltsin was still in power, they said, backed by the Red Army, but Nationalists held the White House. They were barricaded inside, refusing to surrender. The airport remained closed, and it was too dangerous to return to Moscow. The phone lines to Uglich had been cut. There was nothing for us to do but wait.

I introduced Vlad and shared my plans to visit the summer camp. "Just make sure that I always know where you are," said Grigor. "You don't want to miss your ride back to Moscow."

Vlad shook hands all around and gave directions to the camp. "It's easy to find."

The next morning Vlad and I walked two hours on a rambling lane deep into the woods. The road to the camp had been washed away and we detoured to a footbridge across the narrow gorge of the River of Blood.

"There's iron in it from deep springs. That's why the water is red. It's very clean and healthful." Vlad scooped a handful and drank it to demonstrate. "Delicious," he said. "The children drink it for minerals. That's why the lager is located here."

I tried some. It was ice cold and tasted like rusty nails. "Ouch." I startled when I was hit in the head by a pinecone. "Did you hear that?" I asked. Bushes rustled. I heard giggles. "Those kids are throwing pinecones at us."

"Where?"

"Over in the trees. Can't you hear them laughing?"

We followed their voices up a narrow, well-trodden path until we reached a ramshackle assembly of old log cabins and crumbling, moss-covered outbuildings.

"This is the summer camp," said Vlad. "We're coming in the back way."

An old man stepped forward blocking our approach. He wielded a broom like a baseball bat. "Stop right there," he shouted. "I've got a gun."

"That's a broom, Dada Igor. Besides, we come in peace."

"Is that you, Vlad?"

"When are you going to get your glasses fixed, Uncle? I've brought an American guest. Tell the kids to be on their best behavior."

"A guest? A foreigner? I'll fetch Tatyana Safarovna." Dada Igor tossed the broom aside and hurried away. Children peeked at us from the barn door and behind the woodpile. Their heads weren't shaved like at Mishkin and they wore normal clothing. Vlad was right – there were several red-heads.

I felt a tug on my shirt. Two of them stood next to me, an older girl with a blondish ponytail and a little girl with a profusion of bright red curls and freckles across her nose.

"Angela has something for you," said the ponytail.

I knelt to Angela's level. "What do you have little *zolotaya* – golden one?" I asked, suckered by her enormous brown eyes. I suspected from the snorts behind me that it wasn't flowers.

"This is my best friend," she said, unfurling her fingers to reveal a slug. "His name is Boris Yeltsin." She broke into peals of laughter and ran away. The older kids hooted and egged her on.

"That child!" A heavy woman with a Mongolian face that radiated kindness hurried toward us. "Do you know how many red-headed pranksters we're cursed with here in Uglich? Six – enough to try the patience of St. Peter."

"Tatyana Safarovna," said Vlad. "I'd like you to meet Dr. Engel from America."

"Welcome." Tatyana Safarovna engulfed me in her embrace. She was a formidable presence – short, round, and powerful. She propelled me to an open porch along one of the log buildings. A table was spread with freshly baked piroshky and tea fixings. "You are just in time for tea," she said. "Come tell us about America. Then we'll find you a bunk and you'll stay with us. Vlad, go help Dada Igor fix that barn door. The chickens are getting out and the foxes are getting in."

I joined a group of teachers around the table. They introduced themselves while Tatyana poured tea. "We're lucky that the weather's holding," she said. "There's no heating out here." Below us, children laughed and swam in the river, supervised by a man with a whistle. He looked like a coach.

"Your kids look healthy," I remarked. "Not like Mishkin Orphanage."

"Good gracious, poor Mishkin," said Tatyana, crossing herself. "They hide those pitiful incurables out in the woods in places like that. Mikhala Dimitrovna is a saint to stay there. Help her if you can."

"Uglich is a very different case. It's a busy market town," said Anna, the head teacher. "These children have an opportunity to learn trades, even go to high school. Tomorrow, Nina the sewing teacher comes. You'll see how she works wonders training the girls as seamstresses."

"Is there better food here?" I asked. "Mishkin's rations are absurd. No child can grow on such a diet."

"We have the same problem with food rationing, but the local farmers contribute eggs, and we keep chickens and grow our own vegetables. I don't know what we'll do this winter if the rationing gets worse." Tatyana shivered. "The children look good because it's summer. They've been in the fresh air, drinking mineral water, and tanned by the sun. It's hard to see, but they're all small for their ages."

"You do have a lot of red-heads," I remarked, watching Angela's bobbing curls as she ran around the yard. She chased a hen onto the porch and under my seat. Anna shooed it away. Angela climbed onto Tatyana Safarovna's lap, eyeing me wickedly.

Angela (2nd from left) and the red-headed girls at Uglich Orphanage.

"What to do with unlucky children, eh? Red-heads, cleft lips, scoliosis, six-toes, moles – we have them all. We love them too, don't we, Angela?" She looked at the child who was making evil faces. "Don't give Dr. Engel the evil eye, you rascal."

"I was there in the birth house when you were born," I said. "You were named for me."

"Angelova – Angela, yes, I see it. Maybe that'll bring the tyke luck," said Tatyana. "She'll need it."

"I'd like to find an American family to adopt her."

"She isn't adoptable. She has a grandmother who lives in Yaroslavl and takes her on holidays – an awful drunk, sad to say. But she likes her stipend and is happy to have the state raise her grandchild."

"How many of these children are adoptable?"

"Very few, I'm afraid. Only about five percent."

After lunch Anna lent me a bathing suit and I jumped into the river with the kids. I was so glad for relief from the heat that I stayed in the cold water until my fingers and toes wrinkled and went numb. I felt calm for the first time in days – at least until I was ambushed by shrieking boys yelling "bonzai" and cannonballing into the water.

I spent the next few days at the camp and used up my last rolls of film. Tatyana asked me not to pay special attention to Angela because the other kids would pick on her when I left, so I made sure to photograph them all and promised to send copies. I was reassured to see that the children at Uglich were well-socialized and well-dressed. The teachers were kind to the children and welcoming to me. The sewing teacher was extraordinary – they made their own clothes as well as costumes for frequent concerts and plays. Numerous activities kept the kids occupied while the staff worried over events in the local newspaper.

Girls model the costumes they made in sewing class

In the late afternoon of my third day, I was finger-painting with Angela when a neighbor rode up on a bicycle. "Dr. Voronov sent me," he said. "He is heading back to Moscow. You better get to the dacha right away." One of the teachers offered to drive me in his car, but he had just taken pigs to market and the car smelled like pig poop. That stink would not be welcome in the crowded ambulance. I decided to walk. "You better hurry," said Tatyana Safarovna. She pointed to my bandaged hands that were brightly colored with finger-paint – green, purple magenta and yellow. "No time to fix that."

A flock of children escorted me to the end of the dirt driveway. Anna carried Angela, who buried her head and wouldn't look at me. They waved until I had crossed the footbridge and followed the curving road into the forest. Overhead, birch trees formed an arch. Wind gusted, tossing branches and scattering golden leaves, a harbinger of winter.

After walking twenty minutes along meandering lanes, I came to a crossroads and realized I was lost. I tried going back but didn't know which road I had come from – everything looked the same. The only sound was the rush of wind in the trees. I thought about bandits, I thought about bears and wolves, and counterrevolutionaries. Then I heard a motorcycle.

That could be good news or bad news. Should I hide? I decided to stand in the road as if I belonged there. An ancient motorcycle appeared, probably vintage World War I, with a bullet-shaped sidecar. The driver wore an old leather fighter pilot's helmet with goggles, and a sleeveless blue-and-white striped Russian sailor shirt. An unlit cigar drooped out the side of his mouth. He looked about seventy years old. He stopped, surprised. "And where are *you* from, madam?" he asked in elegant Russian, looking at my brightly painted bandages.

"America," I replied, too startled to think of anything else.

"Madam, I believe that you are lost."

I arrived at the Voronov dacha in the sidecar, wearing a leather helmet and goggles. I climbed out, thanking my driver, who refused payment. I grabbed my bag and hopped into the ambulance. They drove directly to Sheremetyevo Airport along a highway littered with smoking debris. Burnt out cars were lying in pieces along the road. Thousands of people had been killed or wounded in the worst fighting that Moscow had seen since the Russian Revolution.

Dr. Voronov waited until I had my new ticket in hand and was in line for Passport Control before he broke the bad news. The equipment I'd brought to Russia had been stored in the office of the Ministry of Health in the White House. The Ministry office was now a burnt-out shell. Everything had been destroyed when the ninth floor was gutted by the Russian Army. I had unknowingly witnessed the destruction of all my hard work from the Puchkovs' balcony.

My tears waited to break loose until the Lufthansa jet lifted off the runway and Russia disappeared under clouds. My body shook with relief – and with grief. The man next to me took my bandaged hands and pressed them gently between his. He was also in tears. Many people were crying on that flight to Frankfurt. Like me, they looked dirty and disheveled. No one knew what the fate of the Russian people would be.

Chapter Twelve

THE MURMANSK HIGHWAY

Seattle to Svir Stroi, Russia – 1993 thru 1996

My first night home in Seattle, I couldn't sleep. I'd doze off, waking up in a sweat to the sound of rolling tanks or shouts from an unknown enemy who banged on the door and threatened to shoot me. I'd have to get up and raise the blinds to assure myself that I was in Seattle, not Moscow, and that the view from my window was the Ballard Bridge and ship canal, not the Kremlin.

In the morning, I drove the kids' carpool to Country Day School in my Jeep Wagoneer. The leaves were turning gold in the October drizzle. Mist rose from the winding streets on Queen Ann Hill as I picked up more children. I drove cautiously. I wasn't adjusting as quickly as I usually did to the eleven time-zone changes between Moscow and Seattle. I'd been snared in a time warp of skewed perceptions and muted sounds. The children's chatter coming from the back seat seemed farther away than the laughter of children splashing in the River of Blood.

I watched my son and daughter race into the red brick school with their friends, their books and papers flying. I'd stayed away too long and too much had happened. Tears filled my eyes – they were growing up and running away from me. I watched them go until the car behind me honked. I left the drive and drove down the steep hill, across the Fremont Bridge and up Stone Way to Green Lake. A brisk three-mile hike around the lake with friends like Carol Hiltner was my healing ritual.

"I can't breathe," I lamented as we walked side by side in the light rain. "The air in America is too thin or something."

"Give yourself a break. You've been through a lot this time," she said.

"And nobody here seems to care. Two thousand people dying in Moscow barely made a sound bite in Seattle." I shuddered. "My family wasn't even worried about me. They're just pissed that I'm a few days late to pick up my kids. I could've been killed."

"Maybe they can't afford to care. Would you rather your kids were scared to death when you're in Russia?" she reasoned. "How are your hands?"

"They hurt like hell. That filthy glass infected my tendons. I'm taking Percocet and a new course of antibiotics. Mix that up with jetlag and I'm in great shape for a board meeting tomorrow night."

"Can't you reschedule?" she asked.

"The three new board members from Magee Womens Hospital are flying in from Pittsburgh. They've changed their tickets twice already and aren't happy about it."

"Don't they realize what happened to you?" I looked at Carol's earnest face and realized that she might be my only American friend who comprehended the recent events in Russia. "Maybe they will be supportive."

"Hardly. They are barracudas in pantyhose."

"Just explain to them that you've been injured. Your hands look miserable."

"If they see me as weak, they'll take over MiraMed, swallow it whole. While I was stuck in Uglich, they were in DC meeting with the State Department and trying to write us out of our own partnership grant. Now that MiraMed has money, we're a plum ripe for picking."

We walked in silence for a while before Carol asked: "I hate to bring up more bad news, but have you told the board about the equipment yet?"

"No – I'll tell them at the meeting." I stopped, feeling winded. In the whirlwind of events, I'd forgotten that the Red Army had blown up millions of dollars of medical equipment stored on the ninth floor of the Russian White House. Suddenly, it was all too much. My head spun. I leaned down with my hands on my knees to catch a breath. "Hold on a minute. I'm dizzy."

"Let's go get a latté and sit for a while." Carol took my arm and led me across the grass to Duke's Chowder House. "I think you're doing too much, too fast."

We ordered lattés. I felt better seated in the leatherette booth with my hands around a warm mug.

"We'll have to inform the donors, as well," I said, "all those medical companies who donated and refurbished the equipment for us. We'll never be able to replace those machines."

"Won't they donate again?"

"Probably, but nothing gets through Customs anymore – it's either stolen or trashed or winds up at an auction in Sevastopol." I sipped my coffee, concentrating on its bitter taste. "The only thing we have left is the fax machine. Yuri had it in his apartment."

"Have you heard from him? Or anyone in Moscow?"

"Not a word. International lines are still down. I don't know if my friends are alive or dead." Exhaustion washed over me. My palms throbbed. I felt like crying. "And Magee expects MiraMed Institute to be handed over to them. We're screwed."

"But you're going to fight, right?"

"For what? A gutted clinic in a crazy country, an apartment next to the nuclear cyclotron, and a burned-up pile of worthless wires and circuit boards?"

I couldn't continue – my throat felt raw. Tears made my nose run. I was too tired to fight the freshly coifed Magee executives and it was too late to bring other board members up to speed on our predicament. Magee was going to offer them an easy way out by canning me. "I just hope that they continue with the birth house. They have the ability and resources to do a great job."

"Give them the birth house, then. But keep MiraMed. You can't just let them walk away with your name and take the credit for all you've done. It's you the Russians trust. You're the one in a position to really do some good there."

I hung my head – the truth was exhausting. "Let's go home."

I could barely manage the two flights of steps to my front door. I ignored the unopened mail that had piled up while I was in Moscow – bills mostly, and IRS notices. I was being audited. MiraMed had eaten through my resources and I was in debt. I'd deal with it later. All I wanted now was sleep.

I lay down on the couch and was out before I could take off my shoes. Immediately, the ground shook, tanks rumbled, cannons fired – I was showered by glass, knocked to the ground with my face pressed against the sidewalk. I couldn't get up. I couldn't breathe. I was bleeding.

Carol Hiltner, my wise friend.

91

The phone rang once and the fax machine chirped next to my head, slowly spewing a roll of shiny paper. I recognized Yuri's handwriting. I grabbed it and said a prayer of thanks. I hadn't heard from Yuri since he and Irina had returned from Siberia.

When the fax stopped printing, I tore it off and read: "Julietta! We are well, but everything is worse since the counter-revolution. Do you remember the orphanages we visited from the ship? They have no money to buy proper food, clothing, or medicine. Hundreds of children will starve if we don't help. You must come back to Russia as quickly as possible." That was all. I would have called him back if I could, but an international call could only be received in a monitored booth in the Central Post Office, which was closed. At least he could send faxes to me.

I thought of Angela's impish face with her bountiful curls and freckles. I recalled the children of Mishkin with shaved heads, dressed in striped jumpsuits that looked like prison uniforms. They were facing starvation without any way to help themselves. How could I be so selfish? Was my life more precious than theirs? My debts, my house, my health were all problems I could handle. God gave me strength and brains and resources. Shame on me if I gave up and didn't use them.

I went upstairs and showered with plastic bags taped over my hands. I stood under the stream of clean, hot water until it ran cold. It was time to pick my kids up from school. We drove through the rain to Tower Records and checked out a Disney video. I couldn't cook with my damaged hands, so my fifteen-year-old son ordered an Olympia pizza, and my twelve-year-old daughter made a big salad with cheese sprinkles.

We snuggled on the couch under our Smoky the Bear blanket, eating Chunky Monkey ice cream and watching *The Little Mermaid*. Rain lashed the windows. Branches scratched the glass. Breathing in the familiar, clean scent of my children's hair and skin, I thanked God for bringing me safely home. I wished that all children could be as healthy and secure as the ones in my arms. I wished that all children could be loved.

The next night, I drove to the Washington Athletic Club for our board meeting. I felt better than I had in days because I had a plan – a humanitarian aid delivery program for orphanages called "Cruise with a Cause." MiraMed would recruit American tourists for cruises on Russian ships and ask them to carry donations of clothing, medicine, and school supplies in an extra suitcase. Russian Customs never inspected the luggage of Western tourists. They could deliver their donations to the orphanages as part of the travel itinerary. The more I thought about it, visualizing every aspect of the program, the more tangible it became.

By the time that the Magee board members announced that MiraMed had lost its funding and that MiraMed Institute now belonged to Magee, I had enough oomph to jump up and say, "No, it doesn't."

I couldn't give Magee a chance to lay out the logic of their proposal to the other twelve board members. I needed to be honest about the loss of the equipment while simultaneously inspiring the board to keep trying. I had to present tragedy as an opportunity.

I launched into my description of "Cruise with a Cause," bringing the children to life as if they were in the room with us. I passed around the photographs I'd taken in Uglich. I wanted everyone to see Angela's wicked grin and curious dark eyes, little buck-toothed Sasha, Lena the bookworm, and Anya with her blond curls. I couldn't stop talking or my energy would flag. They needed to see what I saw – beautiful children in desperate need who were sure to suffer without our help.

"As part of the cruise, the passengers will visit the orphanages and deliver their donations in person. In Uglich, the girls will put on a fashion show of the costumes they make," I said, passing out photographs of sewing class from the summer camp. "In Kostroma and St. Petersburg, we can set up computer labs for job training." I knew we could easily acquire computers and software – there were executives from Adobe and Microsoft on our board.

"Now look at this." I popped a videotape into the VCR. A group of teenaged girls from Svir Stroi danced and lip-synched to the tune, "Life is Life." They wore the school uniforms one of the board members had donated. The girls crowned me with a wreath of leaves while I handed each one a piece of fruit. The film closed with a group shot of the girls waving bananas and shouting, "Spacebo, MiraMed!" – thank you, MiraMed! It was the first time they'd eaten a banana.

"We have to do this," said Doug Howard, our board member from Boeing. The board was hooked. Magee walked away with our money and the birth house, but not our name.

I spent the next three years making "Cruise

Cruise with a Cause passengers sort donations for orphanages.

Children model their new outfits for school.

with a Cause" a reality. We delivered thousands of pounds of medicines and supplies to 23 orphanages including Mishkin and Uglich. The high-end travel consortium Virtuoso promoted the cruises and helped with donations. Our tourists became staunch supporters.

In December 1996, I received an urgent fax from Svir Stroi Orphanage saying that their routine request for winter coats and boots had been denied. The orphanage was in a tiny village on the border with Finland. The temperature was already well below zero. They were desperate and wanted to know if we could help provide warm winter clothes for sixty-five children.

Svir Stroi had been on the front lines between the Germans and the Russians in WWII. The large stone orphanage building had been the northern wartime base for the German Air Force. The old anti-aircraft lights were still in use during the winter when the sun barely rose above the horizon. The main feature of the town square was a monument marking the spot where the last German soldier froze to death in 1945.

Local Seattle churches and Soroptimist Clubs quickly mobilized. I had a list of names, ages, and sizes, and a scrapbook of photographs from our summer visits. Every child was provided with a coat, hat, sweater, boots, and school supplies in an appropriate size and color. Their names were pinned to the jackets and candy hearts placed in each pocket. Everything was assembled and boxed up in the basement of the Magnolia Lutheran Church.

With Doug Howard's influence, Boeing transported me and forty-seven large boxes to St. Petersburg on a new 737 that was being delivered to Aeroflot Russian Airlines. I was met at Pulkovo Airport by Nina Nikolaevna, the orphanage director, and Valeri, an ex-prizefighter turned bus driver. For the next six days we stood stomping our feet in numbing cold, forced to wait outside the Customs shed while the officers inside pretended to be inspecting the boxes. We could hear them playing Pac Man and saw them peek around the corner periodically to see if we had given up and left. At night, we stayed at the Rossiya Hotel, a local hot spot for prostitution and drugs. The nights were rowdy, the beds dubious and I slept in my coat. Every morning we had a breakfast of cold fried eggs, beet salad and black bread with fresh butter. That lasted us until dinner when the meal was repeated. I grew very fond of cold fried eggs. Customs finally let the boxes through when they realized that we weren't going away—but not before they'd stolen the insulin and syringes I'd brought for a diabetic child.

In summer, Svir Stroi was a pleasant four-hour drive from St. Petersburg on the Murmansk Highway. In winter, massive snowbanks narrowed the six-lane highway to a two-lane sheet of ice. Empty logging rigs going north to pick up lumber drove past us much too fast. Trucks coming the other way loaded with as many logs as their axles could bear were slower, but not maneuverable. Deadly pileups were inevitable.

We left St. Petersburg in darkness. Fine, crystalline flakes reflected in the headlights of the little blue orphanage bus that was now loaded with our boxes. Nina and I sat behind Valeri, as close as possible to the feeble heater. A layer of ice coated the windows, rendering them opaque. Cold crept through the floorboards, chilling me despite my insulated boots and full-length down parka. About an hour out of St. Petersburg, the heater gave a final wheeze of warmish air, the engine stalled, and the lights went out. We rolled to a stop in the middle of the road. A logging truck whizzed through the impossibly narrow space between the bus and the sheer wall of ice, horn screaming.

Nina and Valeri scrambled out of the bus, telling me to stay put. Nina hitched a ride to get help and vanished with the next car. Suddenly, the bus jolted forward. I wiped condensation from the windshield and saw Valeri hunched at the front of the bus with his arms locked under the fender. He was pulling the bus to the side of the road. He saw me standing near the steering wheel and signaled for me to put my weight in the back of the bus. I crouched in the back seat, listening to Valeri's grunts and the intermittent roar of trucks racing past us, trying not to think of what would happen when we were hit. I tucked my legs up inside my coat. The cold made me sleepy. The bus inched forward.

I was startled awake when enormous headlamps flashed through the back window. A lumber truck had pulled up, flooding the interior of the bus with light. Doors slammed. Valeri rummaged under the driver's seat, emerging with a length of rope. The truck maneuvered into position ahead of us. The truck drivers hurriedly attached the rope to the front of the bus. Then Valeri signaled for me to get out.

My legs were so cramped and numb with cold that I could barely walk. Valeri grabbed me as I slid from the bus, then frog-marched me to the truck where two young men lifted me into the super-heated cab, plunking me onto the seat between them. Valeri stayed behind to steer the bus. Once we were up to a reasonable speed, the men relaxed.

"Alexei and Denis." The men introduced themselves, pouring tea from a thermos. I accepted the steaming tin cup and told them my name.

"Angel?" laughed Denis, the one on my right, prying open a jar of pickled garlic and offering it with a tin of sardines. "We're *your* angels tonight, Angelova. We grew up in Svir Stroi. We'd know that old bus anywhere."

Angels, I thought, surrendering to the heat, the smell of diesel and fish, and the hypnotic assault of snow on the windshield.

Svir Stroi Orphanage in daylight.

Chapter Thirteen

THE LOST GIRLS

Svir Stroi to Murmansk, Russia and Kirkenes, Norway – Winter 1997

Denis shook me awake. "It's Svir Stroi Orphanage," he said. "We're here." The snow had stopped. Beyond a moonlit field, yellow light shone in the windows of the orphanage, casting shadows on the snow. An old searchlight on the roof shone straight up. "They're waiting for you."

Valeri lost control of the bus on the final turn and plunged into a snowbank. Nothing could be done about it until morning. Alexei told me to stay warm in the cab while they disconnected the rope. Suddenly, a face appeared at one window of the orphanage – then at all the windows. The children were up and waving excitedly. I opened the passenger door and stepped out, dropping straight down over my head into a snowbank.

Alexei and Denis were laughing when they pulled me out of the culvert. Snow had gone up inside my coat and wrapped around my body like an inverted snow cone. "We told you to stay inside," said Denis.

Alexei set me on my feet and said, "Run, Angelova," and I did. The door of the orphanage opened and I ran into the arms of the children.

"Where were you?" Nina Nikolaevna demanded, frantic, tears in her eyes. "I went for the police. When we came back, you were gone. The police looked all over for you. You just disappeared!"

I shrugged, leaving it to Valeri to explain. I lay down on a cot in Nina's office and slept. During the night, all forty-seven boxes of coats, sweaters, boots, scarves, and school supplies were brought into the building. They were sorted, sized, and distributed to the children before they left for school in new outfits.

I woke up late. Someone had laid out a breakfast of cold fried eggs, black bread, and a pot of tea. I enjoyed the silence and the pale winter sun filtering through lace curtains, basking in the sense of well-being that came from accomplishing something difficult. Was Chort watching me? I spit over my left shoulder three times – just in case.

The older children had gone to school. The little ones were playing musical games on the third floor. I walked through the halls looking into empty dormitory rooms with their rows of neatly made beds and climbed upstairs to the fifth-floor storeroom to see what we should bring on the next trip. To my surprise, a rack of fifteen coats still hung in there, all of them for teenaged girls. I checked the names pinned to the collars. These were the same girls who had danced for the "Cruise with a Cause" groups last summer, the ones who'd crowned me with a halo of leaves. There was pink for Katya, purple for Tanya, blue for Yulia. The girls should have worn the coats to school.

I saw Nina's assistant Tatyana sorting a box of shoes. "Why are these coats still here?" I asked, pointing to the rack.

Tatyana put her head down and backed away. I followed her to her office where she slammed the door in my face. I knocked. "Tatyana? Where are the girls?" No answer.

I found Nina and asked the same questions. She burst into tears. "They're gone," she said, her eyes on the floor. "They have been taken."

All of the girls in this summer photo were missing.

"Where?" I persisted.

"Don't ask such questions." She shook her head but wouldn't look at me. "There is nothing that you can do."

"Have you called the police?"

"The police will do nothing." Nina spat on the ground. She disappeared into her office, slamming the door.

"Nina, Nina ... " I pounded on the door, but she didn't answer.

When the other children returned from school, I joined them for their tea. They told me that the girls had won a prize – a camping trip to Finland. They would have picnics, go swimming, do campouts in the woods.

"Swimming in February?"

"They went last summer," was the reply. A bus from Finland came every few years with a foreign man and woman. They would announce the lucky winners for a trip to Helsinki and drive away with all the teenaged girls. No one ever came back.

Dinner was a noisy affair with fifty children in new sweaters celebrating with borscht, piroshky, and chocolate-flavored lard. I tried to look happy, but something was terribly wrong here. Fifteen girls had crossed illegally into Finland and vanished. How could this happen? Why would no one on staff speak to me about this abduction?

The following morning, I walked into Svir Stroi to visit my friends Ada and Ivan, the slough-keepers who managed the locks. They told me that it was common for buses to come from Finland for teenaged girls. None of them ever returned and since they had no families to inquire after them, that was that. The girls left behind eagerly awaited their invitations to go abroad. Wherever their friends were, they reasoned, it had to be better than the orphanage.

I spoke to the Chief of Police in the village of Lodeine Polye, once Peter the Great's shipyard, now a sleepy resort town of 17th century villas. "Those orphanage girls are always going to Scandinavia to work as prostitutes," he said. "Who are we to stop them?"

"They are children," I retorted, my anger rising. "It's your job to stop them. Those girls want careers, marriage, families. Prostitution isn't in their life plans."

"We're just the country police. Why don't you go to Murmansk and talk to the Women's Congress? They have experience with this problem."

In March of 1997 I took the train from Saint Petersburg north to Murmansk and met with members of the Women's Congress of the Kola Peninsula. They had discovered that girls were disappearing from orphanages throughout the region. Buses with Russian girls as young as twelve were crossing the Finnish and Norwegian borders, where they became mobile brothels. The girls were never allowed to leave the buses. Men would pay to board and rape them before the brothel rolled into the next town and over the next border. No one knew what ultimately happened to the girls.

Was this possible? Could something so evil exist? Determined to find out, I traveled four hours from Murmansk across the Russian border to Norway on a local bus crowded with grumpy little Sami people smuggling crates of cigarettes. In Kirkenes, on the northern tip of Norway, I spoke with police who were surprised to see me. They were well aware of the mobile brothels.

"You're American, right?" asked a young constable with a nametag that said Roos. "What do you care about a bunch of Russian prostitutes?"

"They are trafficked children – none more than fifteen years old. The question is: Why don't you care?" I fired back. "Kidnapping, rape, and human trafficking are crimes in Norway, last I heard. What are you doing about it?"

"There is very little that we can do. Your girls are probably dead by now."

"Dead how?" I gasped. I felt like I'd been sucker-punched. Until that instant I'd held the hope of finding them and taking them back. "What if you're wrong? What if they are still alive?"

"If we find any trafficking victims alive, of course we help them. But we find the bodies of girls dumped around here all the time – no names, no papers. We assume they're Russian, so we call them all Natasha. Here, I'll show you." He opened a drawer full of Polaroid head shots of Natashas, all of them young, all of them dead. I looked through the photos, touching their bruised, lifeless faces. Horror churned in the pit of my stomach. The room spun. I thought I would vomit.

"Excuse me," I said, sitting down hard and lowering my head to my knees.

"Shocking, I know," he said, pushing the waste basket in my direction. "If no one claims their bodies, we cremate and bury them. Are any of these your girls?"

I didn't recognize anyone, but death changes a face. "No," I said too quickly. If they weren't in the drawer, I reasoned, they might still be alive.

By the next morning, I realized that I should have looked more carefully at the faces. I'd been too emotional, reacted in haste. I returned to the police department and asked to see the Polaroids again.

Constable Roos had been replaced by Sergeant Ivarson. His response was cool: "What Polaroids?"

I was being stonewalled. I knew it and they knew I knew. There was nothing more I could do. I left the police bureau furious. Violent crimes were being committed against children and those who should be protecting them were indifferent.

I found a small hotel nearby and checked in. I would catch the morning flight to Oslo. I asked the proprietor to recommend a place to eat.

"There's a deli across the street," he said. "But make it quick."

"Why?"

"It's four o'clock," he said, looking at me like I was stupid. "Today is Saturday. The hotel locks its doors and shutters the windows promptly at five."

I still didn't understand. Outside the window, deserted streets stretched to the sea. The sky was bright, the weather fine.

Another guest, an Englishman, filled me in. "Have you ever heard the word 'berserker?'" I nodded in the affirmative. My father was Norwegian. "Tonight, the soldiers come to town on leave. As the saying goes: 'Norwegian boys go berserk on Saturday night and to church on Sunday morning.'"

I made it to the deli just as it was closing and back before lock-down at the hotel. As night descended, the deserted town on the edge of nowhere filled with Norwegian soldiers on weekend leave from the six nearby Russian border garrisons. They drank in the bars, fought in the streets, banged on doors and broke bottles.

I sat with the other guests in the hotel lobby where the proprietor served coffee in front of a fireplace. No one spoke, subdued by the sounds of violence outside. I couldn't eat my shrimp salad. I was horrified by the thought of my missing girls being brought to this place and raped by berserkers. This shouldn't be happening in Norway – or anywhere.

"You think this is bad," said the Englishman. "You should see the submariners on leave in *Tromsø* down the coast. Those sailors go even more berserk after a month at sea." He chuckled and ordered another gin.

I threw my dinner in the trash and walked away in disgust. A mother's rage had been kindled in me – yet I'd never felt so helpless.

Chapter Fourteen

MEETING ZHENYA THE SURVIVOR

Zelenogorod, Russia – In the Fall 1997

In the fall of 1997, my son left for university in California and my daughter decided to live at her sports-minded father's house. My home that had once been crowded with children, their dogs, cats, and friends was empty. It was also in need of repairs. The windows leaked, the hardwood floors were stained and faded, and the garage needed a new door. I had spent the profits from "Cruise with a Cause" on aid for orphanages and taken a second mortgage on the house to fund development of a life-skills program for institutionalized children. The first workbooks for that program titled *We Can Do It Ourselves!* had just been published. I was tremendously proud of it and regretted none of my financial decisions.

There were consequences. The IRS notified me that I owed $256,000 in back taxes for some arbitrage investment from my doctor days that I barely remembered. A few days later, my ex-husband sued me, claiming that the house I'd purchased following our divorce belonged to him. My sinus infections returned, requiring repeated courses of antibiotics and procedures.

Logic dictated that my time in Russia had ended. I should go back into medicine. Dr. Frank Allen, who had purchased my practice, was ready to retire and wanted to sell it back to me. My family would perceive that move as me recovering my senses.. But my children, who were my anchor to Seattle, would still be gone their separate ways. With one at Santa Clara University in California and the other leaving soon for University of Virginia, I had no reason to stay.

I forwarded the IRS notices to my accountant and ignored the threats from my ex-husband's attorney, something which I could only accomplish by plunging head-on into an all-consuming project with impossible demands that would stifle my emotions and divert my attention away from the mundane reality. If I was going to stop the trafficking of Russian children before more were taken, I needed help.

The Internet was an exciting new tool. I learned about search engines and set up an e-mail account at the Speakeasy Café on Second Avenue, the first Internet cafe. I scoured the World Wide Web for organizations that had encountered the sale of Russian girls for sexual slavery and found a report by Dr. Donna M. Hughes at the University of Rhode Island. Her paper, "The Natasha Trade," described the growing exploitation of Russian women and girls by organized crime groups. She referred me to the Foundation Against Trafficking in Women in the Netherlands, who told me that their country had seen a steady increase in the number of women trafficked from the former Soviet Bloc countries by highly organized and extremely violent criminal groups. My resolve strengthened.

I also came across an organization called Global Survival Network. Founders Steven Galster and Gillian Caldwell had been investigating a gang poaching white tigers from Siberia when they had come across another gang smuggling Russian women. Gillian and Steven had gone undercover with cameras hidden in their eyeglasses and met with Russian traffickers who were interested in expanding their US markets. Ultimately, they produced a documentary in Russian and English that exposed a vast network of human traffickers operating in Russia.

I decided that their film, *Bought and Sold*, would be an excellent teaching tool to raise awareness about the risks of trafficking in rural areas of Russia. Gillian told me that it wasn't safe for her to return to Russia. She and Steven had a price on their heads. They agreed to let me show it, but I still needed funding.

About that time, I met Joanne Saunders, the director of UNIFEM – United Nations Development Fund for Women. She informed me about their Violence Against Women Trust Fund. I wrote a grant proposal to purchase videotapes from Global Survival Network and show them in orphanages and villages throughout northwestern Russia.

Even with the grant funds from UNIFEM, I would have to live on credit cards. I bargained with fate: If I received the grant, I would go forward to Russia. If not, I would go back into medical practice in Seattle, fix up my house, and settle. While waiting for the results from UNIFEM, I fended off my ex-husband in court and dealt with the IRS. I worked part time for Dr. Allen, covering my old medical practice – a nice respite. I was happy to be among colleagues and friends and it helped with the bills.

My sinuses were chronically infected. After six weeks on antibiotics, including an intravenous regimen in Swedish Hospital, they were finally clearing about the time UNIFEM announced that they would fund the proposal. Not long after, I won the court battle with my ex and kept my house. Even the IRS admitted its error. I owed nothing.

God's guidance was clear and my life choice was made. I wasn't going to settle – quite the opposite. I packed a portable television with a built-in videotape player into a rolling bag with copies of *Bought and Sold* and, in June 1998, I traveled to northern Russia with a group of "Cruise with a Cause" volunteers. They were spending the summer with MiraMed at the orphanages in Uglich and Svir Stroi, teaching crafts, English, woodworking, and computer skills while doing repairs to the facilities. Three additional Americans came to work with me and Yuri on the UNIFEM project – David Tagliani, Joanne Walby, and Susan Marshall.

Yuri had spent months developing our schedule of presentations while I used my media contacts to set up radio, television, and magazine interviews in each region. One of my contacts was Vladimir Pozner, Russia's most famous journalist, who hosted *Person Behind the Mask* – a weekly news magazine with an audience in the millions. With the help of La Strada, an anti-trafficking organization in Ukraine, we brought a young Russian woman who had been a trafficking victim to appear on the program. *Person Behind the Mask* provided the first national media coverage of trafficking in Russia. It caused such uproar that it was re-broadcast eleven times over the next year.

Susan and Joanne traveled together to speak at universities and to women's groups. I was determined to go to rural areas, where I suspected that traffickers were most active. I wasn't afraid of encountering criminal gangs because I believed, rightly or wrongly, that it would be more trouble than it would be worth for them to harm an American.

I carried the portable player and concentrated on villages with orphanages around St. Petersburg, Yaroslavl, and Nizhny Novgorod, going alone or with Yuri or David. The only requirement for my presentation was electricity for the tape player. My Russian language skills had improved to the point that I didn't need an interpreter. Whole villages turned out for the meetings, which were the social events of the year.

In mid-summer, I traveled by train from Moscow to Yaroslavl and caught the Rocket Boat to Tolga Convent on the Volga River. I boarded the hydrofoil with Russian Orthodox pilgrims who had come from Vladivostok to pray at the ancient chapel of the Virgin of Tolga, a place of healing miracles since the 14th century.

The full ship rode low in the water, buffeted by the current and wind until it rose on its foils and skimmed effortlessly above the surface, flying backward through time. We left behind the industrial silhouette of Yaroslavl and followed a shoreline that had changed little since medieval Rus.

Smoke curled from the chimneys of small wooden houses with brightly painted shutters. Yards were lush with vegetables. Villagers hauled buckets of water from the river to irrigate tomatoes, cucumbers, pumpkins, and squash. Dogs barked, running along the shore. The gold domes of Tolga glinted in the distance.

I had been bringing supplies to Tolga Convent since 1993, when a group of nuns first settled there amidst the ruins of the 600-year-old monastery. The walls were crumbling, the gates hung askew. The ancient church had been dynamited by the KGB and the ceiling collapsed. For the seventy years of Communist rule, Tolga was used as a prison for children whose parents had been executed by the State.

When the sisters dug in the grounds to plant vegetables, they uncovered mass graves of children – nameless little skeletons wrapped in rags and covered with lime. Saying prayers for the souls of the dead, they left the field fallow and sowed the earth with wildflower seeds. Only the calendula germinated because of the lime in the soil. Within a few weeks, bright orange petals blanketed the graves. I could see them now as we neared the shore. The Rocket Boat throttled back, settling into the water for our approach.

We docked at the convent's floating wooden pier. Crew members helped unload my heavy rolling bag. I climbed the hill, following the well-worn path along restored white-washed walls. I waved to the sisters in the vegetable garden. They had helped set up presentations of *Bought and Sold* to schools and orphanages around Yaroslavl. I approached the gate where an ugly brick watchtower still leaned toward the main entrance – the last external trace of Tolga's years as a prison. Inside the walls, the cathedral and refectory were under restoration, the grounds being cleared of debris, and the bell tower repaired. Volunteers from all over Russia worked on the buildings and gardens.

I stashed my bag in the rectory, then crossed the courtyard to the old chapel, a little brick church that had housed the famous healing icon, the Virgin of Tolga, since 1354. Mother Barbara and the sisters were in the church singing prayers. I waited for them in the vestibule, running my fingers over the names carved on the walls by child prisoners – Sasha, Misha, Ira, Tanya and dozens of others. "Remember me," they screamed. "Don't forget us."

Orthodox Church administrators wanted to replaster the walls and restore the original icons. The sisters were fighting to keep the walls as they were to preserve the sad graffiti as a memorial. When the prayers were finished, Mother Barbara invited me to join her for a supper of produce from the garden and cheese from their dairy.

From Tolga, I made daily excursions to nearby villages. That summer was one of the hottest seasons on record, with daily temperatures exceeding 100 degrees. Thermal windstorms tore up trees, broke power lines, and blew away haystacks, but no rain fell. Dust devils coated my clothes and hair with grit and pine needles while I waited to board buses, trams, and trains that would transport me to villages that had changed little since the Russian Revolution.

Vladimir Pozner's *Person Behind the Mask* had played so often that I'd become a familiar face. I must have been an odd sight, wheeling the video player up country lanes in my wide-brimmed straw hat, oversized green cotton sweater, and loose-knit cotton pants that were full in the legs like a black, flowing skirt. The tape player was so heavy that I couldn't manage the weight of any more luggage, so I lived in those clothes. The sweater soon faded to patchy brown like Army camouflage and the pants unraveled along the cuffs.

I was greeted like a rock star when I walked into town. For some reason, the Russian folksong "Shine, Shine, My Fateful Star" was sung to me many times. Everyone wanted me as a guest in their home. They wanted to feed me homegrown vegetables and ply me with moonshine vodka. More than anything, they wanted to touch me. I was always being crowded into a room that was too small or seated on a couch compressed between respectful villagers who poured tea and served plates of sliced tomatoes, apples, *petrushka* (parsley) and onions.

I listened to their stories and learned that they were more afraid of the police than of the local criminals, who were generally well-known members of the community. Every family had suffered at the hands of the Ministry of Internal Affairs, usually through the KGB. That was a serious obstacle in the fight against trafficking because families would wait months before contacting police when a girl went missing. Even then, they restricted their contact to personal connections – a relative or childhood friend whom they trusted.

At the same time, people were always inviting me to meet their son, the village chief of police, or their nephew in the police academy. I began to see how we might be able to build a working relationship with police by utilizing those personal connections to avoid corrupt officials.

I, too, had a personal connection: Once, when I was staying alone at my friend Galina's apartment in Moscow, I woke up in the middle of one night to a commotion in the kitchen. I went out in my pajamas to discover six young, uniformed policemen drinking beer at the kitchen table. I recognized Galina's son Gennady. Galina hadn't told me that he was a police officer.

"Hello, Gennady Alexandrovich," I said. "Hello, boys. Don't get up."

The officers tipped their hats. "Good evening, ma'am."

I went back to bed, knowing that I could call on Gennady if I needed help from the local police, which I soon did.

Summer rolled into autumn and the air cooled abruptly. I left Tolga and traveled to Nizhny Novgorod, where I stayed with musician friends from the balalaika ensemble *Korobeniki* – The Traveling Salesmen. I'd met them on the cruise ships during the "Cruise with a Cause" program and often stayed with Alexei the accordion player and his family.

Dinner with musicians of Korobeniki.

Yuri joined me in Nizhny for more town meetings. They were getting progressively larger and more emotional. Our national media exposure was drawing parents and friends of trafficking victims, and eventually trafficking survivors themselves. I started seeing uniformed police at our meetings, which meant they were attending in an official capacity. I visited so many small towns that they became a blur – but my presentation in the tiny village of Zelenogorod – Green Town – three hours from Nizhny by bus, stood out. It was there I met Zhenya, a trafficking survivor – a lost girl who, against all odds, had come home.

Yuri was busy making a presentation to parliamentarians in Nizhny, so I went alone to Zelenogorod. My bus was met by the city administrator and a group of high school boys who helped with the video player. It was a blustery day with a cold bite to the wind. I had purchased a wool coat in Nizhny Novgorod, but I wasn't warm enough. We walked along muddy streets to the center of the village, passing a general store and a disco. Wild dogs, a blend of mutt and wolf, lounged on the steps, their thick ruffs raised against the wind. They eyed me, panting, but didn't approach. I had seen their cousins in every Russian town I'd visited. Yellow-eyed tabby cats glared at me from windowsills and woodpiles. I had seen their cousins, too.

People came out of wooden houses, pulling on coats and hats. We had quite a crowd when we reached the district school, the only building with electricity. I was escorted to the principal's office and served tea with school officials. I presented them with a packet that included a transcript of *Bought and Sold* in Russian and a copy of the tape in PAL-SECAM, the Russian format.

The group in the auditorium were restless, eager The administrator opened the door to usher me in and the room grew hushed. He introduced me as their distinguished American guest to enthusiastic applause.

I gave a speech about the threat of human trafficking to Russian villages. Then I signaled to the boys to insert *Bought and Sold* into the player and dim the lights. I stayed standing to observe the faces of the crowd, who squinted at the undercover images of young women in slavery, leaning forward as if looking for someone they knew. They listened intently to the stories of Russian girls forced into prostitution and interviews with traffickers and crooked officials with their faces set. No one showed -emotion but their mood was electric.

When the film was over, the boys helped me hand out questionnaires and pencils to the participants so that they could share their personal knowledge about trafficking cases. They took about ten minutes to fill out the papers and hand them back. Then I announced that we would discuss the film and I would be glad to answer their questions.

My invitation was met with predictable silence – it was always that way. I looked at the audience and they avoided my gaze. Soon people were coughing and shifting in their chairs. Usually, I could count on an old woman to break the silence. In Zelenogorod, it was the village matriarch known as Baba Maria – Granny Maria.

"Well," she huffed, shrugging her Astrakhan shawl higher onto her shoulders. "Suddenly you peasants got nothing to say?" She looked back around at the townspeople, "Speak up, you lazy good-for-nothings."

Chaos broke loose, everyone spoke at once. Men swore, women broke into tears bemoaning the fate of their girls who had responded to ads for work overseas and had not been heard from since. Parents recognized the names of businesses that had sent their daughters abroad and berated themselves for letting their daughters go.

After the outpouring of helplessness and despair, I spoke for the first time about the need to develop a network connecting villages and towns across Russia, bringing in trusted personal contacts from the police and government. I told them that with such a network, they would be able to do much to prevent trafficking through education. "Do you want to join me in this fight." I asked. Of course, they did.

Knowing the power of a name, I asked them what we should call our new network. Someone at every presentation wanted to name the network Angel – after me. I liked it, too – not because it was my name, but because of the idea of an overarching coalition, a protective celestial dome, closer to God. Thus, Koalitsia Angel – Angel Coalition, became a living entity even though we had no funding to build it with. Somehow, the Angels had found their wings.

The noise increased in the room until Baba Maria glared over her shoulder again. "Be quiet, you ignorant peasants," she growled. "It sounds like a barnyard in here. Shut up and let Zhenya speak."

The crowd quieted. A slender young woman seated to the right of Baba Maria stood and turned to face the townspeople. After a pause, she spoke in a quavering voice, her eyes to the ground. "I'm so ashamed, Baba."

"Nonsense!" said Baba Maria. "You're back with us. That's all that matters. Now tell these folks what happened."

"Yes, Baba," she said, raising her tear-filled eyes. "Some traffickers came to my school last December. I didn't know that's what they were. I was coming out of class and they were offering girls jobs in Cyprus.

"I wouldn't have spoken to them, but my friend Nadya was with them. She used to go to our school. She looked so tan and well dressed. I stopped to say hi. She handed me a brochure of a beautiful place with sunny skies and blue seas. I had never dreamed that I could work in such a place.

"She took my friend Katya and me for a Pepsi. She told us about working in a resort where rich people go – how they practically give money away. She said I was pretty, and I could have her old job as a waitress if I had an international passport. I didn't, but she said that if I gave her 1300 rubles, she would get me one. It had to be a rush job.

"I took the money from Baba's mattress." Zhenya faltered. "I signed a contract and gave everything to Nadya without telling you." She turned to her grandmother. "Baba, I'm so sorry."

"Young people do foolish things," said Baba Maria handing her a handkerchief. "Carry on, girl. Stop blubbering."

Zhenya dried her eyes. "Nadya and a man took Katya and me to Moscow in a car. We went to Sheremetyevo Airport and joined lots of other girls waiting for the flight to Cyprus. 'This is wonderful,' I thought. Nadya gave us one-way tickets and we flew with an escort. It wasn't Nadya, but some man.

"At the airport in Larnaka, we were told to get into a bus that took us to a health center. We had health inspections. They were terrible. They looked at us naked while a man took pictures. Then we were taken to a brothel called 'Tofias' in Larnaka. We were told that our work would start downstairs at the Kopa Kabbana at 8 o'clock. There were eleven new Russian girls, and we would be doing striptease.

"I said that I didn't want to do it and I wanted to go home. The escort – a pimp named Vegas – told me that I could go as soon as I paid him 8,000 rubles for the plane ticket, 10,000 rubles to the travel agent who escorted us, 5,000 rubles for my health inspection, 11,000 rubles for my training, and 12,000 rubles for a month's rent in a filthy barracks. I had no way to pay the money, so I learned to do striptease.

"After a month, I was skin and bones. After all the deductions from my pay, I had no money left for food. I understood that I would never make enough cash just from stripping to pay my debt and go home. Then Vegas told me that I could make more money by having sex with customers.

"Vegas charged men $50 to sleep with me in a common room or $100 for a private session. From that, I was given $3, that's 90 rubles. It was hopeless. The more I worked, the bigger my debt became. I was giving comfort to twelve men a day and there still wasn't enough money for food. I started to get sick.

"I was coughing so much that Vegas finally took me to a clinic. He told me to lie about my age, to say I was eighteen or he would send someone to burn down Baba's house. I knew he meant it. The doctor said that I had pneumonia and that I would die without antibiotics. He asked me how old I was, I was too sick to lie and told him the truth – that I was fourteen years old.

"The doctor made me stay in the hospital. When I got better, I was deported back to Moscow. I stayed with relatives there until Baba came to get me. Now I'm here." Zhenya broke into tears. "My friend Katya never did come home. I don't know where she is. I never saw Nadya again either."

Baba Maria wrapped the Astrakhan shawl around the girl's heaving shoulders and swept her from the room. The meeting was over. Villagers surrounded me, pressing photographs and passport information into my hands. I tucked them respectfully into my growing dossier of missing daughters, hopeful that I'd be able to help them. At the very least, I could give the information to Interpol.

I was escorted back to the bus stop after turning down invitations to dinner in local homes. While I waited to catch the bus for the three-hour ride to Nizhny Novgorod, the villagers loaded me up with food. "For the train tonight," they said, handing me bags of produce and sausage, thanking me in the only currency they had.

Zhenya brought me a paper bag with piroshky still warm from the oven. "This is Baba's best. There are egg, onion, and potato," she said. "It's for the bus. Eat them while they're hot."

"Thank you for sharing your story with me." I gave her a hug. She felt like a little bird in my arms. "You're a very brave young woman."

"I want to help." She smiled and I saw the glint of spirit in her blue eyes. "Here's your bus. Sit in front, there's more air."

I settled in the second row. When I reached into her bag for a piroshky, I discovered a student's notebook tucked inside. In it, Zhenya had listed the names of all the girls she had met in Cyprus, their hometowns, the clubs where they worked, the names of the traffickers and their addresses. It was enough to open our first cases. This was exactly the kind of detailed information that Interpol was looking for.

Map of Western Russia

111

Chapter Fifteen

THE PLATZKART

Niznhy Novogorod to Moscow, Russia – Winter 1997

R ussia had felt the first bite of winter and Russians were on the move, flooding back into the cities from their summer dachas. Every inch of floor space in the bus from Zelenogorod to Nizhny Novgorod was covered with burlap bags full of potatoes, onions, carrots, bundles of herbs, and wreathes of dried mushrooms. Baskets of carefully wrapped jars of honey, pickles, and preserves were crammed onto the overhead shelves.

The trains would be jammed, too, with Russians returning to apartments and jobs in Moscow. Fortunately, Yuri had booked tickets for us in a first class, two-person compartment before we left Moscow. We'd have clean white sheets and tea served in glasses with ornate metal holders.

I pulled out my notebook and did the final tally. Over the summer, our two teams had traveled through six *oblasts* (states), and met with representatives of 275 school districts, 55 *internats* (special schools for orphans), 32 orphanages, 80 parent/teacher associations, 27 nongovernmental organizations (NGOs), and hundreds of girls, young women, and their parents. It hadn't seemed like so much when I was on the road, but now that it was over, exhaustion seeped into every fiber of my body. I looked forward to resting on the train – making the final leg of our journey in well-deserved comfort. The demon Chort had other plans.

I spotted Yuri pacing, looking anxiously up at the bus windows, when we pulled into the train terminal in Nizhny. He helped me off with the video player and we moved into the milling crowd in the square. In addition to the swell of seasonal travelers, refugees from the civil wars in Georgia, Azerbaijan, and Tajikistan were camped on the open ground.

"It's a good thing we bought our tickets in Moscow," I remarked.

"About that," he said hesitantly. "There is a slight problem with our tickets."

"What do you mean – a slight problem?"

"They've been cancelled," he replied, pushing me ahead of him. "I called to confirm our reservations this morning and was told that everything was fine. We had a first-class compartment. Now I find out that the first-class wagon has been misplaced. They don't know where it is. They think it's in Vladivostok."

"What?" I exclaimed. "The worst travel week of the year and they've lost the whole wagon?"

"Apparently. As it stands, we'll be lucky to get a platzkart on the Siberian Express. Pft ... pft ... pft ... " He spat on Chort and we entered the terminal – a sea of bustling, sweating humanity. People slept in dirty bundles amid piles of plaid shuttle bags. The air was stifling. The remains of smoked fish and greasy wrappers were scattered across the cement floor, contested by motley tabby cats with ripped ears.

Yuri spotted a place for me on a wooden bench and stacked our luggage in front of it. "Sit here and relax," he said. "Give me your documents. I'll be just a moment." I gave him my passport and he hurried off to the ticket line. Yuri was an expert at train haggling. I was a liability.

I groaned at the thought of traveling all the way to Moscow in a sixty-berth platzkart that smelled like urine. I really wanted to sleep in a clean bed and wake up in the morning with the conductor serving me hot, sweet tea. I spit on Chort – too little, too late. At this point, I'd be lucky to get on the train – any train.

The rest of the places on the wooden bench were occupied by other luggage-watchers like me. I nodded to the babushkas on my right and left, then concentrated on the bags. The distractions in the station were many – from the police dragging a struggling, bloody-faced drunk across the stone floor to the pack of snarling dogs fighting over a chicken carcass. Overhead, a uniformed station official stood on a scaffold and wrote the destinations and train numbers on a blackboard. The unmoving air was thick with white chalk dust that settled on my hair and clothes. I sneezed.

Across from me, a heavy, sun-burnt woman with a dirty bandana was slowly rolling thick, cotton hose off her legs, one at a time with chapped hands and dirty, broken nails. Her skirt was pulled up to her hips, revealing fleshy, shapeless thighs the color of bleached flour. She was peddling herself for a train ticket.

The crowd thinned and I spotted a typical train-station trafficking team: a handsome young man accompanied by a matronly older woman who was probably introduced as his aunt or mother. They were working a crowd of refugees from Tajikistan, talking to a group of pretty young girls in headscarves, who were giggling and flirting with their eyes. God help them, I thought, remembering Zhenya.

Yuri returned in about 45 minutes with two tickets. "I was very fortunate," he said. "We have the last berths on today's Siberian Express – in two different platzkarts. Hurry!" He thrust my ticket and passport into my hand and gathered up our luggage. "The train leaves in three minutes."

We hustled along the platform, stopping only to buy bottles of water and beer. Yuri kept talking: "Before I leave you alone, you need to know the 'platzkart rules,' so pay attention. And remember, it's better if they don't know you're a foreigner." He panted and sped up. The conductors were closing the doors. We had to move faster. "Your bed is like your apartment. It's your private space. Consider it locked at all times. No one can enter without permission. That's rule number one. Number two: Never take off your shoes or someone will steal them. Number three: Sleep with your coat on in case someone throws you off the train." He paused and checked my ticket. "Ah, this is your platzkart. I'll take the heavy luggage with me. You take your food bags and some water."

With that, I was handed up to a pair of bearded men with dirty hands who helped with my bags. The door slid closed, locked with a clunk, and the train began to roll. Radio speakers blared Russian pop music, heavy on synthesizer. The heater was on full blast. I stood with my back pressed against the end of the car, holding my overnight bag and two bags of food. Every face seemed to be turned in my direction. I took a deep breath.

"Hello, good folks, good evening," I said politely. "Where is my bunk, please?" I held out my ticket. Several people pointed to an upper berth about halfway down the car. I made my way there, buffeted between the bunks as the train jerked on its tracks. Once there, I climbed up to my bed. We had to stay in our designated spaces until the conductor came through to check tickets.

During the wait, I slipped a gold cap onto my front tooth. My dentist in Seattle had made it for me and I used it when I wanted to be ignored by Russians because it identified me as Eastern European. I could carry off the deception because I still spoke Russian with a Polish accent. The ruse worked until I had to answer questions about Warsaw.

For all their stony stares and silent frowns, Russians thrived on gossip. Once the uniformed conductor left the car, the silence was broken. Babushkas were in the aisles, bossing each other around, jockeying for position as food matriarch. To my relief, there were more women in the car than men. Food parcels were being opened and spread on train tables for all to share. Shirts were off, card games started up, and a bottle of vodka was passed around: "*Domashni* – homemade," someone said.

The babushkas watched me rummage in my bags from Zelenogorod. I pulled out cucumbers, Siberian cheese, boiled eggs, homemade salami, apples, *praenik* (honey cookies), and black bread – a feast. I had finished off Baba's piroshky on the bus and wasn't hungry. I spread everything on the designated table where it met nods of approval. Someone handed me a glass jar filled with malty *kvas*, a home-brewed beer made from fermented black bread. "Fresh from the dacha," I was assured.

When the babushkas were satisfied that we had enough food, the passengers relaxed. Russians did not fear pain, suffering, loneliness, or death, but they did fear hunger and cold. We had plenty to eat and we weren't going to freeze in the overheated platzkart. A group of women started a conversation with me, which led to the inevitable questions about Poland. When I had to admit that I wasn't Polish, but American, they fell silent. Like a single thought transmitted as an electron pulse through a conscious brain, the entire group simultaneously understood who I was and wanted to talk to me. Worse, they wanted to touch me.

It was the familiar ritual, and I was invited to sit as a guest on bunk after bunk, surrounded by a sweaty pile of humanity, bonded together through touch in ways that transcended language. It reminded me of my first hours after landing at Sheremetyevo Airport when I was surrounded and held close by the sleuth of Russian doctors. Then as now, I let go of my desire for personal space and accepted that I had been taken into this new *kolektiv* (team) for the remainder of the trip. What choice did I have?

The members of the kolektiv spun well-worn stories about the Great Patriotic War, the years of violence and famine that followed, the postings of young families to Africa, Asia, and Cuba during the Cold War. I learned that our kolektiv included a novelist, a famous Siberian poet, an astrophysicist, and geologists from the Mirny diamond mine. After a summer of gardening at country dachas, they all looked like peasant farmers and smelled of compost. I was rather ripe myself. I didn't even want to think about what my hair looked like.

Soon my name devolved into the inevitable Angelova as the kolektiv swigged homemade vodka and progressed from polite formal names with patronymics into the intimate universe of Russian nicknames – Alexei evolved to Alyosha and then further into Loshka, Maria to Masha and then Mashinka.

Of all the interesting travelers in that platzkart, one man holds a special place. His wife insisted that I go to his bunk to see him. He apologized for not getting up. At first, he seemed elderly, but at his bedside I saw that he was no older than me. I accepted the invitation to sit on his bed. There was plenty of room because he had no legs. His skin was covered in tumors – ugly black melanomas. He wore a military tunic decorated with rows of medals.

"My husband is a hero of the Soviet Union," said his wife. "He was a helicopter pilot in Kiev when the reactor at Chernobyl exploded. He volunteered to keep flying into the reactor to evacuate people and put out fires. If it weren't for his brave actions the whole plant could have exploded and blown away half of Ukraine."

Other platzkart passengers kissed his hands, remembering that terrible day in 1986 when the Chernobyl nuclear reactor spewed a murderous radioactive cloud.

"The rest of the pilots are dead of cancer. He will die soon. It was his great wish to meet someone from America and now God has sent you. His name is Alexei Gennadiavich Maslennov. You can call him Loshka."

I took Loshka's hand, feeling the power of his soul surge through warm fingers. The two scruffy, bearded fellows who had pulled me up into the car stepped forward, dressed in long, black hassocks with crucifixes around their necks. They were priests. They prayed over us while the other passengers crossed themselves and bowed in the Orthodox way.

Loshka beckoned me to come closer. When his lips were pressed against my ear, he whispered to me. "Angelova," his voice was barely audible, and his breath reeked of internal decay. "Go home and tell your president that I am dying young because I am a free man."

The poet stepped forward to recite well-known patriotic ballads – his own and others. The other passengers joined in the verses. A beautiful basso voice rose from the depths of the wagon and an opera singer climbed down from his upper bunk. An accordion player appeared as if by magic. To cheers, tears, and applause, the musicians launched into an impromptu concert of sad Russian songs about exile, prison trains, and bidding good-bye to warm homes and loving families to face a slow death of cold, hunger, and deprivation in Siberia. The travelers knew these songs well – the oral history of Russia.

More vodka and someone's stash of homemade cognac were passed around and we danced, sang, and cried in the timeless, encapsulated space. We became the partisans, prisoners, exiles, and soldiers, who no longer held any attachment to lives beyond the kolektiv of this train. We could have been moving toward the Western Front, the Ukrainian forests, or destined for labor camps, it made no difference. Platzkart rules were forgotten, or blurred at least, and the party moved from bunk to bunk.

When the Siberian Express rolled into Moscow, harsh overhead lamps switched on automatically, inundating the wagon with intrusive brightness. By then, most of us were stretched out in a stupor from the oxygen-depleted air, homemade vodka, too much food, not enough water, and an emotional purge of stories. A loudspeaker inches from my head chirped and started pounding out the ABBA song "Money, Money, Money." I had been asleep in someone else's bed wrapped in my coat, next to the snoring poet who was wrapped in his coat. I groaned and fumbled for the volume control, but there wasn't one. We were fast approaching the terminal. It was time to go back to my berth and gather my things.

The conductor, whom we hadn't seen since she took our tickets, passed through the car, prodding travelers who were too slow to wake up and kicking a few who had fallen asleep on the floor. As soon as the train came to a screeching stop, the door slid open to a blast of cold and a swirl of snow. We stood in a disheveled line down the center of the car, clutching our bags like refugees. Then we shuffled toward the open door to the ABBA chorus of, "Money, money, money! It's always sunny – in a rich man's world."

A detail of uniformed soldiers boarded and carried Loshka from the train. On the platform, I barely had time for hurried farewells, a few hugs and kisses before Yuri took my arm and guided me down the stairs into the maze of tunnels connecting the train station with the Moscow Metro. He shook his head in disapproval.

"Most people just get into their beds and go to sleep," he scolded. "You let them know that you're American, didn't you?"

I was too tired to retort that I could only carry off the Polish deception to a point and that Russians could suss out a faker in a blink. The most I could muster was a grunt before I fell asleep on the Green Line Metro train with my head on his shoulder.

Chapter Sixteen

ANGELS IN CYBERSPACE

Seattle to Moscow – 1999

I stayed awake at Yuri and Irina's apartment long enough to eat scrambled eggs with *sprots*-on-toast (sardines) before crashing on their sofa. Irina woke me at 3 A.M. for the drive to Sheremetyevo for my Aeroflot flight to Seattle. Ours was the only car on the road. The air of Moscow smelled cool and clean as we raced at breakneck speed through the center of the city. We skidded past St. Basil's and turned sharply onto Tverskaya Street. A light snowfall dusted Red Square.

Irina dropped me at Departures, and I passed through ticketing and customs like a zombie. Once airborne, I stretched across three seats in the Ilyushin and tried to sleep, but my head pounded to the rhythm of "Money, Money, Money!" I finally drank a vodka, swallowed half a Halcyon sleeping pill, and slept, waking a few times confused by the roar of jet engines that sounded like the wheels of the Siberian Express. I kept my coat and shoes on, adhering to "platzkart rules."

Friends who'd been house-sitting picked me up at SeaTac. I'd forgotten to remove my fake gold tooth and they inquired if I'd had dental work done in Russia. They carried my luggage up the two flights of stairs to my front door and left me standing on the sunlit porch.

I took in the warm fall day with its promise of rain. Seattle's skyscrapers glinted above the city to the south, but a lenticular cloud over Mount Rainier boded brisk winds and precipitation by tomorrow. The Cascade Mountains rose snowless in the east. Bright spinnakers dotted Lake Union. A tug and barge slid between the raised spans of the Fremont Bridge. I inhaled and coughed. American air seemed too thin after the thick Russian atmosphere.

I didn't enter my house, but walked around the garden, reminding myself that this was where I belonged. Yellow chrysanthemums and orange nasturtiums overflowed the flowerpots. "I planted those," I thought aloud. "And the alyssum, sweet William, lobelia, and dusty miller." Wild pinks bloomed on long stalks, splashing the yard with color. I unlocked the French doors to the kitchen and found a warm pan of lasagna on the stove.

I woke the next morning with sunlight flooding the bedroom and the wind howling around Queen Anne Hill. The gale recalled the hot, dry cyclones that had whipped the trees in Yaroslavl. But in Seattle, there would be rain. The first drops gusted against my window like a fist full of pebbles. I stopped caring where I was. I burrowed into my pillows and slept all day. Around midnight, the phone rang.

I sat up. "Allo? Hello?" I said into the receiver.

"I have an emergency," said Yuri. "I am at Russian Parliament. They don't know how to contact NATO. I need your help before there's an incident."

I switched on my bedside lamp. "Are you nuts? I'm in my pajamas." My first reaction was to laugh, but Yuri often consulted with parliament.

"Julietta, pay attention," he shouted over the sounds of an argument. "They are going to start a war. Please do as I ask. Find NATO."

He was serious. I shook myself awake, ordering my brain to function. "Stay on the line. I have to figure this out," I said.

I decided to call the Pentagon and dialed information in Washington DC on my other line. The operator asked if I wanted the 24-hour Pentagon hotline. I said yes and a young male voice answered.

"I have Russian Parliament holding," I said. "They need to contact the head of NATO in Moscow and don't know how to do it. It's an emergency."

"Don't be ridiculous," was the snide reply. "Of course, they know how to do it."

I held up the phone to the other handset so that he could hear the shouting in Russian.

"Just a minute." He put me on hold.

A few minutes later he confirmed that it wasn't so easy to contact NATO in Moscow. Although the NATO commander was American, he could only be reached through the German Embassy. He gave me the emergency number of the German Military Attaché.

I explained the process to Yuri and gave him the number. He thanked me. "Sorry to disturb your rest," he said. "Go back to sleep."

Impossible. I was wide awake. Beyond the adrenalin rush from the phone call, day and night were reversed in my body clock by the eleven time-zone changes and would be for days. I pulled on my robe and padded barefoot through the dark house, peering into rooms illuminated by moonlight. With my children gone, there were too many. In the room that had been my daughter's, everything was just the way she'd left it. She'd moved to the University of Virginia and chosen to make her Seattle home at her father's waterfront mansion. She'd made it clear that she wasn't coming back.

I stood at her gabled window recalling the day that we had painted her walls Dutch blue and her furniture white. I would sit on her bed at night while she settled into sleep, telling stories about Alabaster, the flying white horse, who came to her window and carried her off on great adventures.

Wind rustled through bare branches that scratched at the glass. The lights of Seattle – bridges, waterways, and distant skyscrapers – twinkled on turbulent water. Headlights sped across the Aurora Bridge. I turned away, unable to remain in that space where her scent lingered. Her absence was an ache that had no relief.

I sat cross-legged on my bedroom floor and opened a suitcase. My green sweater and black pants were too faded and threadbare for Goodwill. Their dusty, sweaty smell brought back memories of the trains, buses, and grimy villages. I recalled the feral dogs that followed me with yellow eyes, panting in the heat, and villagers hurrying from their wooden houses to greet me and touch my hands. I held up the shoes that had walked so far. The soles were nearly worn through. I had a closet full of expensive clothes and shoes, barely worn. They didn't seem to belong to me anymore, but rather to someone I once knew.

I sorted through folders stuffed with photographs and information about girls who had disappeared. I looked through Zhenya's notebook, running my fingers down its ruled pages. The tiny Cyrillic script was written with dull pencil. It would require a translator to decipher. I should have left it with Yuri, but I knew people in Seattle who would do it.

As dawn approached, the winds quieted. I dressed and prepared to join joggers and cyclists on the three-mile trail around Green Lake. Rowing shells glided across the water, their cockswains shouting, "Pull, pull." Mallards and Canada geese made a ruckus on Duck Island. I tightened my laces and walked at a brisk pace through the drizzle. I had learned to reset my biological clock by exercising at daybreak – either at Green Lake in Seattle or along the Moscow River in Russia.

I needed a sharp mind to face the financial problems that I'd put off all summer. I had plugged the shortfalls in MiraMed's budget with credit card accounts left over from my doctor days. Now I had debts of over $300,000 and no way to pay them without going back into medical practice – or selling my house. My house was an asset, but also a burden. The empty rooms had become a sad reminder that my children had grown up and gone.

I wished that I could adopt little Angela and bring her to Seattle. I'd like to give her the same opportunities in life that my children had. I checked on her whenever I was in Uglich and kept in touch with Tatyana Safarovna. Angela was a smart girl, doing well in school. She was artistic and liked making clothes for her dolls. But she remained unadoptable. The best way that I could see to help all my Russian children was with education and health programs administered through the orphanages. I had made a soul commitment to the missing girls and that meant spending more time in Russia.

I called a realtor and put my house on the market. I didn't want it anymore. My friends were shocked to see me letting go of a comfortable, respectable life in a beautiful home. I was being irrational, they argued. It wasn't too late for me to go back into practice and give up this obsession with Russia.

I went to work fund-raising – connecting with donors and speaking to groups of former passengers from "Cruise with a Cause." I gave presentations to community groups, churches, and at the Russian Consulate. I shared the story of my winter pilgrimage on the Murmansk Highway and of my terrible discoveries in Svir Stroi, Murmansk, and Kirkenes. People opened their hearts and gave generously.

My proposals for federal grant funds were well received in Washington DC and I was invited to speak at the State Department and before Congress and then at the United Nations in New York. The US Information Agency – USIA – agreed to fund the first meeting of twenty Russian anti-trafficking coalition leaders in Moscow. I had proposed that as the launch of a counter-trafficking campaign in Russia.

While in DC, I did an interview for Voice of America (VOA). Their bulky headsets and 1950s-style microphones reminded me of broadcasting from the Peace Committee years before. VOA asked me to talk about the progress that MiraMed had made in Russia, with our expanding programs of orphan life-skills education and our summer program on preventing human trafficking.

VOA programs were broadcast across Russia and were often the only programs a village radio could receive. They were giving me an opportunity to talk to girls like Zhenya who had survived and returned. I had no other way of reaching them. Thousands would be listening to this broadcast. Surely Zhenya was in the Zelenogorod Library with Baba Maria right now. I could see her with the other villagers, gathered around the radio as I told her story and lauded her courage. "Do not lose heart," I said. "The international community will not tolerate this despicable crime of human trafficking any longer. We know what has to be done and we're going to help."

I looked at the VOA producer to see if she were about to cut me off. She smiled and signaled to keep going. "I've never told you how I came to be in your villages where I met such warm, generous people. That story begins in the middle of winter when I was traveling north on the Murmansk Highway in a logging truck … "

At the end of the broadcast, I took off my headset and left the darkened studio. Had I done the right thing? Had I made an unrealistic promise? I recalled the words of Bella Abzug: "Forge ahead. Worry about the details later."

After Washington, I traveled on Amtrak to New York and presented the results of our trafficking education program at the United Nations Commission on the Status of Women. My unconventional Voice of America broadcast had been monitored by the UN and I was invited to participate in a global videoconference linking women's groups from North America, Europe, Africa, and Asia to discuss human trafficking. I wondered if videoconferencing might be something that we could use to bring together our anti-trafficking network without the need for travel, post, or telephones.

It wasn't. Even in the high-tech studios in the basement of the United Nations building, the conference was fraught with problems. The technology was unreliable and, even in developed countries, the visual quality was poor. When women from rural India finally made it to the video screen, they covered their faces, fearful of being identified.

After the all-night broadcast, I joined the UN technicians in the cafeteria for scrambled eggs and coffee. Two of them were Russian. I told them about our trafficking network. "We need some way to bring people together across huge distances using technology similar to the videoconference, but it has to be simpler, cheaper, and widely available. I need to know who the participants are without showing their faces or real names."

"You're right that videoconferencing won't work in Russia," said the bald one named Vitaly. "But there's something new that might. The universities are nearly all hardwired for Internet now. They have a mandate to train the public on using it and setting up free e-mail accounts," he said.

"What does that do for us?"

"Haven't you ever heard of a chat room?" the younger one, Maxim, asked.

"Sure," I said. "That's where hot guys like you hook up with hot babes in bars, right?"

"Funny," he said.

"A chat room is a low-tech version of the videoconference," said Vitaly. "There is no audio or video – just text. If your Russians can type, they can participate and use any code name they want."

Maxim added, "We could only have eight people at a time with the video. The chat room is pretty much unlimited. You can have hundreds."

"All at once? The whole country?"

Vitaly considered the question. "Why not set a time for each of the eleven time zones you have to cover. That way you could have thousands over an eighteen-hour period. Start with Vladivostok and work your way west with the sun."

This was great news. "How do I set that up?" I asked. "Can we do it from here?"

"Everything the UN does is too expensive. You're better off using a Russian Internet provider. The biggest and most reliable is Glasnet in central Moscow. I can introduce you to the president if you like."

I still had to raise the funds to make it all work. "Think about it," I told Soroptimists International at their yearly gathering a week later. I had joined them as a guest speaker in Helsinki. "How do we bring people together across a country that spans two continents and eleven time zones? The answer is cyberspace, and the best news is that it's practically free. We just have to teach the Russians how to use it."

I didn't mention that most of our activists were from remote villages and had no knowledge of computers or the Internet. Many didn't have electricity or own a telephone. Most lived a full day's travel from the nearest university. We had no way to reach them except the unreliable post, community bulletin boards, and Voice of America. My modest goal was to achieve 200 participants and gather information on trafficking from at least five regions.

We got the funding.

In January 1999, I sold my house, paid off my debts, and moved to Moscow. Yuri had found me a two-room apartment with high ceilings on Kosmodamianskaya Embankment for $500 a month. The flat was tucked into a corner of a huge Stalin-era building that ran for a full city block along the Moscow River. It had good cross ventilation and excellent light.

A balcony overlooked the Kornet Champagne Factory on one side and the Headquarters of the Military District of Moscow on the other.

I would wake up at dawn to the tinkling of champagne bottles, the air redolent with fermenting grapes. At night, I fell asleep to the patriotic songs of the Red Army Chorus rehearsing next door. Ironically, the apartment's previous occupant had been the NATO Commander's fiancé. It would have been easy for the Duma to find him there, if I had only known.

That small flat became the first international headquarters of MiraMed Institute in Russia. Yuri left his job at the All-Union Center to be our full-time Country Director. Vlad moved from Uglich to Moscow to assist him.

I pitched the chat room to Glasnet's board of directors. They signed on and gave us a generous discount, agreeing to let our team run the chat room from inside their headquarters on *Khlebny* (Bread) Street next to MacDonald's.

With the help of the technology department of Moscow State University we developed a proposal and sent it to all Russian universities, asking that their Internet centers conduct the chat room in their conference facility. We asked that they start by teaching a class on cyber-technology and set everyone up with e-mail accounts. Participants would complete our questionnaires. When their time-zone came online, they would take turns giving information to an onsite moderator who would enter the text and send it for posting in the chat. Our administrators at Glasnet would translate if necessary.

Twenty-six universities and thirty-five Internet centers responded positively. They sent out invitations to their communities through the local schools and Palaces of Culture. No one had ever done anything like this before, but everyone thought it could work – if people came. There was no feedback mechanism, so we had no way of knowing who got the message in the villages and whether they were coming. So far, Russians had been reluctant to use the Internet and mistrusted e-mail.

I could understand why. Cyberspace was a huge reach for people in places like Zelenogorod. In addition to the learning curve, we were asking them to travel for hours on a bus to a university center, then share personal information online with strangers – very un-Russian.

In the meantime, I worked with the Forum Foundation of Seattle to design a special questionnaire called the Opinionnaire™. Each questionnaire would provide 500 data points about human trafficking in each region based on the knowledge and opinions of participants. The responses were marked with a No. 2 pencil on a computer answer sheet – something else that was new to Russians.

Our whole team joined the effort to send the bulky packages of Opinionnaires, answer sheets, and pencils to the university Internet centers. We used the trains – paying conductors to take the packages, then calling ahead and providing the scheduled time of arrival and the number of the car – very Russian.

The night before the chat room, I was too anxious to sleep. The idea of relying on Russian villagers to travel on buses for a day to sign up for Internet accounts suddenly seemed absurd. I had risked my credibility on the presumption that at least some of them would. What if none did?

Chort snickered in my left ear. "You're pretty cocky, aren't you?"

"Pft … pft … pft … " I spit on him. He shut up, but I still couldn't sleep.

By first light, I was on the Green Line Metro to Tverskaya Station. I walked through deserted pedestrian tunnels, emerging near Pushkin Square, still trying to convince myself that Russia wouldn't let me down. Lights were on in the offices of ITAR-TASS News Agency, but other buildings on Pushkin Square were dark. The only sounds were my footsteps on the sidewalk, a cascade of water in the fountain where lovers met, and the swish of a street-sweeper's broom.

My staff and I were set up and ready to run the chat room by 6:30 A.M. While we waited for Vladivostok in the Russian Far East to sign on first, I recalled the evening, years before, when I'd sat at the empty tables in the Hotel Prague, wondering if anyone would come to our banquet, then worrying that too many people might come.

We didn't have to wait long. "Greetings from Vladivostok Women's Center and House of Culture." They began at exactly 7 A.M. Then Irkutsk and Barnaul were on. Siberia was jumping the gun with city after city signing on early. Soon we had Tomsk, Krasnoyarsk, and Bratsk. So many people were online that the translators couldn't keep up. The Russian language flashed past so quickly in Cyrillic that I couldn't follow it. I told our staff to stop trying to translate. We were recording everything – I would read it later.

Suddenly, a group from Novosibirsk with the name GirlsForSale broke into our chat with the opening line of, "*Yob tvoi mat* – Fuck your mother." We'd been hacked! The Glasnet techs revved into action with a special gatekeeping function they'd developed that blocked the intruders. We cheered our success but forgot to spit on Chort. Immediately, the power grid in central Moscow cut out. Half the city went dark.

When Glasnet re-booted twenty minutes later, the discussion had continued without us and more cities were signed in. Around 4 P.M., Europe and the United States started coming online and our interpreters were kept busy translating between Russian and English.

By the end of the day, over 2,500 people from Russia and the former Soviet republics of Kazakhstan, Armenia, Azerbaijan, Tajikistan, Ukraine, Moldova, and Republic of Georgia had participated. Most had gathered at university centers, but many facilities had joined the chat room without contacting us in advance. They had obtained copies of the questionnaire and answer sheet from other universities. We'd have no way of knowing how much data we had until everything was collected.

The next morning, the process of retrieval began. Regions without train service sent in their questionnaires by bus. Packets arrived on commercial trucks. And every center returned the No. 2 pencils as well. The last package came on a watermelon truck from the Republic of Georgia. The driver apologized profusely for being so late and gave us a complimentary watermelon. He had been trapped for a week by gas shortages in the Pankisi Gorge.

I was elated by the response. We retrieved over 4,000 questionnaires from 55 regions of Russia and 7 former Soviet republics – quadruple what we had sent out. That provided us with 1,250,000 pieces of data that revealed the vast extent of human trafficking in each region – involving up to 27% of families in some areas.

We now had a statistically significant sampling of the Russian population as defined by the Russian Parliament, the State Duma. Yuri and Vlad prepared the material to present to Alexander Lisichkin, the Chairman of the Legislation Committee, to be used in drafting an anti-trafficking law.

Reviewing the transcripts, I scrolled through the leading participants to assemble our list of invitees to the first meeting of the Angel Coalition. I was pleased to find Zhenya signed on as ZhenyaZ in Nizhny Novgorod. She had shared her story online and encouraged other survivors to come forward and help build a support network for trafficking victims.

"I won't let you down," I exclaimed aloud.

I added, "Pft ... pft ... pft ... " and spit on my left shoulder for good measure.

Chapter Seventeen

SHADOWS OF HISTORY

Moscow, Russia to Kiev, Ukraine – Fall 1999

On September 13, 1999, I sat at my desk sipping a cup of freshly brewed coffee, enjoying the early morning quiet. I had just switched on my computer, dialed up the Internet using Glasnet, and started reading the news when the earth cracked. Plaster fell from the ceiling. Hot coffee splashed into my lap. Windows shattered and bottles splintered in the courtyard of the champagne factory. Car alarms shrieked across the city. The power went out.

I ran to the balcony, recalling the sound of tanks firing at the White House six years before. Smoke billowed over southern Moscow. Fire engines and police cars raced along the embankment on both sides of the river, sirens wailing. They were followed by ambulances that turned and headed south on the Ring Road toward the plume of darkening sky.

The lights came back on. With shaking hands, I re-booted my computer and dialed up the Internet again. The CNN headline ticker read: "A bomb has exploded in an apartment block on Kashirskoe Boulevard. The fire department is battling a massive blaze that ignited when the explosion broke the central gas main." I looked up Kashirskoe on my city map. It was three kilometers to the south, mere blocks from Yuri and Irina's place. I tried to call them but got a busy signal.

I stared at the computer, shivering in my coffee-soaked pajamas, afraid to take my eyes off the news ticker to go change. I didn't want to shut the balcony doors either and lose the sound of my neighbors' voices. They were shouting updates as they heard them. I finally dressed hurriedly. When I came back, the CNN ticker read: "Moscow authorities confirm that a bomb has exploded in the basement of an eight-story apartment complex in southeastern Moscow. The central tower has collapsed. Hundreds are trapped inside, an unknown number have been killed … This act of terrorism follows the same method as a bomb placed in the basement of an apartment on Guryanova Street on September 9, killing 94 people and injuring 249 … Chechen terrorists are suspected … " The ticker stopped. Glasnet had shut down.

The telephones didn't work. I took the bus to Yuri and Irina's and found them getting into their car. I climbed in back and Yuri drove to the destroyed building – a naked gash in the lives of hundreds of people. The central third of a block-long complex was gone, blown into a pile of smoldering rubble. Occupants were crushed in their beds when the concrete floors pancaked on top of one another.

The Fire Brigade was hosing the burning wreckage. Ambulances and fire engines lined the street. Dogs sniffed for survivors. The air reeked of methane and cement dust. A policeman approached the car. Yuri rolled down the window and presented his parliamentary ID card. "How many poor souls gone?" he asked.

"Three hundred and counting," said the officer, handing it back.

"Any survivors?"

"A few. Can't dig until the gas fire's out." The cop lit a cigarette and tossed the match. "Goddamn Chechens," he said. "Time we taught them another lesson, eh? Now move along."

No one spoke as we edged our way through traffic and onto a boulevard. Finally, Irina said, "That's bomb number four this year – Okhotny Ryad, Buynatsk, Guryanova, and now Kashirskoe Shosse. Terrible, terrible."

Yuri shook his head. "This is going to mean another war with Chechnya."

"Chechnya is still part of Russia, isn't it?" I asked. "Why didn't Chechnya become independent with the rest of the republics, like Georgia or Ukraine? That's what they want, isn't it?"

"Chechnya and the other Caucasus republics comprise the treacherous underbelly of Russia." Yuri swerved and swore, narrowly missing an ambulance. "We cannot let the Chechens form alliances with foreign militants or Russia will be overrun by Islamic jihadists. It is the gravest threat to our national security."

"You should read the history of the Caucasus," said Irina. "It is the past and future of our country and probably yours as well."

I recalled our Chechen partners from Grozny – Fatima and Gul. They had participated in the chat room and brought in groups from Dagestan and Kabardino-Balkaria. I'd gone to the Chechen capital to show *Bought and Sold*. We'd picnicked in a grove of avocado trees on the Terek River, looking across the border at the Republic of Georgia. It had been a hot, clear day. "Chechnya is a beautiful place," I said.

"But the people are violent. They hate Russians," said Yuri. "Chechens have been nothing but trouble since before the time of Shamil, the Lion of Dagestan. You should read about him, too."

"That's why the Tsar sent the Cossacks to Ukraine. They were the only warriors fierce enough to fight the Chechens," Irina said. "In the 1930s, Stalin exiled the Cossacks to places like Turkmenistan thinking they would die in the desert. Incomprehensible. They wound up running the place."

"Our Vlad is from Turkmenistan," I said. "But he claims that he's Russian."

"Our young Vlad is a Kubansky Cossack," said Yuri, turning onto Andropovsky Boulevard and picking up speed. "Those Cossacks were fierce fighters and excellent farmers. Once they were exiled, the stupid Ukrainian peasants ate their own seed-grain and starved for generations."

"Mark my words," said Irina, "This next Chechen war will be the end of that Jew, Boris Yeltsin. Watch the new man Putin – the Orthodox Christian from St. Petersburg. He's on the way up."

"I met Vladimir Putin at Pulkovo Airport a few months ago," I said. "We were both doing interviews for ORT TV." I recalled a quiet, sturdy man of about my age who shook my hand politely – the opposite of the garrulous Yeltsin, who had kissed me on the lips. "He seems steady and smart. I talked to him about trafficking."

"The Soloviki will use Yeltsin's family scandals to push old Boris out of office and into the grave," said Yuri.

"Soloviki?"

"The shadow government – the ten men who control Russia from behind the curtain. The only time you see them on TV is in the front row at the State of the Nation address in the Hall of Columns," said Yuri. "That ambitious young Putin sat with them this year. That means he's next in line. He'll be our first Russian Orthodox president. The rest were all Jews."

"I wonder what that will mean for our anti-trafficking work."

"Who knows?" Irina shrugged.

"Our first trafficking conference is a month from now," I said. "Do you think the participants will be afraid to come to Moscow?"

"Perhaps. It's not too late to change the venue, though. It doesn't need to be held in Moscow," said Yuri. "We can go someplace peaceful – like Ukraine. Kiev is just a pleasant night on the train."

"Here's your building." Irina stopped the car. "Shall we walk you in?"

"Not necessary," I kissed them good-bye and stepped through broken champagne bottles on the way to the steel entry door.

Two weeks later, on October 1st, Russia mobilized against its own Republic of Chechnya and carpet-bombed the capital, Grozny. Prominent Chechens who lived in Moscow and owned businesses including luxury hotels took their objections to the State Duma. They presented compelling evidence that the bombs in the Moscow apartments had been false flags, set by the KGB, re-named the FSB, to ensure the election of Vladimir Putin. The arguments fell on deaf ears. Russian troops invaded Chechnya. Chechen militias were rumored to be operating in the forests around Yaroslavl to protect their own people. Terror attacks were imminent.

Vlad called. "I'm not coming in today. They've cut the phone lines to Uglich. I have to make sure my family's okay."

"How are you getting there?"

"My friend is driving. Do you want to come? I don't know what the status of the orphanage is. They were at the lager, last I heard. But the woods are full of Chechens. They've been driven out of the town and are living rough."

"Yes," I said. "I'm coming."

"Get the Metro and meet us at the River Station in one hour. We can't drive into Moscow with Yaroslavl plates."

I found Angela and the kids at the Uglich orphanage in town. The gates were locked, guarded by Dada Igor. "Angelova," he greeted me through a slot in the steel door. He opened it a crack. "Come in."

"Julietta!" Tatyana Safarovna engulfed me in her embrace. "Come in for tea." I spotted a flurry of activity at the upstairs window. The door flew open and Angela wrapped herself around my legs. I ran my fingers through her tangled corona of red hair. There was a brush caught in it.

"She won't let us cut it," said Anna. "Puts up an awful fuss."

"At least finish combing it." Tatyana Safarovna said to the older girls. To Angela she said, "Go make yourself pretty. You don't want Dr. Engel to think you're a fuzzy-wuzzy, do you?" Angela shook her head no and scampered off. "She's nearly ten and smart as a whip – but so tiny. She gets away with all kinds of mischief."

"I just came to make sure you're safe. I was worried when Vlad said the phone lines were cut."

"It's true. We had to come back to town early. All the Chechen families have been driven out of Uglich. They're living at the lager, eating our chickens and vegetables. Ptoo," she spat.

I spent the night on a sofa bed in the orphanage dining room, awakened early by the clatter of pots in the kitchen. I opened my eyes and found myself nose-to-nose with Angela.

"I want to go here," she said, pointing to a picture of London. She had covered the sofa bed and me with *National Geographic* magazines that were left by one of our "Cruise with a Cause" tourists. There were torn paper bookmarks in each magazine. "Where is this?"

"That's London," I said. "The capitol of England."

"What about here?" She opened another and pointed to lions and elephants.

"That's a game park in Tanzania," I said, reading the caption. "In Africa."

She plunked herself onto the bed and nestled close. "How do I get to Africa?"

"You go to school. You get a job," I said. "I'll help you go to an institute in Yaroslavl or St. Petersburg. You can be a nurse or a teacher."

"I want to be a pilot," she said.

The cook rang a cowbell announcing breakfast. The room filled with hungry children. Angela fought for her place at the table, elbowing aside two bigger boys, and held up her dish for kasha.

After a few days, I went with Vlad back to Moscow. We had a lot of preparation ahead for the upcoming anti-trafficking conference. Two weeks later, amidst mounting tensions and military buildup in Moscow, twenty human rights leaders from across Russia met Yuri and me at Sheremetyevo Airport.

We barely knew one another from the chat room and couldn't put names to faces yet. A few of us had met in Huairou, China, at the United Nations Conference on Women in 1995. Others had been part of the summer program, organizing town meetings where one of our team had spoken and shown the film *Bought and Sold*. From the airport, we traveled by charter bus to *Kievsky Vokzal* – Kiev Station – to board the night train to Ukraine and the first gathering of our anti-trafficking network in the Ukrainian capital.

I had polled the participants and we decided that Kiev was a safer environment than Moscow. La Strada, a Russian-speaking Ukrainian NGO with considerable expertise in human trafficking, had agreed to do an intensive ten-day training.

Kiev Station was Moscow's busiest train depot and an obvious terror target. We arrived to find the main entrance barricaded. Armed soldiers waved our bus to the opposite side of the square. We waited nearly an hour while they inspected the luggage compartment with sniffer dogs. The bus was silent – no one spoke while soldiers walked the aisle with dogs.

Once we'd retrieved our suitcases, a policeman led us down a darkened side road lined by more soldiers in camouflage gear and balaclavas, armed with Kalashnikovs. German shepherds sniffed at our clothes and luggage as we lifted our bags onto the waiting train. We boarded and found our ticketed cabins. Yuri and I shared a two-berth compartment. We paid the conductor an extra 200 rubles for clean sheets and scratchy little square towels, then struggled to stow the baggage on the overhead racks and under the seats. Yuri brandished his handkerchief and mopped his brow. The air in the compartment was hot and stale. I tried to open the window. It wouldn't budge. The radio speaker blasted ubiquitous pop music.

The trip would take fourteen hours. It was an express, which meant bypassing the smaller stations where passengers had a chance to jump off to buy smoked chicken, fish, and homemade beer from the locals. Irina had sent us off with cheese, salami, apples, bread, and water. Yuri had stocked up on his usual Baltika Beer No. 9, which was closer to cognac than beer. Throughout our journeys together he liked to drink two Baltika No. 9s, read the newspaper, and go to sleep, snoring loudly.

The train screeched and jerked forward, rolling slowly through a junk-yard of rusting, twisted scraps of steel and broken wagon-cars, then abandoned factories with shattered windows and into flat farmland. This was dacha country. Little log houses with gingerbread windows and geraniums in flower boxes lined the tracks.

The conductor tapped on the door for our tickets. When she left, Yuri opened his first bottle of Baltika and spread the newspaper on his bunk. Before long, our new colleagues found us, arriving with bags of food. They were smiling and chatting, getting to know one another. Within minutes, food was everywhere. People had brought their regional specialties. It was my first experience of sweet *chakchak* pastry from Tatarstan and smoked *omul* fish from Lake Baikal in Siberia. The delegation from Karelia poured their local plum brandy into train glasses with metal handles. From Udmurtia in the Ural Mountains came slices of spicy kolbasa.

The upper bunks were lowered so that more newcomers could sit up top. Eventually the radio music faded, and the cabin lights dimmed to a blue glow, signaling sleep-time, but we were just warming up for a *vecherinka* – an evening party. Our health, happiness, and the future of our project were toasted.

The Russians chugged their glasses of vodka while I sipped mine. Yuri was telling a joke about two hunters, a dentist, and a bear on a bicycle. Our new kolektiv laughed themselves into tears. I sat to one side, feeling like an *inostranka* – a stranger, a foreigner. I seldom understood Russian humor although I tried to laugh in the right places.

The train slowed and passed through another village. In the glare of streetlights, young couples walked hand in hand along the tracks. Women rocked children on porches. Men sat on doorsteps and smoked, their cigarettes glowing orange as they enjoyed the unseasonably warm fall weather.

We accelerated again and Yuri closed the window shade against the night. One after the other, the Russians introduced themselves and told family stories. When it was my turn to share, I hesitated. I understood that no one would trust me until I revealed my true self – or at least as close as I could get. I didn't know much about my secretive family. I'd have to fill in the blanks with imagination.

I began: "My grandmother Mema was an opera singer. She sang at the Metropolitan Opera in New York and later at the Hollywood Bowl," I began. That much was documented fact. "I remember her sweeping into the living room in a long black dress and a hat with a black veil.

"I would beg her to tell us stories about her younger days, even though her stories never had happy endings. She would only say, 'They all died in the terrible war.' Under her bed, she kept a hatbox full of old photographs.

"'I brought these to America – from France,' she'd say, pulling one out. 'Look at this postcard. That is the Place d'Opera. And that is Les Invalides. Here is my precious Papa as a medical student with his classmates in front of the Arc de Triomphe. Wasn't he handsome?'

"There were photos of Mema singing opera in the costumes of Carmen and Norma, or dressed as Margarita, posing with your famous Russian baritone, Feodor Chaliapin as Mephisto. They sang *Mephistopheles* in New York – also true.

"Then there was her handsome, mustachioed father, my great-grandfather, in an officer's

Mema, the opera diva circa 1930.

uniform. He was a surgeon in 'the terrible war.' She'd had a ring made from a button of his dress coat. I have it now." I lifted my right hand to show everyone the blue and white enamel button mounted on a band of cast silver. Everyone bent close to examine the ring.

"Years later in medical school, I visited Paris. What a shock. It wasn't the city of my memory – not at all like Mema's pictures. The Arc de Triomphe was too big and in the wrong place. The architecture was wrong. The rivers were wrong. The streets were wrong. The trees were wrong.

"I went to the Paris Medical School, looking for my great grandfather's name among the graduates. No Eugene Chabrison was recorded. There was, however, a Yevgeniy Chabridov, a Russian student from Moscow. I was sure that he couldn't be the one, so I stopped thinking about it and got on with my life.

"I was forty years old when I started coming to Russia. On one of my winter trips, I was booked in a hotel on Kutuzovsky Square. At daybreak, I stood in the window and saw the Arc de Triomphe looking exactly the way I remembered it – the statues on the top, the graceful proportions of the triumphal arch below. It floated like a ghost in the swirling snow. I blinked and it vanished.

"A few days later, I went to my first concert at the Bolshoi Theater. I stepped out of the car and came around the corner into the lighted square and froze – before me stood the great Opera House of Paris. I looked around me and, sure enough, I saw Les Invalides and the Place Vendôme from Mema's pictures.

"Yevgeny Chabridov *was* my great-grandfather. I took this ring to the curator of the Armory Museum in the Kremlin. She identified it as a button from the uniform of the *Tzarsky Okrana* – the Tsar's Guard. She found a book of photographs of the officers of the Okrana from 1880 to 1917. Dozens of handsome young men rode on horseback and posed with swords, most with mustaches. I searched for the face most like my own, but it was hopeless. They all had high cheekbones and pale eyes.

"My grandmother was Russian."

The cabin was hushed, and I wondered: Had they understood my peculiar Russian-Polish accent? Maybe they didn't believe me. It was a story full of half-truths that had bubbled up from an unknown place and flashed before me in familiar vignettes with questions that I could not answer. Did Russian blood explain why I felt such passion for this country?

Before anyone could ask, Yuri started to sing, softly and off key, one of the long, sad songs that Russians sang on trains. Soon everyone in the cabin was singing. Our voices drew a crowd from other cabins and people came down the corridor to join the well-known lament. We sang the same songs about war, suffering, and exile that the kolektiv had sung in the platzkart.

More vodka was passed, and we devolved into boisterous rounds of "Katusha" and "Moscow Nights" – the one song to which I knew all of the words. It had been taught to me by Korobeniki, the balalaika ensemble from Nizhny Novgorod on the "Cruise with a Cause" ship. Yuri insisted that I sing the solo parts with the rest joining in the chorus. "Just this once," I said. A little drunk, I gave it my full voice. The boisterous crowd cheered and clapped their hands at the high notes.

Yuri finally dozed off and started snoring. The kolektiv took the hint. They gathered their bottles and food wrappers and wandered back to their berths after kissing me good night. The barriers between us had melted away. I made up my bunk and lay down, exhausted. I'd had Baltika No. 9 and vodka. Nothing was going to keep me from sleeping.

We reached the Ukrainian border in the early morning hours. Border guards came onto the train and made everyone get up and stand in the corridor while they searched our cabins. Everyone, that is, except me – or so I was told later. They couldn't wake me. I was shaken, threatened, and bright lights were shone onto my face while the guards searched the cabin around me. Eventually someone paid a bribe, and the guards gave up, letting everyone return to their beds.

When I heard about it from Yuri the next morning, I thought he was joking – but too many people confirmed what he'd said. What no one knew was that I was carrying $20,000 in hundred-dollar bills in a money belt around my waist – an amount that was illegal to take across the border. It was the money for our hotel, transportation, meals, and training. There was no way to wire the money or pay with credit cards. Travelers were forced to carry cash and the border guards knew it. If they'd found it on me, I would have woken in a Ukrainian jail.

Chapter Eighteen

THE BIRTH OF THE ANGEL COALITION

Kiev, Ukraine – Fall 1999

Moscow was balmy when we left. Kiev, five hundred miles to the south, should have been warmer. It wasn't. We stepped off the train into a blizzard. Icy wind blasted us as we hurried to waiting cars wearing thin sweaters. None of us had brought coats for cold weather – we wouldn't make it five days in sub-zero temperatures.

Yuri made inquiries and had the taxis drive us to a local coat factory. In their outlet shop we found racks of warm, woolen coats in rich colors – brown, green, purple, black, and gold. There was only one style – ankle-length with a monk's hook trimmed in black faux fur. The price was right at $25. We each bought one, twenty coats in all. Wrapped in the luxurious soft wool, we walked to our hotel. The wind gusted on Maidan Square, blowing us through the ancient heart of Rus like fallen leaves, or robed priestesses arrayed in the colors of autumn.

We were surprised to find La Strada's office located in an unguarded building. They seemed unconcerned by their frequent death threats. This led to long discussions about security, laws, and judicial procedures. LaStrada answered our questions on dealing with local mafias and maintaining personal safety. The next five days of training with NGOs, government actors, police, and trafficking survivors were intense. Back at the hotel each night, we packed into one another's rooms to discuss how to adapt the Ukrainian successes to the Russian scenario while avoiding their mistakes.

Midway through the week, the Deputy Minister of Internal Affairs of Ukraine gave a lecture on how traffickers and other criminal gangs were structured, specifically the way that they were always protected by a *krysha* – roof – composed of corrupt government and law enforcement officials at the top and local criminal enterprises at the bottom.

That night, I suggested mirroring the mafia model and building our own roof using the new free technology of cyberspace. We didn't have the money or muscle that the criminal groups had, but if each of us built a lo-

Angel Coalition in Kiev, 1999.)

cal sphere of influence based on trusted personal relationships, and acted in support of all the others, we could create a national network of NGOs, law enforcement, government officials, educators, media, and sympathetic businesses to fight human trafficking. We would have our own krysha.

The Russians embraced the plan and lawyers in the group prepared a charter with our organizations listed as members. Koalitsia Angel or Angel Coalition was chosen unanimously as our name. From that point forward, we were The Angels. When we walked down the streets of Kiev in our identical coats, we called each other Angel 1, Angel 2, Angel 3, etc. Our lives would depend on the trust we were building once we were back in Russia and operating openly.

After Kiev, we kept in touch through e-mail and regularly scheduled chat rooms. We decided that our first collective project would be a multi-regional public information campaign to warn the Russian public about the dangers of trafficking. We applied to the US Bureau of Educational and Cultural Affairs – BECA for funding. I met with their staff in the Public Affairs section of the US Embassy in Moscow.

"This kind of public information campaign will be a first for Russia," I told the assembled staff. "And it will work because we'll be doing it under the umbrella of the Angel Coalition."

"Aren't Russian NGOs afraid of blowback from traffickers and local government?" asked Helen Szpakowski, Head of Public Affairs.

"As Angels, they stay anonymous. This way a tiny NGO without so much as a telephone becomes a powerful voice for human rights."

"What about local police? They'll be a problem, won't they?" asked Natalia Ivanova, Helen's aide.

"We've asked that the NGOs invite trusted police and government officials to become part of the planning process. So far, this has guaranteed police protection and government participation with everything we've done."

"What about the local mafias? Anything you do that's public will draw their attention?"

"That's why we've hired Robert Aronson," I said, gesturing to the man sitting next to me. "He's a media specialist with years of experience doing controversial campaigns with civic groups in various countries."

"The Angels want to stay as anonymous as possible," said Robert. "Each region will create its own public action and media events. We'll be working to maximize media coverage and minimize risk."

"As soon as you start marching through town or whatever you're going to do, you've got the mafia on your neck, don't you?" asked Natalia.

"Newsworthy events can be very short and still be powerful," Robert answered. "All that matters is that the news cameras are snapping and rolling. Our goal is to have each regional event televised on the national news on May 16, 2001, launch day."

"How will you get media attention at all?" asked Natalia. "They expect to be paid and we don't fund bribes."

"We'll make them part of the Angel Coalition and involve them in the planning process from day one. Journalists will be personally invested and do this because they care. We'll give them free food, but not payoffs."

"You know we only fund training," said Helen.

"That's all we need," I said.

BECA approved funding for the training of six regions and the expansion of the Angel Coalition to twenty more NGOs for a total of forty. Soroptomist International funded material development and printing for the 2001 campaign. We now had enough to start with. Over the next year, Robert, Yuri, and I conducted five-day training sessions in each region.

In October 2000, we had our second annual Angel Coalition meeting in Moscow with forty NGOs. The Moscow City Administration donated meeting facilities and a secure training center. Attendance exceeded one hundred participants and included high-level Russian government officials, parliamentarians, and law enforcement.

Angel Coalition in Moscow, 2000.

We invited representatives from the US and other embassies, European Union, International Organization of Migration, and Interpol – all key partners for the Angel Coalition krysha, or roof. When the conference opened, the Angel Coalition welcomed twenty new NGO members, primarily from the Caucasus and Central Asia.

I was standing behind the registration table when Nadezhda Belik, our dynamic Angel from the Palace of Culture in Nizhny Novgorod, arrived with her delegation.

"Julietta!" she exclaimed, grabbing me around the middle and lifting me off my feet. "Look who I brought. It's your young friend from Zelenogorod. She works for me now."

"Zhenya!" I greeted the young woman. "You've grown up." I gave her a hug.

"I'm eighteen," she replied. "I'm studying at the Polytechnic Institute and volunteer for Dr. Belik now."

"She's a great little worker," said Nadezhda. "She's teaching classes at orphanages and has a group of trafficking survivors that meet at the Palace of Culture several times a week. Who could guess there'd be so many?"

"Good for you, Zhenya." I handed her a registration packet and slipped a nametag lanyard around her neck. "We'll talk more. I want to hear about your survivor group."

Zhenya and her trafficking survivors group.

Zhenya and Nadezhda moved on, replaced by delegates fresh off the train from Irkutsk and Barnaul in Siberia. I was engulfed by more Russian bear hugs.

The weeklong conference was a whirlwind of energy, creativity, and enthusiasm. Duma Deputy Alexander Lisichkin presented his draft counter-trafficking law at a press conference after the opening plenary, followed by interviews with radio, television, and newspapers. The Angels Coalition was spreading its wings. The krysha was growing more powerful.

At our banquet on the last night of the event, the tables were packed and the noise level rose steadily as the Angels ate, drank, danced to the band, and toasted their success with key Russian and international partners.

I sat at the head table between Yuri and Vlad, exhausted but elated. Our momentum was undeniable. Yuri wanted to dance, but I was too tired. When I turned him down, Nadhezda Belik grabbed his hand and swept him onto the dance floor. I spotted Zhenya at a table with other young women – her group of survivors. I was starting to go to her when I felt a hand on my shoulder.

"You've done good work, Angelova," said the Colonel, taking Yuri's seat beside me. I had seen Ivan Ivanovich at the conference, but not the Colonel.

"Welcome, Colonel," I said. "Have you had something to eat?"

"I can only stay a moment," he said. "I wished to inform you that the Duma will pass a preliminary law making it possible for the Ministry of Interior to prosecute trafficking cases."

"Yes, and in a few months, we'll launch our anti-trafficking campaign in six regions. Next year, we do the same in the Caucasus," I said, flushed with pride and wine. "Pft, pft, pft," I added.

"I wish that spitting on Chort was enough to protect you from that devil," he said. "I'm afraid you're going to be very disappointed."

"What do you mean?"

"You've gone too far too quickly. You've drawn unwanted attention."

"You mean the traffickers? The mafia?"

"Not at all." He laughed. "You are not even a fleabite on their hairy arses."

"Then who?"

"Your embassy," he said, gesturing to the tables where a group of Americans lingered over drinks and dessert. "They do not want you in the Caucasus."

"Why not? The southern border areas have a huge trafficking problem. The embassy is helping us." I pointed to the Americans. "The Deputy Ambassador, the heads of USAID and BECA, the law enforcement team ... "

"Don't be naïve. They're not here to help you." His voice was flat. "The Americans will ruin you before they allow you to build the Angel Coalition in the Caucasus."

I was stunned. I'd been at the embassy every few weeks to brief Public Affairs on our progress. They'd seemed supportive of our plans to expand into the southern border regions and the Muslim Caucasus. "Why?"

Ivan Ivanovich appeared with the Colonel's coat. The Colonel stood and slipped it on. "You'll have a new ambassador soon," he said. "The new man, Vershbow, is from NATO. He isn't so in love with helping the Russian people." He bowed and kissed my hand. "Be careful!" he said. "You have encountered what we call in our business Factor X." He turned and left.

I had little time to consider the Colonel's warning, although I did recall Irina's admonition to study the history of the Muslim Caucasus. "It is the past and future of Russia, and your country as well." she'd said. Yuri had called it the treacherous underbelly of Russia.

Zhenya approached in her coat, towing a suitcase. "I've come to thank you and to say good-bye."

"I wanted to hear about your survivor group," I said, fatigue settling into my bones.

"I'm afraid there's no time – we're catching the Siberian Express back to Nizhny." I hugged her, feeling fragile shoulders beneath the thick wool coat. "I have a project to propose to you," she said, handing me a neatly typed document. "We can discuss it by e-mail."

I kissed her cheek and watched her walk away with Nadezhda Belik. They joined the other Angels riding the night train to Nizhny Novgorod, or beyond to Kazan and Perm – then further still to Siberia.

Chapter Nineteen

PUBLIC AFFAIRS

Moscow, Russia – 2001

At the end of 2000, Yuri retired and the Puchkovs went to live with Irina's daughter in Oregon. They left Russia over the Christmas holidays while I was in Seattle. I returned to Moscow in January, uncertain how I could continue without Yuri. We had traveled the length and breadth of Russia together. I had relied on his assessments of every situation. Our projects were growing in scope and impact.

We had funding commitments for the next three years and I hoped that Vlad would be able to assume Yuri's role as MiraMed's Country Director. Vlad was in his mid-twenties, but smart, loyal, and unflappable. We had worked together long enough that he could simultaneously translate for me.

We now had twelve employees and it was time to rent a real office for our growing staff and a bigger apartment for me – one that could allow me some privacy and still accommodate the constant flow of visitors. Fortunately, Moscow was in the throes of a rare renters' market. Paying in euros or dollars could land desirable spaces at reasonable rents. I haggled while fingering three thousand dollars in new $100 bills, which I stacked in front of me. Potential landlords proved unable to take their eyes off the money and deals were settled.

For myself, I rented an old apartment on Goncharnaya Embankment overlooking the Moscow River. It had once been a communal apartment – with three big bedrooms, high ceilings, a huge kitchen by Russian standards, and a balcony with a view upriver to Red Square.

I also found a perfect office space a short walk along the riverbank in the *Vysotka* (Skyscraper) a building that had once housed the elite of the Communist Party. Completed in 1953, the year of Stalin's death, it was the last and largest of seven massive buildings known as "Stalin's wedding cakes" encircling old Moscow. In the center, Stalin planned a towering monument to Communism – the Palace of Soviets – topped with a statue of Vladimir Lenin taller than the Eiffel Tower.

The Second World War disrupted those plans, but the Vysotka remained the preferred home of the rich and famous until they started moving to Moscow City, an island of modern skyscrapers in the middle of the Moscow River that Muscovites called the City of Gold. The Vysotka was officially an apartment building, but we had permission from the city government to have our nonprofit office there.

Walking with Vlad in front of the Vysotka.

In my office with Vlad and Angel staff

While the staff moved into the office, I transported my boxes from the furnished flat on Kosmodamianskaya to the larger, unfurnished flat on Goncharnaya. I bought a bed and an elaborately carved rectory table with eight chairs at a Romanian furniture store. It fit perfectly in the kitchen. Soon, friends and guests would be seated in every chair, passing bowls of buttered potatoes and roast beef.

For now, it was stacked with boxes, waiting for my new landlord, Alexander Sergeivich, to paint the apartment. It was difficult to get any colors other than bile green and mud brown in Moscow, so I'd bought rich Behr pigments at the Irish House and cans of white mixing paint at a hardware store. I explained to him how I wanted the paints mixed, providing swatches of the soft, pastel colors that I'd visualized on the apartment walls. I could hardly wait to cover the walls with the folk art that I'd collected during my travels.

We were fast approaching the May 16th launch of the Angel Coalition's Anti-Trafficking Public Information Campaign in Moscow, Petrozavodsk, Yaroslavl, Nizhny Novgorod, Veliky Novgorod, and St. Petersburg. I would have to trust my landlord to oversee the painters while I was away working on it.

I met regularly with the Public Affairs staff at the US Embassy. The American diplomats were friendly and supportive both at the embassy and after-hours social events. Surely the Colonel must have had that one wrong. Or so I thought until I contacted the office of the new ambassador, Alexander Vershbow, and asked for a meeting. A civil rights action of this scale had never been done in Russia before and I wanted to brief him personally on activities that would be drawing national and international attention. He declined. I invited him to participate in the Moscow press conference or to send someone to represent the embassy. He declined.

I didn't have time to think about what that meant. Robert, Vlad, and I were shuttling back and forth to the various regions on rattle-trap airplanes, local trains, and buses. I still wanted to keep our embassy informed, so I set up a meeting for the Monday before our Wednesday launch with the staff of Public Affairs. In the meantime, I had some free time and a vast expanse of blank wall space begging for art. I decided to go to the outdoor art market across the Ring Road from Gorky Park called Krimsky Val.

I caught the "b" bus – my favorite means of transport when I wasn't in a hurry. The rambling old electric buses circled the inner city on the Ring Road, dragging a length of grounding chain that sounded like sleigh bells. I sat by the window and watched traffic whiz past in a frenzy while

145

I relaxed into the lazy rhythm of the bus. In winter, I'd ride the "b" bus wrapped in head-to-toe furs, taking a seat with the Russian ladies in their furs. We looked like bears with purses. But on that warm day in May, the passengers wore shirtsleeves and dresses.

We crossed the Red Stone Bridge over the Moscow River, which was swollen by snowmelt and threatening to flood the shoreline. Downriver to the south, the domes of Novospassky Monastery glinted gold where the river curved to the west.

Across the river, the Russian Philharmonic concert hall was under construction – a graceful cylinder rising against the backdrop of the International Business Center. The bus stopped at Paveletskaya Square where the neon sign for the Mount Carmel Restaurant still flickered. I'd been there with Sasha and the Peace Committee my second night in Russia when I met the Colonel for the first time. Beyond Paveletskaya, the next stop was Krimsky Val and the New Tretyakov Gallery, a huge building made up of dozens of private galleries selling museum-quality Russian art. Local artists sold their less expensive work from tents outside. Artists from other regions or former Soviet Republics were relegated to open space down along the river.

I walked the length of the outdoor bazaar and bought a brightly colored Armenian painting of Nut traversing the ocean on a reed boat, bearing the moon across the sky. In the last booth, a leather maker was selling hats appliqued with suede and brimmed with nutria fur. I bought one – destined to become my forever favorite.

I brought home my treasures wrapped in newspaper. Later, I sat at my new kitchen table reviewing the upcoming events. The national campaign would kick off at 9:00 A.M. on Wednesday with simultaneously televised civic actions in each region. The events would be followed by press conferences announcing the opening of regional hotlines for trafficking victims and their families. The telephone numbers printed on posters, stickers, plastic packets, and bus/metro placards were unique to each city. I was tasked with helping in Nizhny Novgorod where I'd be working with Nadezhda and Zhenya.

On Monday morning, I carried samples of all the campaign materials to the embassy. I was the first to arrive in the conference room, so I used the time to decorate. I mounted six of our posters showing the different regional hotline numbers on their white board with magnets. I spread more of them around the large conference table. I did the same with a dozen bus/metro placards. I hung a printed plastic bag on the back of each chair and laid a copy of our printed booklet, Plain Speaking About Trafficking, at each place. Additionally, I tossed stickers and campaign buttons onto the table like party favors.

By the time the Public Affairs staff filed in and took their seats, the materials were everywhere. I waited with anticipation for their reaction. To my surprise, the ten people who had been so enthusiastic during the previous weeks sat looking at their hands, notebooks, or pens, acting as if the materials weren't there.

I was stunned. I cleared my throat and asked: "What do you think?" No one responded. I continued, "Next week the Angel Coalition will be on television, radio, and on the streets in six regions, campaigning against human trafficking. It'll be the first action of its kind in Russia." I expected smiles. This wasn't news to these people – yet they struggled to not notice the posters and placards and pretended they didn't see me. Their deadpan silence would have been comical if it weren't so bizarre.

I reached into the portfolio and pulled out the videocassette of our television spot, slipped it into their VCR and turned on the television monitor. A puppet trafficker appeared on screen, fishing for a mermaid with a hook baited with an ad that promised a great job overseas. She was wary at first, but when she bit the hook, he yanked her from the water and she screamed, "Save me!" Then a voiceover said, "Don't get hooked by false promises – get the facts," and the local Moscow hotline number appeared on the screen.

"Puppets? Really?" Helen Szpakowski perked up. "Russians aren't going to like that," she snorted.

"Of course, they will," I rebutted. "The Gorky Theater puppeteers are famous here. Everyone knows their voices. They're like the Muppets of Russia. Robert Aronson worked with Theater for a Change in Nizhny Novgorod to produce this one-minute commercial for $1500."

"That doesn't sound very effective," said Helen. "We didn't pay for that, did we?"

"Don't get hooked by false promises. Get the facts!"

"No," I said. "BECA funded the regional trainings and the expansion of the Angel Coalition. That's all been completed successfully, as you know. These campaign materials were paid for by Soroptimist International. Global Ministries and private donors from several countries paid for the TV and radio spots. The entire budget for the six-region campaign is only $200,000 – an amount that would normally buy a single television spot."

What was wrong with these people? Producing a huge campaign for very little money should have earned us kudos. Instead, even Helen refused to meet my eyes. I continued, "The posters, bus and metro placards, the stickers, buttons, and bags all give the same message." I picked them up one by one. "You see? The slogan of the campaign is, 'Don't get hooked by false promises. Get the facts.' We kept the design simple – black and red against a white background. The fishing hook is baited with a typical newspaper ad – the kind you can find in any Russian newspaper, promising high-paying jobs abroad with no language skills required."

"Can you prove that none of this is being paid for by US government?" asked Natalia Ivanova, Helen's assistant.

"You mean, this?" I held up a poster and shook it, losing my patience. "Or this, or this?" I held up brochures, bus placards, and plastic bags and waved them around. "No American taxpayer dollars were used. You know that. You have the grant reports."

"And you allege that these printed materials are in a warehouse in Moscow now?" asked Helen, opening a manila folder on her lap.

"Allege? The trucks are picking them up tonight," I responded. "They'll be delivered to each region in time for the campaign launch on Wednesday. You can watch it on the news."

"I have a report here that says the warehouse is empty." Helen tapped the folder accusingly. "There are no materials, are there? This is all a scam."

I was floored, I recalled the similar experience of our Angel partner in Tajikistan. Her NGO had printed materials for a campaign in Dushanbe. US Embassy representatives then went to her printer and forced him to sign a statement saying that he'd printed nothing – in spite of the fact that the very same materials were posted all over the city, including the US Embassy. Was this some kind of standard script that embassies used to undermine their own NGOs? Had I just run headlong into the Colonel's Factor X?

"There are floor-to-ceiling piles of printed materials, lorries full. Go see for yourself." I looked around the table. Now Helen was smiling. I had the sick feeling that I had fallen into a trap.

"I want the address of your warehouse," she said. "We'll go see for ourselves and talk to your printer."

"You'd better hurry. The trucks are coming tonight at 8:00 P.M. to take everything."

"Tell them to delay. We won't be able to visit until May 25th."

"That will be too late," I said. "And since you didn't pay for the materials, we have no obligation to hold up the campaign for you."

"So, there's nothing there," said Helen, making a note in her file. "You admit it."

"I do not. Just look around you. Here are posters, placards, buttons, stickers and bags printed with six different hotline numbers, one for each region. Are you going to deny that they exist because you won't look at them?" From the looks on their faces, I understood that that was exactly what they were going to do.

I stood up. "One more thing before I go." I inserted a tape of our radio commercial in a cassette player and cranked up the volume. It started like an ad for a trafficking recruitment firm. A soft, low, male voice wove enticing images of the wonderful, carefree life overseas where money grew on trees and jobs were plentiful. Suddenly a female voice boomed, "Stop! Don't get hooked by false promises. Get the facts. Call the Angel Coalition."

The audience looked pained. Finally, Helen scoffed. "And you think you can get this on Russian radio? It will cost tens of thousands of dollars."

"Not so. Our partners have developed personal relationships with media. They've done a bang-up job convincing the producers that, by supporting the Angel Coalition, they help protect their own sisters and daughters. Nearly every station has promised us prime-time exposure." I should have spit on Chort three times and shut up, but I couldn't stop myself: "Our best media recruiters have been from our Angel survivor group."

"You mean your little super-girl Zhenya?" said Natalia. "Are you serious?"

"Of course. Now if you will excuse me," I looked at my watch and stood up. "I have a plane to catch for Nizhny Novgorod."

"You'll be running the campaign from there, will you?" asked Helen.

"Certainly not," I retorted. "This is an Angel Coalition event. MiraMed staff will be out of sight, in support roles only. We'll help with troubleshooting behind the scenes."

"I certainly hope so," said Helen, standing. "This meeting is over."

I left the materials strewn across the table and the tape in the player. I was escorted to the embassy gate grateful for fresh air and glad to get away. I hurried to catch the "b" bus back to Taganskaya. I found a seat near the back where I could pretend that the rattle of the grounding chain was jangling of sleigh bells. What did it mean to our future now that Factor X was clearly in play? I decided to set my concerns aside and focus on the challenge of getting myself packed and to the airport.

Chapter Twenty

ANGELS IN NIZHNY NOVGOROD

Nizhny Novgorod, Russia – May 2001

Nizhny Novgorod, Russia's third largest city, is a one-hour flight from Moscow. I flew there in a wood-paneled prop plane that was older than me. The Nizhny campaign had been organized by Nadezhda Belik and Nina Dernova of the Russian Children's Fund, two iron ladies who had been pillars of that community since the Communist era. As schoolteachers, they had known most of the region's key political figures since they were children and called them by their grade-school nicknames. Nadezhda felt no hesitation in phoning "Bori" Nemtsov or "Seryosha" Kiriyenko, both currently Deputy Prime Ministers under Vladimir Putin. If they didn't respond promptly, she would call their mothers.

I deplaned on the tarmac. "Over here!" Zhenya was waving her hat above a crowd at the chain-link fence. "I have my new car."

Once through the gate, a young man took my bag and rolled it to the open trunk of a beat-up red Zhiguli that had seen better days. Zhenya introduced him as Gennady. "He's a police cadet from our village. The cadets are helping with the parade. Look who's waiting for you in my car."

Baba Maria sat on the backseat, wrapped in her Astrakhan shawl. Nizhny was generally colder than Moscow. I joined her. Zhenya slid onto the driver's seat, Gennady beside her.

"Now," said Gennady. "Shift out of neutral and put it in first."

"Insanity!" scoffed Baba loudly. "If girls were meant to drive, they'd have been born with gear shifts." The car jerked forward and stalled.

Zhenya started it again, this time shifting cautiously from first to second and turning into traffic. "Baba's a reactionary." She laughed. "Old Farmer Mirozov died and left me this car. Gennady and I fixed it up. Now I can visit Zelenogorod on weekends to see my granny. Still, she complains."

"She's learning to drive really fast." Gennady smiled. "Zhenya's not afraid of anything. She's always been a daredevil. Even when we were kids in Young Pioneers."

We drove to Nadezhda Belik's apartment where I was staying. It was an hour's drive from Strigino Airport past miles of buildings, factories, and parks that blurred in the gathering darkness.

"Oojastna ... dai bogh – Help me God," Baba complained at every bump while Zhenya and Gennady went over last-minute details for the parade with me. First thing Wednesday morning, two dozen school buses would deliver four hundred children to the center of the Nizhny shopping district – a long pedestrian street – for a march against human trafficking. They would parade through town accompanied by two dozen police cadets from the Nizhny Novgorod Academy of Internal Affairs. We would finish at the Gorky Puppet Theater for a special performance and ice cream.

We arrived at the apartment complex on Radialnaya Street and climbed three flights of dark, dank stairs to Nadezhda's apartment. Zhenya rang the bell. The door flung open, flooding the hallway with welcoming light and kitchen smells.

"Angelova!" Nadezhda lifted me off the ground with her hug. "Come in! Come in!" she boomed, leading us into the flat, where soup simmered on a gas stove, steaming the windows. We took off our shoes and put on *tapichky* – slippers. Nadezhda introduced her husband Viacheslav and other women from the campaign.

I washed my hands while the Russians put the finishing touches on a make-shift table set for a dinner party with platters of salads, piroshky, cheese, and home-made pickles. Viacheslav, the lone male, opened bottles of Crimean champagne, Georgian wine, and Russian vodka. We sat on every available piece of furniture, which had all been pushed to the table, and raised our glasses to toast peace between our countries and the success of our campaign. After a late night and more food and liquor than I was used to, I slept *kak ubit* (like death) on Nadezhda's sofa.

The Nizhny campaign kicked off on schedule at 9 A.M. on May 16th with a well-attended press conference led by Nina Dernova with the deputy mayor and the chief of police. I never saw it. I was busy downtown with Zhenya and the four hundred children, who paraded through the shopping district with balloons and flowers, handing out stickers, buttons, and plastic shopping bags. Police officers, many of them parents, turned out to assist the cadets. The day was glorious and clear. The children were having such fun that the event was more of a celebration than a protest.

Local television crews had cameras on-site. I was filming from the front of the parade with my own camera, trying to stay ahead by running

Children's protest parade.

several yards forward and then turning around to shoot. Every time I did that, the children would start running with me. Our parade moved down Gorky Street at such a rapid pace that we arrived at the theater while the puppeteers were still setting up. Larissa Trannina kept the kids happy by singing folksongs and telling fairytales until Sergei Nuzhin and the other puppeteers were ready to perform. Zhenya and I handed out ice cream sandwiches donated by the local grocery.

Meanwhile, Angel volunteers hit the streets to put up posters around the city. In spite of our having permits, the police took them down because someone in the Ministry of Internal Affairs had detected a political tone. The police were apologetic, leaving them up long enough for news teams to film them and interview the Angels. Our posters were then neatly stacked and returned to us at the end of the day.

After the parade, I did a newspaper interview with some photos, after which Nadezhda and I were transported in a police car to the Great Hall of the Nizhny Novgorod Yarmarka – the international trade center. I had no idea what was coming, only that Nadezhda and I would make an appearance at an event hosted by the governor.

"This is a special surprise for you," said Nadezhda, pulling a comb from her purse and running it through my windblown hair.

"Don't you think I should go back to the apartment and change?" I said, trying to smooth my rumpled clothes. I was still in jeans, sweatshirt, and sneakers.

"No time," she said. "Put some color on your lips. This will just take a minute." She handed me her compact and bright red lipstick.

We entered the hall of the newly restored Yarmarka complex, built four centuries before to showcase the wealth of Nizhny Novgorod. It was then a thriving trade center at the confluence of the Volga, Aka, and Kama Rivers. The deputy mayor was waiting inside. His face lit up when he saw me. "Nadezhda has told us all about your grandmother, the famous Russian opera star who sang with Feodor Chaliapin. Feodor was from Nizhny Novgorod, you know." Taking my arm, he led me to the front of the hall. "We are honored that you agreed to sing for us."

I stopped and turned to Nadezhda – stunned. "What?"

"I told them that you'd sing 'Moscow Nights,'" she proclaimed, squeezing my shoulder. "Just like you did on the train to Kiev."

Panic left me speechless. The deputy mayor pulled me forward through the crowd of beautifully dressed luminaries holding wine glasses and nibbling hors d'oeuvres. Then I heard familiar music and recognized the Korobeniki Balalaika Ensemble – I knew them well. They had played every night on the cruise ships for the "Cruise with a Cause" program. They had taught me to sing "Moscow Nights" in the first place. Now they were on stage in their hometown of Nizhny Novgorod and I knew exactly how they would play "Moscow Nights." I was familiar with their arrangement, their unique changes in tempo and shifts in key. Their lead singer, Vladimir Kubasov, was also onstage. I had sung with him many times on the river cruises. He winked at me and I felt better.

The deputy mayor led me up three steps to center stage, placing me next to Vladimir. Nadezhda was at the microphone making an introduction. "You can do this," Vladimir whispered in my ear. I ignored Nadezhda, focusing on Vladimir's hand pressing into my back – and his hushed words: "Forget all those people. They won't hear me, but you will. Sing with me like you did on the boat."

Nadezhda finished, the audience applauded, and Korobeniki launched into the long, complicated, but familiar introduction to "Moscow Nights." I stepped to the microphone and closed my eyes, transported back to summer on the river when Vladimir, the musicians, and I sat on the fantail of the river ship, drinking vodka and singing to the sky.

Vladimir tapped my arm, counting down to the start of the song. "Open your eyes and smile. Think of something happy."

I couldn't see the audience beyond the stage lights, so I stared at the magnificent ceiling of the great hall, replaying this perfect day – running down the central shopping street of Nizhny with hundreds of laughing children, their clothes covered with our stickers and buttons, handing out booklets, balloons, plastic bags, and flowers. "That's right – big deep breath," said Vladimir. "Now sing!"

I spread my arms, homed in on Vladimir's voice, and gave it my all. He signaled when to slow down or speed up by squeezing my arm. The audience had no way of knowing that I'd sung "Moscow Nights" dozens of times with these same musicians. I launched into the complicated series of key changes between verses and finally the emotional crescendo that ended the song on a long, high note. The audience was clapping and shouting, "Urra, malodyets," followed by the dreaded words, "Encore, encore."

I took my bows but declined requests for another song. I had pulled off "Moscow Nights" through a confluence of fortunate circumstances, exhausting my voice and my courage, not to mention my repertoire. I had no idea that the concert was being televised until I saw Nadezhda Belik in front of the cameras giving an interview. She was spinning a tale about me as the granddaughter of an exiled Russian diva returning to sing in triumph.

"Beautiful, beautiful!" declared the deputy mayor, kissing my hand. "The governor is most grateful. This program is being broadcast from Vladivostok to Kaliningrad. You are famous!"

The parade was aired on local news that night along with interviews by

Interview with Nadezhda after performance. I look shellshocked

Zhenya, Nadezhda, and the chief of police. The morning newspaper headlined with a full-page photograph of me holding up a poster, my cheeks flushed and hair in a tangle. I'd thought that the cameras were focused on the poster – not me. In any case, the results were positive, and doors began to open. Newspapers that had been demanding money to run stories offered to run them for free, and the local transportation board decided to put our placards and hotline numbers inside every bus and Metro car in the region – thousands of pieces.

Newspapers from across Russia.)

One of the first calls on the hotline was from the deputy minister of internal affairs whose daughter was about to take a job as a hostess overseas. Nadezhda took his call, confirming that the employment agency was a known recruiter for international traffickers. The deputy minister tore up his daughter's contract and started the first prosecution of a trafficking ring in Russia. That afternoon, their recruiting agency burned to the ground.

On the night-flight back to Moscow, I wondered if the American Embassy would take note of the newspaper headlines, my appearance in the parade, or singing on national television. I wasn't sure why it mattered, but I kept thinking back over my strange meeting with Public Affairs. I still couldn't make sense of their reaction. Why wasn't the embassy proud of our successful efforts to promote democracy in Russia? Strengthening civil society was an American priority, wasn't it? Maybe I had misinterpreted their reaction. Maybe Helen had just had a bad day and our next meeting would be back to normal.

I arrived home about midnight, making my way through the series of codes and locks that secured my apartment. Lights were on inside and voices came from the kitchen. Robert and Vlad were eating soup at the table.

"Check out your living room." Robert laughed. "It's almost as bad as your bedroom."

I flipped the light switch in the main room. The walls were brilliant cerulean blue. The painters had used the undiluted pigment. The cans of white paint for mixing were unopened. They had done the same in my bedroom, which was fire-engine red. The rest of the rooms were unchanged because they'd run out of color. "It's kind of cheerful," I called toward the kitchen. *Shto delat?* (what to do?)

Vlad served up a bowl of his famous Ukrainian borscht for me – prunes were an ingredient. I sat at the table and picked up my spoon.

"Not the usual colors for a Russian apartment," said Vlad, passing a plate of black bread and cheese. "Rather bright."

"We've got bigger problems," said Robert. "With the embassy."

"Didn't you meet with them before Nizhny?" asked Vlad. "To show them the printed materials? Was everything okay with them?"

"Absolutely not. I took examples of all the materials, including media, to Public Affairs and they refused to look or listen. They pretended to be deaf, dumb, and blind. It was bizarre."

"They did the same to us," said Vlad. "They called us in for a meeting, but it was actually what we Russians call a hostile interrogation."

"It was awful." Robert scowled. "Your friends shone a light in my eyes and grilled me for three hours about the Angel Coalition. They kept asking the same questions over and over about how it was legally structured, who the officers were, when and where they met? I kept saying that I didn't know. It wasn't my department. I tried to show the campaign materials and talk about how successful the campaign was, but they wouldn't look and didn't want to hear."

"Then it was my turn," said Vlad. "They demanded to know about the Caucasus. Who have we seen there? What officials have we talked to? What is our plan for that campaign? I said that everything was in our report right there on the desk in front of Helen – but they pretended not to hear and asked the same questions again. They acted like I was invisible."

"This must be Factor X," I said.

"Factor what?" Robert raised his eyebrows.

"The Colonel warned me that the embassy would ruin us if we tried to go into the Caucasus."

"How can that possibly be? That's one of their preferred grant regions. We're just following their guidelines. Now they're doing a one-eighty and turning on us? Why would they do that?" Robert was warming up for an argument that I didn't want to have.

"How should I know? It doesn't make any sense. That's why it's Factor X," I snapped, willing him to go away and let me bask in the warmth of success in Nizhny Novgorod – at least until Monday.

"There's more, I'm afraid," said Vlad. "The embassy has been calling the Angels and telling them not to work with us."

"I can't believe it." I stood and paced, furious. "This is insane!"

Robert added: "The Angels are being asked to write letters against us if they ever want American grant funds."

"Has anyone pulled out of the Angel Coalition? Any letters?"

"One that I know of – Novocherkask. They called me to apologize and faxed me a copy of the threatening letter from the embassy and their reply. They didn't say anything negative about us – just that they are withdrawing from the Angel Coalition. They have a number of debts and are desperate for money," said Vlad.

"And they think the American Embassy will bail them out?" asked Robert.

"They said big grants will be available for anti-trafficking NGOs, but only if they work with a new American organization called IREX – International Research and Educational Exchange," said Vlad. "They're taking over trafficking prevention."

"IREX?" I scoffed. "They do student exchanges, not human rights work."

"I am telling you what Novocherkask told me." Vlad shrugged defensively.

"Has anyone else been called?" I asked.

Vlad's phone vibrated on the table. "All of them have," he said looking at caller ID. "Here's Khodyrieva calling now. You can ask her about it." He answered his phone and spoke to Angel Coalition president Natalia Khodyrieva in St. Petersburg. I tumbled down from my Nizhny high, sagging back into my chair, too tired to follow his rapid speech. I didn't want to have to say one more word in Russian.

"Here's Julietta." Vlad handed me the phone. Natalia, who spoke no English, reiterated what Vlad had said. Each Angel partner had been contacted by the embassy or by IREX with the same threats. Maybe if I'd had some sleep, I wouldn't have made the mistake of whining to her that perhaps it was time for me to give up and go home.

"What?!" the phone squawked in my ear. "You are going to turn tail and run because of a little pressure from that wussy embassy? What kind of weak-kneed, candy-assed American pussy are you?" I grimaced, realizing my terrible mistake. In Russian culture, you endured every insult and inconvenience in stoic silence. Russians do not whine. They have no words for twitchy, irritable, or ants-in-the-pants. There is, however, a rich vocabulary far beyond anything in English for coward, traitor, betrayer, weak-hearted, treacherous worm, lower than a steaming heap of bear dung.

She called me all those smelly things and it got progressively worse from there. Personal weakness and the betrayal of your friends – people who would die for you – were unforgivable sins. Natalia's "pep talk" was a wake-up slap. I may have been many things, but a quitter – or any of the other steaming piles of things she was calling me – I wasn't.

Soon we were both having a good laugh.

Chapter Twenty-one

THE ANGEL ROOF

Republic of Karelia, Northwestern Russia – Summer 2001

The anti-trafficking campaign ran from the middle of May to the middle of August. A few weeks into it I traveled by overnight train to the capital of the Republic of Karelia on the northern border with Finland. I was met in the morning by Larisa Boizhenko, our Angel partner in one of my favorite Russian cities, Petrozavodsk, that stretched along the shores of Lake Onega. We'd planned a series of afternoon meetings with local media, and a televised panel at the University of Karelia Law Faculty where she was a professor. For our free time, she had booked a rocket boat to take us across Lake Onega to Kizhi Island for a private tour of the famous wooden cathedral. Her friend was the curator for the Kizhi Wooden Museum, a UNESCO World Heritage Site.

The hydrofoil rose on its stabilizers and flew above glassy water toward the northeast where Lake Onega bordered Finland. I could see the weather-silvered domes of Kizhi Cathedral silhouetted in the distance.

Larisa shouted above the engine's roar, "Do you like lamb chops?"

Kizhi wooden cathedral.

"What? I can't hear you."

"A friend of Viktor's wants to meet you. His lamb chops are exceptional."

"Your Viktor? The chief of police? Lamb chops?"

"We've been invited to dine at the headquarters of the Azerbaijani grocery king. His name is Camille. He's from Baku." She patted my knee. "Viktor is in business with him now."

"You mean the Azeri godfather – that Camille? The one who's been shooting it out with Armenians over who sells groceries has invited me to dinner?"

"Yes, the same."

"I thought he was in prison."

"Not anymore," she said. "Camille's family has cornered food distribution in northwest Russia. No need for bullets now – just good business. He gives grocery stores to local officials if they agree to buy their meat and produce from him exclusively."

"Bribery?"

"It's called franchising. It's perfectly legal."

"So Viktor isn't police chief anymore?"

"Of course not." She chuckled. "He has no time – not with two grocery stores to run."

"Why would Camille want to meet me?"

"I'm not sure." She shrugged. "Here we are." The boat settled into the water and bumped against a wooden pier. We were greeted warmly by the curator of Kizhi Island.

That evening, I was picked up at the Miska Hotel by Camille's cousin Akhmed – a tall, swarthy man with a sidearm bulging beneath his tight leather jacket. I slid into the backseat of the Mercedes next to Larisa. Viktor greeted me from the front seat. We drove through miles of forest while Akhmed and Viktor chatted about fishing in Lake Onega versus the Caspian Sea. The car sped, but time stood still, frozen in daylight. During the White Nights of summer, the sun never set in Karelia.

We reached a clearing. Armed guards with German shepherds patrolled a walled compound surrounded by rolls of barbed wire. We were waved through sliding gates into a courtyard where mountains of bright red tomatoes, green grapes, apples, oranges, and pears were being sorted and packed by women in colorful headscarves. They looked like gypsies – a sharp contrast to the pale blondes of Karelia.

"These are Roma people," said Akhmed. "They come and go with the seasons."

He parked and opened my door. "The *abattoir* – slaughterhouse – is over there." He pointed to the largest building, where cattle, goats, and sheep milled in crowded pens. "Follow me, please." We climbed an outdoor staircase to the second floor.

A portly, balding man waited on the landing. He threw his arms open to greet me – all smiles. "Welcome to my home. I am Camille." He beamed, showing a gold tooth. "And you must be my special guest, the doctor from America." He kissed my hand and led us into his elegant office-apartment. He pulled out a red plush chair for me at a carved table and sat next to me. Viktor, Larisa, and Akhmed took their seats. "I hope you like lamb chops."

"Yes," I said. "Larisa tells me that yours are exceptional."

"Absolutely true. There are none better." Fresh fruit was piled on long-stemmed glass platters that floated above a white lace tablecloth set with salads, cheeses, and cold fish. "These are all specialties from Azerbaijan," he said. "We sell them in our groceries."

He snapped his fingers. White-shirted young waiters entered to fill our glasses from bottles of red and white Azeri wine. "Now you shall have your lamb chops," said Camille, signaling to a lad who opened the window and shouted something. A disturbance echoed up from the abattoir. Frantic bleating was followed by a loud thud and the buzz of an electric saw. Within minutes, we were served a wooden plank of sizzling lamb chops. "The freshest meat you'll ever eat." Camille flashed a smile, pushing chops onto my plate. "No seasoning needed."

After the meal and a round of thirty-year-old Baku-Jeyhan cognac, the table was cleared. Akhmed poured tea into delicate porcelain cups. I held the cup to the light – the tea was blue. "This is my own special blend," said Camille. "I make it from wildflowers that grow around the burning springs of Yanar Gulaq."

"That's a mountain near the gas fields with many unique species of plants," said Akhmed. "The stones have burned like torches since the days of Abraham."

"Have you been to our country?" Camille asked.

"Not yet," I said. "It sounds extraordinary."

"We have everything from high mountains to sandy beaches on the Caspian Sea. It is the biblical land of milk and honey, the Garden of Eden with oil wells."

"We grow all of the products you see here," said Akhmed.

"We're planning another Angel Coalition campaign in the Caucasus next year," I said. "Maybe we can include Baku?"

"What a good idea," said Larisa. "Yerevan in Armenia is participating. Why not Baku in Azerbaijan?"

Camille thumped his fist on the table. "Precisely! We will introduce you to the mayor of Baku and the president of Azerbaijan – whomever you wish. You will have their full cooperation and I will cover all your expenses in Azerbaijan. You will be the guest of my family." He paused. His smile fell away, and he wiped his eyes with a handkerchief. "Something must be done to stop these barbarian slavers. Akhmed, show them the file on Raina."

Akhmed retrieved a brown envelope from the sideboard. It contained a police report with the photograph of a lovely young woman in a nurse's uniform. "This is my daughter, Raina – the pride of my life," he said. "An intelligent, well-educated girl raised in a good Muslim family."

"I remember her well," said Larisa. "An outstanding student. She studied medicine and drove an ambulance as a volunteer."

"High spirits, not afraid of anything." Camille touched the photo. "She took a job in Turkey to be a nurse. She was supposed to stay with my sister in Marmara, but never arrived."

Akhmed scowled. "The job was a ruse. She was locked in a container and taken to Egypt. We traced her to Cairo."

"Do you want us to help you find her?" I said, uncertain as to what they wanted me to do. "The Angel Coalition can activate Interpol. We have good relations with them now. They can help bring her back."

"Too late. Her mother and I buried our child last week," he said.

"And now," Camille thumped the table again, "something must be done about those criminals. We will start here in Petrozavodsk. From now on, every grocery store in Karelia will have the Angel Coalition poster in the window. We will print your information on our grocery bags and hand out brochures. Young women and their families must be warned."

Larisa looked determined. "Yes, they must. Pour more cognac," she said. "I propose a toast to the Angel Coalition and the new and very important member of our roof, our krysha – Camille."

"To the Angel Coalition," I said. We clinked the fine crystal.

"What about the traffickers? The ones who took Raina?" asked Viktor. "Should the police be investigating?"

"Forget about them." Akhmed scowled. "We buried them."

Camille draped his arm around my shoulders and said, "How would you like to own a grocery store?"

A week later, I was back in Moscow working on a budget so that we could add Baku to the Caucasus campaign. I didn't accept Camille's offer of a store. I settled for a packet of his special blue-green tea, a bottle of Baku-Jeyhan, and a basket of pomegranates. Having the Azeri grocery cartel on board to assist the Angels was a major step forward. Camille pledged to provide food to Larisa's new shelter for trafficking survivors. I wondered if other powerful mafia groups would come out in opposition of human trafficking.

I didn't have to wait long. I got a voice message that afternoon from Valentina Shelkova, our Angel in Yaroslavl. She was shouting excitedly over the sounds of traffic and I couldn't understand her – I was worried. Yaroslavl was notorious as a mafia-controlled city. Traffickers were particularly active there, so Robert had coached the local Angels to do a short, powerful action for the news cameras to open their campaign.

On the morning of May 16, six young women dressed in black stood bound and gagged in front of the mayor's office. Signs around their necks read, "I was a trafficking victim in Bulgaria," "I was a trafficking victim in USA," " … Great Britain," " … Turkey," etc.

Protest in Yaroslavl, May 16, 2001.

The action lasted all of ten minutes and drew a hefty crowd of surprised pedestrians walking to work. It was so visually striking that it made newspaper headlines and newsreels across the country, quickly becoming an iconic image.

I called three times before Valentina answered her cell phone. "Allo?"

"Valya?" I shouted. "Is everyone okay?"

"We're okay," she said. "But we had a good fright."

"Why? What happened?"

"We were handing out booklets in front of McDonald's – the one where traffickers recruit high school girls." She paused to catch her breath. "A big, green car pulled up. It was foreign with a cat on the hood."

"A Jaguar?"

"Maybe. Three big guys got out. Ugly guys with shaved heads, all in black leather and gold chains. Scared us to death. We just stood there while they took some brochures and went inside."

"Was that it? Did you run?"

"Of course not. We weren't going to let them scare us off. They came out again – with ice cream for us. They started asking questions."

"Who were they?"

"I'll read their business card to you. It's in English: 'High-end Imported Used Cars.'"

"The used car mafia." I gasped. "They steal cars all over the world and ship them to Russia. Be careful, they're brutal."

"They said they'd seen the campaign and didn't want their sisters and daughters victimized by the 'steaming scumbag traffickers.' They showed us where the traffickers have their office – it's just up the street from McDonald's. They left a guard with us and said to call if the scumbags give us any trouble. They said they would display our materials in automobile showrooms. They'll drive us in chauffeured cars if we need protection."

While the regional campaigns were popping with the same high energy, making connections, and growing the Angel Coalition krysha, our roof, Moscow was slower to launch. Fifty-three Moscow organizations participated in the campaign activities, but not one dared to operate a hotline. MiraMed had to purchase two cellular telephones for the Moscow hotline and rent a small apartment where volunteers could work. It quickly became the target of a police investigation and was closed down by the local militia for "suspicious activities." The neighbors overheard our staff discussing "human trafficking" in the hallway and turned them in. At least we knew the TV and radio spots were having an effect.

We thanked the concerned neighbors for their vigilance and moved the hotline operation into an abandoned school provided by the Moscow Department of Education.

Even with a support letter from the office of the mayor and legal permit numbers stamped on all materials, posters were taken down as quickly as they were put up. Volunteers distributing materials suffered constant harassment by police. Despite months of appeals through the various levels of city government, permission could not be obtained to post the bus/metro placards in city transport without paying considerable bribes.

We kept trying and eventually our persistence paid off. Moscow, once activated, gave outstanding support, which grew into long-term cooperation. Permission was finally given to post materials for free on all major train routes to and from the city. Mayor Yuri Lushkov signed an order to have the radio commercial played on Moscow trams every twenty minutes for five days.

Posters were put up and brochures distributed in all government buildings, including the lobby of 36 Novy Arbat, the city administration building and office of the mayor. The Moscow Committee on Education distributed posters, stickers, and booklets throughout the system of high schools, internats, and orphanages. Booklets and posters were distributed throughout all the unemployment offices in the city – places frequented by women seeking work.

Moscow City Duma – the city government – formed a working committee on prevention of trafficking and sponsored Angel Coalition billboards on the roads approaching each Moscow airport and in areas with high concentrations of students. They printed large posters and installed them at most bus stops through the city's distribution system as well as posting placards in buses frequented by students and young working women.

Our media segments ran on four national television stations and four national radio stations. Stories ran through ten newspaper syndicates, including *Kommersant, Pravda, Interfax, Itar-Tass,* and nearly all regional media outlets. The press conferences and fol-

Posters at Moscow bus stop and Metro station

low-on activities were reported throughout the three-month campaign in regional papers and distributed to over 500 newspapers via Interfax. The media was pro bono.

The public actions were covered in a ten-minute segment on Vladimir Pozner's nationally-broadcast weekly news program *Vremya* (*Time*) with an estimated audience of 40 million. German, Spanish, Japanese, and Dutch television, AP, BBC, NBC, CBS, CNN, Washington Post, LA Times, *and* Christian Science Monitor did feature stories.

From May 16 through August 30, 2001, the combined total of calls to the six regional hotlines was 1,562. The leading country used for bait was the United States, followed by Germany and Finland. Callers were surprisingly open with information on how traffickers advertised, the names of their companies, how they recruited, etc.

We compiled our data and sent it to the Ministry of Internal Affairs and the Russian State Duma. Although the purpose of our campaign was prevention, we were also able to rescue fourteen women who called the hotline and asked for help.

Two percent of calls were death threats against us. We reported the threats immediately, but the police were unconcerned. I spoke to our contact in the Moscow Ministry of Internal Affairs – GUVD. He expressed surprise that we didn't get more threats. "If the traffickers want you dead," he reasoned, "they're hardly going to call you first."

I spent August in Seattle. On September 11, 2001, I flew back to Moscow, sleeping through most of the eleven-hour flight. I was jolted awake when the Ilyushin decelerated on the Sheremetyevo runway and deplaned into chaos. Armed guards were everywhere. Rumors flew: Eleven American planes had been hijacked, multiple buildings were hit, thousands of Americans were dead. Moscow would be attacked next.

Roadblocks were up around the city. My taxi was stopped, and my passport checked twice on the way to my apartment. I tried to call Vlad, but the exchanges were jammed. At home, I couldn't get on the Internet. I didn't have a television set and it was midnight, too late to knock on my neighbors' doors. I tried the radio but was frustrated by the fast speech. I finally tuned in Voice of America and learned that the World Trade Center buildings in New York City had collapsed and a plane had struck the Pentagon, killing hundreds.

First thing in the morning, I joined my neighbors who were buying flowers at a kiosk. We boarded the "b" bus to the American Embassy to leave the bouquets in the Russian tradition of sympathy. My neighbor Ludmila sat next to me, holding white carnations wrapped in clear cellophane. "Terrible." She sniffed back tears. "Who could do such a terrible thing?"

We stepped off the bus on Novinsky Boulevard and joined a long queue of Muscovites who'd come to pay their respects. When it was my turn, I laid my bouquet of roses on a wall of flowers three feet high and three feet thick stretched the length of the American Embassy. Muscovites spoke in hushed tones, concern in their voices: "What will the Americans do now?"

I left my Russian friend and entered the embassy through American Citizens Services. I found a seat in the crowded Manila Bar to watch CNN with my countrymen. The bar stayed open late while we shared our shock and sorrow, our need for answers.

Chapter Twenty-two

FACTOR X

Moscow, Russia – Winter 2001

December was a hectic month. The Russian New Year's holidays were fast approaching, when the entire country would shut down for ten days in an epidemic of binge drinking called the "dead season." Banks, shops, businesses, theaters were closed every year from New Year's Day through the weekend after Russian Orthodox Christmas on January 8. Television stations would broadcast endless re-runs of New Year's Eve parties from the past while the nation sank into a collective hangover. I had a lot to do before leaving Russia to spend Christmas with my family in Seattle.

I was at the Russian State Duma, discussing the draft anti-trafficking law with Deputy Lisichkin when Vlad called from the office: Helen Szpakowski and Natalia Ivanova wanted to see me at the embassy – now.

"You look unhappy," said the parliamentarian when I hung up.

"It's the embassy," I said. "They want to talk to me, and I'd better go. They've been threatening to block our funding."

"Can they do that? After your successful civic action?"

"Of course. The embassy can block BECA grants and, if they do that, we won't have enough for the campaign in the Caucasus."

"Ah, the Caucasus." He narrowed his eyes. "The Americans have their own agenda for our southern border. I've heard rumors that they're arming militant jihadis in exchange for oil rights in Central Asia."

"I don't know anything about that," I said.

"You should inform yourself. Read *The Grand Chessboard* by that fake Polish count, Zbigniew Brzezhinski," he said. "Every Russian has read it – why not every American? It's your nation's devious plan."

"I have read it. But I'm not sure what it has to do with MiraMed or the Angel Coalition." I sensed Factor X looming. "We aren't part of anybody's politics."

"That doesn't matter. If you're present in the Caucasus, the press will be with you – am I not correct? I saw you on television singing for the governor of Nizhny Novgorod. You don't go unnoticed."

"That wasn't planned," I said defensively.

"Best you go along to the embassy and not be late. My assistant Vladimir Popov will drive you. Maybe he'll be allowed into the meeting. I'd like to know what they say."

"I'll ask if he can stay," I said.

"You might also ask about the trafficking law that your new Ambassador Vershbow is proposing."

"I don't know anything about it," I said. "He refuses to meet with me."

"Not surprising," he replied. "Here's the draft we obtained from your embassy this morning. I can't let you take it, but it's in English. Read it quickly, and please don't mention that I showed it to you."

I scanned through the pages, horrified. "This would make prostitution legal in Russia and require any trafficked woman to prove that she didn't go abroad knowing that she would be a prostitute. That's impossible for the women and a free pass for traffickers. Surely the Russian government won't fall for this?"

"The Moscow City Duma already has. American lobbyists have whispered in the ministers' ears, enticing them with the revenue they'll make from taxing prostitutes. They also claim that legalizing prostitution will reduce the spread of HIV-AIDS."

"That's absurd."

"The Minister of Health of Moscow is buying it. If the Moscow City Duma votes for the law, the Russian State Duma and federal government will follow – they always do. After all, several members of Parliament own brothels in Europe. This would be good for their business."

"I'll see what I can find out because this can't be right. This law contradicts Bush Administration policy which opposes prostitution. Has the embassy gone rogue?"

"Certainly not." He chuckled, buzzing for his aide.

At the embassy, I introduced Vladimir Popov as our legislative liaison from Russian Parliament. He and I were given badges and escorted to Public Affairs. Helen seated me in front of her desk and aimed a high-intensity lamp at my face. Vladimir Popov was seated behind me. I'd thought that Robert had exaggerated about his "hostile interrogation." He hadn't. I told them to turn off the light or I was leaving.

"You walk out of here and you'll never get another American penny," said Helen.

"Can Mr. Popov please leave? He works for the State Duma and has nothing to do with this."

"No, he may not."

Natalia dimmed the room lights and Helen began a droning inquisition about the legal structure of the Angel Coalition – the same questions she had asked Robert and Vlad. I gave the same answers: "You've got all of that information in the report in front of you," I said, pointing to her desk. "Angel Coalition is Russian. All of the translated legal documentation is in there. We wrote ten pages of responses to all the questions you asked Robert. Did you read it?" Helen stared at the report as if she'd never seen it before, then started the same questions again.

The session ended three hours later when a Marine opened the door and announced that Public Affairs was closing for the weekend. Helen stood and announced, "Your funding's been pulled. Go home and get a real job."

"What about the information campaign in the Caucasus? Everyone is trained and ready to launch in the spring."

"Canceled," said Helen.

"What about the rescues that we've started through Zhenya's network. We can't just abandon those girls," I pleaded.

"You shouldn't make promises you can't keep," said Helen, leaving the room.

Natalia brought up the room lights. "Please remember," she said nervously. "This is objective, not subjective."

"What does that mean?" I demanded, but she followed Helen from the room.

I mulled over Natalia's words in Vladimir Popov's car on the drive home. "Your embassy doesn't like you very much," Vladimir remarked, stopping in front of my apartment building.

"They'll get over it," I replied, trying my best not to reveal my emotional turmoil. "Besides, BECA is not the only source of funds. We have applications pending with the new Trafficking in Persons office at the State Department."

That night I lay awake, unable to construct any reasonable explanation why the embassy would turn on us. Everything we had accomplished so successfully was in line with the stated policies of the State Department and the Bush Administration.

I could only conclude that the embassy was acting on its own to push a law that was counter to US policy, but that made no sense. If the United States was serious about stopping human trafficking with maximum "bang for the buck," we had just demonstrated the way to do it – making history in the process.

I stared at the ceiling, searching for the words to explain to the Angels how their stunning success had resulted in failure. "On what basis?" they would ask me.

"Factor X," I murmured aloud, spiraling into another round of obsessing that led nowhere.

Worst of all was imagining Zhenya's disappointment when I told her that the Angel Survivors' Network had lost its funding. "What about those girls in Cyprus? We're not going to leave them behind, are we?" She would ask, trembling with rage, her eyes huge and sad.

Monday morning, I walked to the office along the riverbank. The staff was assembled at our conference table, which was unusual – I normally got there first. I poured myself coffee, but before I could sit down, Marianna said, "The Angels from Rostov, Nalchik, and Taganrog in the Caucasus called me. IREX told them that they control the BECA money now and they've cancelled the information campaign. If the Russians want American grant money in the future, they can't work with us anymore."

Afsona Kadyrova, the Angels' attorney, shook her head and asked, "Why are the Americans trying to kill the Angel Coalition?" she asked. "There's no legal basis for their actions against us."

All I could do was shrug and say, "I don't understand it at all. I'm sorry."

"Nadezhda Belik called me on Saturday," said Oleg Kouzbit, the Angel Coalition director, who lived in Nizhny Novgorod and commuted home on weekends. "IREX told her that rescues would no longer be funded, and the survivors' group has been cut. Zhenya is very upset."

"I'll have to call her right away." I picked up my cell phone.

"No need," said Oleg. "She's asleep in your office. I brought her on the train with me. Poor kid's exhausted. She's in the middle of her exams for law school."

"The news isn't all bad," said Vlad, handing me a fax. "It seems we've been approved for funding from the World Childhood Foundation for the Babushka Brigade. Your single mothers' program can begin next month. Congratulations."

I read the fax. "The Americans may not like us, but the Swedes sure do." We had also just been funded by the Swedish International Development Agency (SIDA) for a project with the Swedish NGO Kvinnoforum to conduct Russian law enforcement training on trafficking prevention. "We've got plenty to keep us busy. When Zhenya wakes up, I'll see if she wants to be our intern for the summer. She can stay at my place and come to Stockholm with the Angels. There are other ways to get funding."

"And the two girls waiting to be rescued in Cyprus?"

"We'll do it ourselves. Call the Turkish Embassy. Get in touch with our law enforcement contacts in Cyprus. It's time to talk to the Russian Consular Services. Get them to process the paperwork and send the girls home. It's their legal obligation to assist Russian citizens who are victims of crimes."

"Will it work?" asked Marianna.

"We won't know until we try," I said. "According to the Foreign Ministry, Russian consulates are required to repatriate victims. Let's get them activated."

An hour later, Zhenya was still asleep on my couch when two bull-necked agents from the Russian Federal Tax Police arrived in our office. They presented their credentials and said they'd had a call on their anonymous tip line that we were operating a foreign NGO illegally in an apartment builing – a serious administrative offense.

Vlad and our accountant Murat Vafin brought out the notarized agreement with the city and let them examine our up-to-date tax filings. Before they left, they asked to have a word with me in private. We stepped out on the balcony.

"We have found that everything is satisfactory," said the tall one.

"Thank you," I replied, waiting for them to go. They didn't budge. Did they want a bribe?

Finally, the short one said, "You have a legal right to ask us who reported you. Don't you want to know? It's quite interesting."

"I thought that your rat line was anonymous."

"That is left to our discretion."

"Who called?"

"The call was routed through the main switchboard of the American Embassy."

"What?" I gasped.

"It seems they don't like you." He smirked.

"So I've heard," I said. I struggled to sound nonchalant. I was seething inside. Vladimir Popov had surely reported my interrogation at the embassy to Lisichkin and word would be spreading around the Duma. Now the Tax Police were chuckling over the rat line call. What would the Russians think of an organization that was disparaged by its own government? Or was that part of their plan to ruin us?

I sat at my desk and thought back to the scorching summer of 1998 when I'd bought the book *The Grand Chessboard* by Zbigniew Brzezinski at Shakepeare and Co., the English language bookstore near Novy Arbat. It was a bestseller in Moscow, and I'd needed something to read on the bus to Yaroslavl.

I read the tedious, rambling narrative cover to cover because there was nothing else to do on the four-hour ride. It seemed absurd, a grandiose plan to undermine and ultimately destroy Russia from the inside by balkanizing the former Soviet republics and causing a Muslim uprising in the Caucasus. Now I wondered if the odd behavior at the American Embassy was related to their plan to do something like that.

Zhenya stirred on the sofa, looking small under the crocheted throw. The courage of this brave girl standing up against the armed power of organized crime brought me to tears of frustration. The American Embassy should be supporting her work, not belittling her and cutting her funding. And what about me? I was no different from Zhenya – just older, a little more battle-hardened. I'd believed in the goodness of my country. I'd convinced Russians to believe it as well. I'd made promises on the basis of that conviction.

The Colonel had warned me that trouble was coming, saying it in the oblique way that I found so irritating with Russians and calling it Factor X. Why didn't he just come out and say, "Global agendas are afoot. The American embassy has been ordered to sweep you out of the way. A war is coming to the Middle East and the Caucasus that will destroy the lives of millions. There's nothing you can do about it."

Actually, he *had* implied that there was nothing I could do to influence decisions made in my government and the best thing I could do was stay out of the crosshairs of pending conflict. I stepped from my office onto the stone balcony and observed the crazy mess of Moscow traffic. It was the start of rush hour. The balcony faced northwest along the Moscow River and into the heart of the Kremlin, which was brightly lit in the twilight. I wondered, as I often did at the end of another day, if I really belonged here. This wasn't my country, was it really my fight?

"Julietta?" I heard my name and turned to see Zhenya shivering in the doorway. It was time to head home for the night.

We walked back to my apartment along the snowy embankment. I heated the big pot of chicken chili borscht I'd made for the week. Zhenya cut thick slices from a loaf of black Borodinsky bread that smelled like cardamom. She had always been thin, but now she looked gaunt.

"I shouldn't have come," she said, her eyes red-rimmed "I was so upset – I made Oleg take me. I've got exams to study for."

"I'm glad you're here. You're always welcome." I watched her peck at the food and placed my hand over hers. Her fingers were cold. "You look pale. Are you ill?"

"You sound like Baba Maria." She pulled her hand away, avoiding my gaze. "I'm in the middle of exams, that's all."

"Finish dinner and get a good night's sleep," I said. "We'll send you back to Nizhny tomorrow."

"What about the girls in Cyprus? I promised I'd get them home." Her lip trembled and the brave front collapsed. Tears broke free, her shoulders heaved. "It's my fault. I failed them. I failed you. If I'd only been better … "

"Hush. You just leave that to me."

My cell phone rang. I took the call in my bedroom in case it was bad news. It wasn't. I came back to the kitchen and said, "That was Oleg on the phone. The girls in Cyprus are safe at the Russian Consulate. The Foreign Ministry has agreed to give them new passports and pay for their tickets home. You'll see them in Nizhny in a few days."

"*Slava Bogu* – thank God," she said, kissing her crucifix. We ate in silence until she yawned.

"Go to bed," I said. "You know where everything is." She gave me a hug and snapped on the lights in the guest bedroom.

I checked on her a few minutes later. The lights were still on and she was asleep in her clothes. There was too much tension in her slender body. Her eyes were moving under the lids – she was dreaming, groaning softly as if in pain.

I covered her with a quilt and turned out the light.

Chapter Twenty-three

RUSSIANS IN SEATTLE

Seattle – Winter 2001

I flew to the US a few weeks later to spend Christmas with my children. My first stop was the Russian Consulate to accept an award from the American and Russian Associations of University Women.

My flight was late arriving. By the time I cleared security, there was no time to go home and change. I was jetlagged, rumpled, and exhausted after flying eleven hours, but took a cab directly from Sea-Tac to the Russian Consul's residence in Madison Park, a tony neighborhood on Lake Washington. Most of the attendees appeared to be Russian diplomats.

"Congratulations, Angelova," said a voice that belonged to another time and place. "You have made quite a name for yourself in our country."

"Sasha!" I exclaimed, recognizing my former KGB shadow. "What are you doing in Seattle? I haven't seen you since the Peace Committee broke up."

Sasha kissed my hand, looking plaintive. "Those were better days, eh? Lots of leg work, personal contact, dinners out. Now it's all pimply kids on computers intercepting electronic thoughts before they become deeds. What's the skill in that? I'm a businessman now. I advise the commercial department of the consulate." He raised his wine glass. "Can I get you a drink? Wine? Vodka?"

"Mineral water, I think."

Sasha made his way expertly toward the bar, looking stylish in his tailored suit. He paused to shake hands with other men and to light the cigarette of a grizzly bear. *Oh no!* It was Igor, the man who'd tried to shake me down for $25,000. I hadn't seen him since the night that I'd unplugged his microphone on national television and flown off to Simferopol with Sergei Popov. He was coming straight at me, arms open wide.

"Angelova!" He wrapped himself around me and smooched me on the lips.

I tried to pull away, but he crushed me against his chest. When he released me, I sucked in air and said, "Igor – how nice to see you again."

Sasha handed me a glass of sparkling water. "It's Borjomi from Georgia – your favorite."

I sipped the warm, salty liquid and made a face – seashells. It was as bad as I remembered. "Thanks," I said.

Igor and Sasha took turns telling me about their new business venture – some kind of import/export scheme. I smiled politely. Their presence was disorienting. I felt like I was flying backwards aboard a rattling old Ilyushin that smelled like Stoli cigarettes and chicken poop on a course that defied time and space to Moscow in the 1990's. The KGB shouldn't be in Seattle. My worlds had collided.

"Are you enjoying your stay in America?" I interrupted, my eyes sweeping the room. I needed to get out of there, or at least find an American friend to latch onto. "Where have you been?"

"New York and Washington DC," said Igor, munching hors d'oeuvres. "Catching up with old friends like you."

"Quite frankly, we are looking for investors," said Sasha. He continued talking about fertilizer and concrete, cargo ships and boxcars. Pressure built in the center of my forehead, at the point behind my third eye. The intersection of past, present, and future began to tangle and burn. I recalled Sergei Popov. He was back at the Shamanic Center in Moscow after writing a best-seller. He'd just sent me an e-mail inviting me to the Altai Republic with his grandmother for a shamanic winter retreat. Baba Lydia had added a note requesting my measurements. She was ordering me a set of squirrel-skin insulated underwear for Siberia.

"You seem distracted. Perhaps we are boring you?" Igor leaned forward until his breath was in my face, taking me back to the night in the Slavyanskaya Bazaar restaurant when he made his pitch for our cash.

"It's just jetlag, I came here straight from the airport," I said. "Sorry."

"By the way," said Sasha. "The Colonel sends his regards to you … and your family."

"My family?" Alarm flashed. We had never spoken about family. That was taboo. I didn't want them made part of any interchange I had with these men.

"Your two beautiful children – your son and daughter at university." Sasha grinned. "You must be very proud of their success in athletics and scholarship."

"They are fine, thank you." I felt sick. Their words didn't sound threatening, but they were. This was happening too close to my nest. Had I flown home trailing these birds of prey? I shook off my paranoia. The Russians had every right to be in their own consulate.

"When your son and daughter visit you in Russia, I can arrange a tour of the Kremlin, or the Bolshoi Theater – front row seats." Igor handed me his card. "Just call your old friend, Uncle Igor. Any time. No favor is too small."

"They have no interest in coming to Russia," I responded too quickly, feeling my clutch of disappointment in their lack of interest. The heart pain that haunted me showed on my face, reflecting back in Igor's eyes. I tried to cover my slip by sipping the water that smelled like the Pacific Ocean. The sharks circled me, smelling blood. Igor leaned closer.

"How terribly lonely for you," he said. "How do you manage to live all alone in a foreign land apart from loved ones? How can you look after them properly when you are so far away?"

Now I felt panic. I couldn't meet his eyes.

Sasha saved me. "Perhaps it is the Russian in her blood." He laughed. "She can't stay away from us. It's in their blood too – her children."

"No, it's not." I retorted when I should have said nothing. I was playing chess with half a brain.

"I am referring to your Russian grandmother and the fond memories she shared with you as a child – the old photographs, the music, and so forth." How did Sasha know the story that I'd told on the train? "And then there is your uncle."

"My uncle?" I swallowed their hook. My uncle, my mother's brother, worked for the National Security Agency. He was a mystery to me.

"*Gospodi,*" Igor exclaimed, his mouth full of cheese – goodness gracious. "She doesn't know. Tell her, Sash."

"The 'Colonel,' as you call him, was an acquaintance of your uncle during the Great Patriotic War," said Sasha. "They met in England when they were very young. That's why he wanted to meet you when you arrived in Russia."

"I thought the Colonel wanted me to work on birthing reform. I was told he'd lost a daughter at Hospital 70."

"Very tragic and also true." Igor shook his head. "That's why he let you stay."

"How did he know my Uncle Wally?"

"They both worked at Bletchley Park, members of the international team that decoded the Enigma machine. The Colonel has often remarked how perfectly your uncle spoke Russian. He was the youngest OSS officer and a rising star in intelligence," said Igor. "Later he became a founder of the National Security Agency and visited Russia – always in an official capacity."

"You know more about my uncle than I do," I said dryly, recalling my stout, chain-smoking, anglophile uncle in his waistcoat and tweed hunting jacket. "He died a long time ago."

"Twenty years. And here you are, following in his footsteps."

"Hardly, I'm a doctor not a spy."

"Following him to Russia, I mean," he added hastily. "He spoke of you fondly, or so I've been told."

"He barely knew me."

"Are you sure?" Sasha lowered his eyes and smiled in a way that said: *I see right through you into all the impenetrable secrets that even you don't know.*

A welcome burst of English chatter at the door broke the spell. The Americans had finally arrived. They greeted me. When I turned back, Sasha and Igor were working the crowd. I finished the day on autopilot, my face frozen in an insincere smile.

That night, I lay awake. The Colonel knew my uncle – what did that mean? Was it even true? All I knew of my mother's brother was that he worked for the NSA, had been at Bletchley Park and was often overseas. Where could I go for more information? My family was closed-mouthed about the past. As to the NSA, most Americans had never heard of the huge government agency that spied on them. I knew it was located at Fort Meade in Maryland, but nothing more.

My Uncle Wally – the spy.

My one memory of Uncle Wally was from high school when I visited Washington DC and we sat in his den watching *Secret Agent* starring Patrick McGoohan. "That's not really how it is," he'd said in his posh English accent. "Not at all."

Ignorance of my family origins suddenly felt dangerous, not only for me but for my children. The same snarled jumble of DNA that I carried on my chromosomes was also coursing through their veins. I'd always felt reassured, knowing that they were safe at home while I was fighting the battles that would better the world, but was that true? Had they been threatened today? No – Sasha and Igor were looking for investors, doing their obscure dance of non-threatening coercion. I'm sure they enjoyed watching me squirm. But above them was the Colonel and all that he represented, about which I knew nothing. Now I'd learned that he knew who I was before I arrived in Moscow. My invitation had come from the Soviet Peace Committee, but had he sent it?

A new undercurrent of Factor X – the unseen tide that shaped my destiny, the knot in my third eye, was unwinding to reveal a portal into the unknown and beyond that a rabbit hole into the childhood I could not remember.

Chapter Twenty-four

ANGELS IN ACTION

Moscow, Russia – 2002

Within a few months our Moscow-based international help lines were open, connecting the Angel Coalition Rescue Center to Europe, Middle East, North America, and North Africa. Of our Russian partners who'd been told to withdraw by the embassy and IREX, only Novocherkask had left the Angel Coalition. Their director called me to complain. "They lied to me," she said. "Those embassy friends of yours said we'd get money if we sent that letter against you. We got nothing."

"Who promised you money?" I asked. "Was it IREX?"

"Natalia Ivanova from your embassy. I wrote the letter like she asked me to. Now she pretends like she doesn't know who I am."

"I really can't talk now," I said impatiently.

"But I've got debts. What am I going to do? I owe the mafia money."

"What do you think that *I* can do?"

"I want to move to Moscow. I can't stay in Novocherkask. I want you to speak to the American Embassy on my behalf."

"I have no influence with the embassy – that should be obvious," I said, disconnecting.

The Angel Coalition Victim Assistance Protocol was completed and sent to Russian Parliament, and from there to all Russian embassies and consulates. The anti-trafficking law itself remained in play. NGOs supported by the Soros Open Society Institute were energetically lobbying the deputies of the Moscow Duma for the American Embassy version of the law along with legalization of drugs and prostitution.

As Deputy Lisichkin had indicated, if the Moscow Duma approved the American version of the law, the State Duma would most likely follow suit. We needed to convince the Minister of Health of Moscow, but how? We had limited funds, time, and manpower to fight against multi-million–dollar international lobbyists. However, now that we were funded by the State Department through the Trafficking in Persons office (GTIP), we did have some clout in Washington.

I requested that the State Department clarify the Bush Administration policy with Ambassador Vershbow, since he still refused to meet me. Over the next months, they sent three envoys to discuss this with the ambassador. I was never included in the discussions and nothing seemed to be resolved. Everything I knew came from Deputy Lisichkin who kept me apprised of the embassy's updated versions of the law, which were basically unchanged.

Fortunately, our Swedish supporters understood how legalization of prostitution in Russia would create a nightmare for trafficking victims in destination countries like Sweden. A week before the Moscow Duma was set to pass the American Embassy version of the law, the Swedish Institute – the public relations arm of the Swedish Embassy – sent us Gunilla Ekberg, a fiery human rights lawyer. Gunilla came with a copy of the soon-to-be-released feature film *Lilya4ever* – a devastating indictment of the effects of prostitution and trafficking on Russian girls in Sweden.

With help from sympathetic Moscow deputies, we were invited to show the film and speak at a meeting of the city duma. This was our last chance to convince the minister of health of Moscow, who was vigorously supporting legalization, to change his mind before the Moscow Duma voted.

I was thrilled when he burst into tears halfway through *Lilya4ever*. Pretty much all the ministers and deputies were in tears by the end, and so was I. From that moment forward, any version of the law that put the burden of proof on the trafficking victim was defeated.

By summer five Angel Coalition safe houses were established – two in St. Petersburg, one in Petrozavodsk, one in Kazan, and one in Murmansk – constituting the first shelters for trafficking victims in Russia. Each safe house program began working within its community to build a support network of funding and services to victims, providing training for staff and community stakeholders as well as the physical structure of a safe place to stay. The Angel Coalition krysha or protective roof continued to expand.

Working with the Moscow city administration, we printed tens of thousands of pamphlets with our help line numbers to be distributed at airports and train stations. The pocket-sized booklets described human trafficking and urged young women to call

Young boys rescued in Siberia.)

our toll-free number if they found themselves in unexpected destinations, if their passports were taken away, or if they were forced to work in prostitution. The Federal Migration Service put them in racks between passport control and security. A thousand women took them each day.

I was commuting between Moscow, Stockholm, New York, and Washington DC, building support for the programs and searching for funding to fill in the holes left by grantors who never wanted to provide enough funding for staff. They would fund 10% of this person and 17.5% of that person, making it virtually impossible to run a project. Our staff had to work on multiple projects sponsored by many different funders and agencies.

Everyone worked on human trafficking, orphanage life skills development, law enforcement training, and eventually HIV/AIDS prevention programs for schools and orphanages. We adapted by growing our individual capacities and, because of it, became an ever more efficient and closely knit team. We worked long hours together, traveled constantly, and met daily challenges.

Interns came to us from the US, Canada, UK, Germany, Sweden, Poland, and Russia. We'd become an approved site for graduate level accreditation. Major universities including Princeton, Harvard, Yale, Oxford, Stockholm, and Cambridge contacted me to place interns. I didn't have resources to run a formal program, so I adopted the philosophy that if a prospective intern were doggedly persistent enough to get my attention, he or she would probably be a good intern. We needed people with Russian language skills, courage, and determination. Those were precisely the people who fought their way to my door.

Angel staff and interns from US, Poland and Sweden.

Our first intern was American Angela Bortel, fluent in Russian and studying at Moscow State University – MGU. She rode around Moscow in all-weather on a bicycle with her dog Bianca barking in the basket. After leaving Moscow to attend UC Berkeley Law School, Angie became a human rights and immigration lawyer, later joining the MiraMed Board of Directors.

She was followed by Shonda Werry from the University of Chicago, also studying graduate-level Russian at MGU. Shonda would come into the office and ask what I needed her to do. I would say something like, "I need you to do a survey of Russian university students to see if they ever engage in prostitution." Shonda would nod a few times, make a few notes, ask one or two questions, then disappear for a couple of weeks. When she reappeared, it was with the completed survey ready to publish. When Shonda joined us later as Program Director, I could say to her: "We need law enforcement training in Almaty for high level Russian and Kazakh police." She would nod, make a few notes, and work with the Russian staff to manifest the event.

The Survivors Network was once again funded and Zhenya was often in Moscow working in the Angel Coalition office and doing trafficking prevention in orphanages. In March, she was staying at my apartment doing a series of trainings between Moscow and Yaroslavl, including Uglich Orphanage. I asked her how the trainings had gone and had she seen Angela?

"That little Angela is a pepper pot," she said at breakfast. "She took all of the materials and asked a zillion questions."

"Do you think the girls are getting the message?"

"I hope so. Anything outside of the orphanage sounds wonderful. Those kids watch American TV shows like *Dallas* and *Santa Barbara*. They think the whole world lives like that – except for them in Russia."

Outside, noisy crowds were passing on the embankment. Music played in Red Square. Today was *Maslinitsa* – the spring butter festival, the last chance to eat, drink, fight, and party before Lent and forty days of fasting. Straw effigies of the crone Winter would soon be set alight on bonfires from Kaliningrad to Vladivostok. Russian spirits were high. The days of darkness and below-zero temperatures were coming to an end.

"This is my favorite holiday," I said when Zhenya joined me on the balcony, wrapped in the light green terrycloth robe I'd bought for her in Istanbul. Steam rose from our mugs of coffee. Our breath hung in the still air. A pale sun hugged the horizon and painted the sky yellow. "They're already stuffing their faces with pancakes." I pointed toward Red Square.

Rising smoke meant that coal braziers were alight. Muscovites would gorge all day on little red pancakes called *blini*, slathering them with butter, jam, and honey. A balalaika band clashed with the music of a merry-go-ground and the screaming from a roller-coaster assembled especially for the day. Children ice-skated on a rink poured in front of GUM department store.

Zhenya pointed to a group of sailors staggering along the embankment of the frozen river. "Sunday morning and they're already drunk," she said.

"Let's hope they don't run into any paratroopers," I replied. "Last year a bunch of them got into a fight on the river and fell through the ice. They nearly drowned."

"It's the same in Zelenogorod. Men like a good fight after being cooped up all winter."

"And that is why we'll spend today in Tsaritsyno with the Babushka Brigade – no drunken sailors, just moms, babies, and our wonderful babushkas. It will be the babies' first Maslinitsa. We'll have sledding, pony rides, and outdoor games."

"And blini?"

"With homemade jam. The babushkas have been working on it all week. There'll be music and clowns with balloons. They've made an ice slide."

"How will you keep all the drunks out?"

"We've got a very high wall and a police guard courtesy of the Mayor of Moscow. We talked the Moscow government into co-sponsoring the festival. They're sending a poet and a pianist and maybe the deputy mayor. Reporters are coming – we'll be on TV."

It was snowing lightly when Zhenya and I boarded the "b" bus with the grounding chain jangling behind us. The windows were frosted on the inside, enhancing the illusion of

Baby's first blini. & Pony rides in the snow.

183

time travel. At Paveletskaya Square, we caught the Green Line Metro to Tsaritsyno Community Center in southwest Moscow.

The cares of the city slipped away when we entered the gate of the community center. Fur-clad grannies of the Babushka Brigade pushed prams along the shoveled walkways, fussing over the bundled-up babies in their care. They waved a greeting. Behind the guard house Shetland ponies were being brushed, feedbags over their faces.

An Orthodox priest in a long, black hassock swept out of the freshly painted yellow building. Over his head a banner decorated with balloons read, "Maslinitsa at Tsaritsyno."

"Bless you, Julietta," Father Gregori said. "Come in, come in, please. Stepan Ivanovich is waiting for you. He's making sure everything is ready. The Deputy Mayor and the Minister of Education have both agreed to come."

Inside, the center had been scrubbed, polished, and decorated with photographs and children's artwork. The babushka choir, dressed in traditional Russian costumes, was rehearsing with an accordionist in the auditorium. In the crafts room, young mothers were feeding babies and toddlers. We climbed to the third floor. Stepan Ivanovich Butyrnik, the center director, looked flustered, but happy to see me. I introduced Zhenya, then inquired about the accordionist.

"He's new. The babushka choir is happy and, if they're happy, we're all happy." He turned to address Zhenya: "A few years ago, this was just another rundown community center full of old people waiting to die. It was Julietta's idea to bring in the single mothers and their babies. She was sure that the abandoned old people and struggling young people could work together to raise happy babies. Now we are supported by Queen Sylvia of Sweden and the World Childhood Foundation."

"It looks like it's working," Zhenya remarked.

"I wasn't so sure at first. This was a very un-Russian idea – helping people who aren't part of your clan. The babushkas weren't interested until MiraMed donated the costumes for their choir and asked them to do a concert for the children. Of course, as soon as the moms and babies arrived, our sleeping old people woke up and decided to live a while longer. Now they're too busy dishing out advice to die. Right now, they're in the kitchen teaching the young moms how to make jam.

"Smells delicious," I said. "This is my favorite of all our programs. In less than a year, it's been replicated in four other community centers. We even have a bi-monthly reality TV show."

The babushka choir.

Stepan Ivanich continued: "Father Gregori will be baptizing the new babies later today. The church is down the street and you're welcome to come. That's new a new program for the church. Until now, children born out of wedlock were never baptized."

"I want to be baptized," said Zhenya. "Will God accept me after what I've done?"

I put my arm around her shoulders. "Of course He will."

"A visit to Father Gregori should take care of you," said Stepan Ivanich. "Now, here comes the motorcade with the deputy mayor and the minister of education with his wife. Excuse me, ladies. I must go introduce our honored guests and open the festivities." He turned back and winked: "Maybe our patroness, Queen Silvia of Sweden, will honor us with a visit one day."

"I'll ask when I'm in Sweden," I promised.

In September, Her Majesty Queen Silvia did come for a visit, accompanied by members of the board of the World Childhood Foundation. To prevent the Russian government from seizing control of her schedule and possibly preventing her visit to Tsaritsyno, we kept her pending visit a secret. The conspiracy of silence was vast, involving our staff, the Swedish Embassy, the staff of Tsaritsyno, over 100 young mothers and their babies, Father Gregori's parish, and dozens of babushkas. Nobody leaked.

On the day before her arrival, the Russian government was informed by the Swedish Ambassador. Tsaritsyno was deluged by police, FSB (formerly KGB, OMON), Special Forces, and German shepherd bomb-sniffing dogs. The babushkas took the invasion in stride, greeting me when I stepped through the gates-turned-military-checkpoint. A few hours later, the police retreated to the outer walls and the courtyard was once again a place of peace.

The Queen arrived, accompanied by the Swedish ambassador and an entourage of European oligarchs. The Babushka Choir, who had been stuck in a traffic jam and threatened to kill the bus driver if he didn't get them to the center in time, sang a welcome and the program began.

Queen Sylvia of Sweden visits the Babushka Brigade.

That evening, the Queen hosted an intimate dinner at the Swedish Embassy for Russian oligarchs – millionaires and billionaires from the City of Gold – and Yuri Lushkov, the Mayor of Moscow. At the dinner, she introduced MiraMed, endorsing our work and encouraging the Russians to support us financially.

I had my doubts that that would ever happen. Through the years, I had come to know steel magnates, grocery kings, hotel moguls, and heads of commercial empires of all sorts. They were extremely generous with time, resources, and commodities. We could always get services, clothing, food, and transportation in support of our rescues or orphanage programs. I could make a phone call and get plane tickets, hotel rooms, boxes of food, and vitamins. Russian companies bought holiday cards that we made from children's artwork – our largest annual fundraiser – and gave us event space whenever we needed it, but cash donations rarely shook loose. They did listen politely while their Swedish counterparts gave inspirational speeches on the importance of giving.

After that evening, I became a regular invitee to society events sponsored by the Russian elites. I did my best to expand our support base among the wealthy. A few weeks later, I was attending a spectacular exhibition of Romantic Art at the New Tretyakov Gallery sponsored by Russian oligarch Alexey Mordashev of *Severstal* – Northern Steel. I had been invited as his personal guest to the opening night gala. It was a sumptuous private party, and the inner circle of wealth and power was out in their finery.

I was standing in front of Henri Rousseau's painting "The Snake Charmer" – a huge, dark, jungle painting that I'd last seen at Musée d'Orsay in Paris. It had intrigued me since childhood. A naked, dark-skinned dancer played a flute at the edge of a jungle teeming with serpents. I was drinking champagne, lost in the painting, swaying to the wistful tune of the flute, about to feel the dangerous flick of a snake tongue when the man standing next to me asked, "Do you like Africa?"

I gasped, splashing some champagne. "Never been there," I answered dabbing at my jumper, wishing he'd go away.

"This painting makes me think of Africa," said the man. "I go there often."

I turned to take him in. "You're wearing a gold earring," I exclaimed. He also had a ponytail.

"I'm a pirate." He laughed. He wore a weathered, brown leather flight jacket, faded blue jeans, and laced up boots. He looked as out of place among the tuxedos and ball gowns as I did in my linen jumper, clogs, and colorful Papier-mâché necklace made by Angela in art class.

I knew that his name was Ruslan Ulyanov and he lived in the Vysotka on the two floors above our office. I saw him sometimes in the elevator. His rags-to-riches story as a gun trafficker was a local legend, a favorite told by the babushkas who sat by the front entrance when I stopped to share a paper cone of pistachios. Ruslan was a billionaire, they told me. A pirate who had gorged himself on the spoils of Africa.

The party flowed around us. We stood side by side, entranced by Henri Rousseau's erotic portrayal of temptation at the junction of daylight and darkness, a boundary penetrated only by serpents. Fortunately, a cell phone mogul took my arm and guided me to the buffet, breaking the spell. As I moved away Ruslan said, "Someday, Angelova, I will show you my Africa."

I didn't think that Ruslan's Africa was something I wanted to see. The Africa of my childhood dreams had been destroyed by death merchants like him. After the breakup of the USSR, highly connected FSB and GRU agents working with Special Forces – *Spetznatz* – had gained easy access to stockpiled weapons and cargo planes. Since then, they'd been flying to every corner of the world, selling guns and bombs to demagogues and rebels. Payment was received in gold, blood diamonds, or rare ores like coltan, used to manufacture cell phones. The Russian arms traders suffered no qualms about selling weapons to both sides of a conflict.

I forgot about Ruslan until a few weeks later. At that time, we didn't have a functioning lock on the inside of the office – just a very sticky door that required a serious shove to open. The lock mechanism required an irreplaceable key that had been lost long ago. One day Ruslan applied his shoulder and burst in while I was pulling on my boots. He grabbed my arm to keep from knocking me over. "This is the day," he said, excitedly. "I've come to show you Africa."

I wasn't having any. He'd caught me on a really … bad … day. Marianna and I had gone to Sheremetyevo Airport to meet a trafficking victim deported from Israel only to have her spirited away by traffickers before our eyes. I ranted at Ruslan about the criminal oligarchs who thought they could just come crashing through a person's door without ringing the bell like polite, normal people.

"Don't be angry with me – it's my birthday," he said with a lopsided grin. "I came to invite you to my little party. You said you wanted to see Africa?"

"Happy birthday," I said as he helped me into my coat, thinking for a horrible moment that he was talking about flying me to Africa.

"I'm showing some slides I think you will find interesting. Come and have some cake."

I was curious to see his apartment. I'd heard all about it from the babushkas – how he'd bought two old apartments in the tower and converted them into a single two-story mansion joined by a staircase. "He has a gold-plated Jacuzzi tub with diamond-studded faucets in his bedroom," the babushkas in the lobby had marveled. I needed to see that with my own eyes.

"Okay," I said. "Just some slides. Then I've got to go." I was also wondering if he could help the Angel Coalition with rescue operations, maybe by flying trafficked women home.

We entered the elevator, and he pushed the up button to his apartment. As soon as we walked through his door and saw his Ukrainian flight crew, I changed my mind. Ruslan pulled off my coat before I could escape.

"This is my crew," he said, flashing a smile that revealed gold–capped incisors, "We're going to look at some pictures and drink some beer. We'll be flying tomorrow. Maybe we'll crash. You'd be sorry if you never saw me again, wouldn't you?"

He proceeded to introduce me to the eight tattooed men. Some had shaved heads and sported Cossack forelocks, others had ponytails. Several wore jumpsuits, all were drinking bottles of Tusker Beer with an elephant's head on the yellow label. I was invited to sit in a zebra-skin chair that still smelled like the zebra.

"Thanks." I said when the ponytail named Taras handed me a beer. "I'd love to see your pictures."

I looked around the room, trying to be nonchalant, recalling the night in Galina's flat when I'd awakened to find my kitchen full of policemen. A projector sat on a coffee table. One of the Ukrainians known as Motorola, the radioman, keyed up a slide show on his laptop. The lights dimmed. The slides started and I was captivated. They were set to music by Ladysmith Black Mambazo – opening with "African Skies." Sweeping vistas filled the screen – aerial views of deserts, jungle, river deltas, and savannahs.

Ruslan and his crew reminisced over every photograph, describing how they lived out of their Ilyushin and Antonov cargo planes, flying the hulking behemoths from Russia to Pakistan, Bulgaria to Kosovo to Sudan, crisscrossing the continents of Europe, Asia, and Africa to deliver long, green, military-looking crates to Liberia and Cote d'Ivoire – returning with cargos of fruit, flowers, or furniture. In several photos, men were resting in hammocks slung under the wings of aircraft, drinking vodka. Some of the airports were so small that I couldn't imagine how the forty-ton cargo ships could have landed. The crew had the esprit de corps of a well-honed team that had faced and defeated death. I gathered that they had all been in the same elite Spetznatz forces unit before the breakup of the USSR.

I searched for clues in each slide as to what the cargo boxes contained, hoping to spot open crates of AK-47s being handed out to child soldiers, or something else incriminating. I looked for company names or logos. Not even identifying numbers for the aircraft were visible. The only photograph showing cargo other than the green boxes was of the interior of an Ilyushin packed end-to-end with palm trees. After the final slide of empty vodka bottles littering the runway, the lights came up. "That's a lot of vodka bottles," I said.

"It's just for effect," said Motorola. "We never drink when we fly. The natives expect us to be drunkards, so we toss a few bottles and take a picture."

"For our image," laughed the bull-necked Ukrainian with a forelock, thumping his chest, "our reputation as Cossacks."

After the show, we piled into two waiting black vans and drove to Chita Grita, an upscale Georgian restaurant a few blocks away. Ruslan ordered Caucasian dishes – steaming cheese bread or *katchipuri*, hot and cold bean dishes called *lobio*, and marinated chicken, pork, and fish kebobs or *shashlik*, grilled on an open fire. After dinner and toasts for Ruslan's fortieth birthday, we ate Georgian fruit cake dowsed with cognac.

I wasn't in a hurry to get home. My apartment had been taken over by a group of American volunteers coming back from a summer at Uglich Orphanage. I'd been at the camp several times with them and met Angela's grandmother when she came to visit. She was a sweet woman, bent with arthritis. We talked about Angela's future and I promised to help with her education. Now my apartment floors were littered with carpentry tools and the beds with mounds of dirty clothes. Everything smelled like camp-fires and sweat.

Ruslan and his crew spread maps on the table and planned their morning flight. They would take off from Ramenskoye Airfield in Zhukovsky and fly to Burgas, Bulgaria. Ruslan had his arm over the back of my chair, making sure that I was listening – tapping my shoulder if I stopped paying attention. He seemed to be saying something about himself in code, while telling me nothing. The babushkas said that he had a movie starlet girlfriend, a supermodel named Eleanora. I wondered if she'd seen Africa.

I listened for evil intent but heard only the love they had for one another and their passion for flying. They never spoke about huge profits or lavish lifestyles. There was no talk of war or death, child soldiers or civil war. They looked like the same scruffy group of pilots and mechanics as they'd been when the USSR collapsed – stranding them amidst the largest unregulated weapons stockpile in the history of the world. It had made them billionaires.

After dinner, they dropped me off at my building. I watched their sleek black SUVs cross over the *Krasnokholmsky* (Red Stone) Bridge, heading south toward Zhukovsky. They'd be airborne by first light.

Chapter Twenty-five

GOD'S ROSES

My Moscow kitchen on a quiet day.

Moscow, Russia – 2003

"Hello," I called from my front door, stepping over backpacks, tools, and piles of trash. Voices and the smell of soup wafted from the kitchen.

Eric Schempp, who had come to us from the Peace Corps, peered out and said, "Hey! We're cooking a stew with everything we have left over from Uglich. Do you want some?"

"I've eaten," I said. "I'll sit with you, though."

I put the kettle on for tea, then joined the six volunteers at the table. I had chosen this rambling old apartment rather than a modern one with better plumbing because of its enormous kitchen and four bedrooms. My extra rooms were usually filled with Angels passing through Moscow, interns and orphanage volunteers, journalists, my relatives and other assorted Americans – and trafficking survivors. When a journalist from CNN asked if I was lonely living in Moscow by myself, I'd laughed and said, "I haven't been alone since 1999."

Dianne Gruty handed me a scroll of thick paper. "It's a gift from Angela," she said. It proved to be painting – a happy family scene. Father, mother, children, and pets around a Christmas tree – everything Angela's heart yearned for, the dream I'd longed to give her. "It won first prize in the Uglich Art Fair."

"It's lovely," I said, tracing my fingers over the colorful tree decorated with raised globs of paint and glitter. I stuck it on my refrigerator with magnets. "Do you have any photos that I can put with this?"

Everyone had pictures. Angela and the girls had spent the summer sewing elaborate fashion collections that they modeled for our tourists. They'd even come to Moscow for an American Chamber of Commerce sponsored fashion show at the Ararat Hotel to raise money for scholarships. I stuck photos of Angela on the fridge modeling Princess Leia, Snow White, and Victorian Lady costumes that she'd artfully constructed from fabric scraps. Angela was thirteen now, a petite beauty with exuberant curls tied back in a ponytail.

Angela modeling costumes at the Ararat Hotel, Moscow.

"Here's one," said Walter, handing me a picture of Angela leading a line of little ones in rubber boots. They carried buckets.

"Berry picking?" I asked.

"Shrooming," said Walter. "White mushrooms mostly. She was teaching them what's safe to eat and what's not."

"Here's one of the orphanage. Angel Coalition posters are all over the place. Zhenya did a good job teaching the dangers of trafficking. The kids seemed to listen."

"That's good. The girls have to understand the risks," I said with a yawn. "I'm going to bed."

The volunteers stayed up most of the night, packing and chatting. I dozed to the comforting sound of their voices, waking at dawn to make pancakes. I watched from the balcony as their van disappeared

Angela teaches mushroom picking class.

toward Sheremetyevo Airport and the flight to Seattle. The place was mine.

I lingered over coffee, catching up on the Internet news before my taxi arrived to drive me to one of our busiest program sites – a shelter for rescued children near the Kremlin. Sixteen little girls were being treated by our Swedish-trained psychologists using new sandbox play techniques developed in Stockhom. The girls were from Central Asia – Tajikistan or Kazakhstan, mostly. It was impossible to know for sure. They ranged in age from 5 to 9 years. Some of them had been rescued from the child brothels on Yaroslavl Road. Others were referred from Altufevo Prison for Children after they'd been picked up for petty theft. I'd bought special therapy hand-puppets on my latest trip to Stockholm. The girls dug them out of the shopping bags and played with the mice, the rabbit, and the teddy bear, but cowered away from the tyrannosaurus rex – all except for little Gul. She went nose to nose with it and roared.

Gul, God's little rose.

Her name in Farsi meant "God's Rose." She was picked up for stealing food at a local market. She didn't know how old she was. Based on her teeth, the shelter doctor estimated her age at 8–9 years. By size, she looked about 4. Children wore out quickly in that violent life and the ones who survived the brothels were sent onto the streets to beg and steal. I saw something special in Gul – a spark in her brown eyes. I tickled her tummy with the tyrannosaurus puppet. She rolled on her back, shrieking with laughter. God's Little Rose was a survivor.

Play therapy and a few puppets made for a pleasant afternoon but did little to improve the life prognosis for this girl and the thousands like her who were destined for children's prisons and lives as criminal outcasts. To save them meant systemic changes at every point where they interacted with society – starting with police and child detention centers.

In September 2003, Ambassador John Miller, Director of the State Department Office to Monitor and Combat Trafficking in Persons, our major sponsor, was coming to Moscow for an official visit. Zhenya and another woman from the Survivors Network named Rosa were staying at my flat in anticipation.

Rosa was a striking Siberian blonde, about six feet tall, who'd been repatriated from the Netherlands three days before. Zhenya had been her contact during her six-month imprisonment in Amsterdam for working without a passport – the usual charge. We could have brought her back sooner except that she'd organized a hunger strike and refused to leave until all the trafficked women were released. Eventually, she left under protest, making us promise to help the rest of the women.

We sat up late together, drinking tea in the kitchen. "You must be a strong woman," I said. "You took on the Dutch legal system and won."

"I was strong once," she said. "I had to be. My husband and I were structural engineers for hydroelectric projects in the Russian Far East. We built dams and power plants in Northern China. I used to be an athlete, too, before I slammed my motorcycle into a tree and had to crawl ten kilometers through the snow with a broken leg."

"Very strong," said Zhenya.

"Things were hard in Siberia, but they became impossible during the financial crash. The big projects shut down. My husband and I had to find other jobs. He started drinking and gambling, running up debts with bad people. I didn't know about it until they threw him from the roof of our building. I was hanging wash on our balcony. I saw him go – screaming and falling."

"How awful," Zhenya exclaimed. "What did you do?"

"I grabbed my daughters from school, and we fled like refugees. There wasn't time to bury him. We left him in the street." She paused with a blank look, clutching a worn, pocket-sized Bible to her chest, thumbing the pages absently. Tiny Cyrillic script was crammed onto the margins. Was this a record like Zhenya had kept? "May God forgive me," she whispered.

The hall clock chimed. "Midnight," I said. "We've got a busy day tomorrow." We stacked our cups and plates in the sink. "Breakfast is at seven. I've had my shower, so you and Zhenya decide who showers tonight and who gets the hot water in the morning."

I walked to the office early to catch up on e-mail and phone calls and finish a grant proposal for juvenile police training. When I looked up from my computer, Rosa was standing in the doorway. She'd brought me a mug of tea. Even dressed in donated clothing – an old black sweater, a pair of jeans, and hand-knit socks – she was stunning.

I invited her to sit on the little sofa. It was important to take information about a case soon after a survivor returned to Russia, but Rosa looked spent. I answered e-mails while she stared out the window in the direction of the Kremlin – its gold dome and Russian flag visible through light snowfall.

"Are you okay?" I asked. "You seem far away."

"I can't believe I'm back in Russia. Maybe I'll blink and be in that prison again." She wiped away tears. "It was filthy and cold – ten women to a cell. The guards treated us like animals. Of course, we stank!" She met my eyes. "I feel guilty that I'm here and the other girls are still in cages."

"We'll fix that soon. Your hunger strike has hit the media. The Dutch want to send the rest of the Russian trouble-makers home."

"Will you tell me as soon as they arrive?"

"Of course."

"Am I hallucinating?" Rosa sniffed the air. "I smell *pelmeni*. Is someone cooking Siberian dumplings?"

"Just for you," I said.

Olga Shtul and Tatyana Uzakova were boiling the dumplings in the office kitchen. I invited Rosa to bring her tea to the conference table where salads, bread, and salami were laid out. After a heavy Russian lunch, Rosa fell asleep on my sofa. I woke her at about 5 P.M. It was already dark, so we caught the bus home. Zhenya would join us later.

I showed Rosa how to operate my satellite TV and left her curled up on the couch under the Smoky-the-Bear blanket while I took a shower. Later, we watched the Russian version of *Dancing with the Stars*, called *Figure Skating with the Stars*. Rosa kept her Bible in her lap.

"The name of the club was Petrushka," she said, lowering the sound with the remote. I picked up my notebook and pen. "I was staying in Voronesh south of Moscow with my sister Nastya. After a couple of months there, she talked me into going out to a new club. There was a long line to get in, but the bouncer said that we were very pretty. He waved us inside. There was a good band and lots of people dancing. It seemed like harmless fun.

"A man was staring at me. He wore gold chains and looked rich. Nastya said he was a famous gangsta' rapper with clubs in Europe. He had a recording studio in Berlin.

"He sent a bottle of champagne to our table and came over. I told him how much I admired his music, though I'd never heard of gangsta' rap before. I thought maybe he could get me a job in Germany for a few months.

"He said I was gorgeous, that I'd make a good hostess. He asked if I'd like to come to Berlin.

"'What about the ticket?' I asked. 'I haven't any money.' I remember his exact words.

"'Don't worry, beautiful,' he said. 'We'll buy the ticket, and you'll make so much money that you'll pay me back in a few days.'

"He met my train in Berlin. 'This is such a good scam,' he said once we were driving through the city in his Mercedes. 'You stupid Russian girls keep signing up and I keep selling you to German brothels. Get used to it, baby, you're now a whore.' He turned on the CD player – it was his own music. The words to the rap were fast – staccato, like gunfire." Rosa mimicked the beat of the music, accenting it by pretending her finger was a gun. "Bang-bang-bang. They were strings of women's names – Russian women – all the foolish girls who had signed his contracts. I started to cry, and he hit me in the face. He knocked my front teeth out. 'You're not so pretty anymore,' he said. I fainted."

Rosa pulled out the plastic bridge that filled the space where her front teeth had been and set it on the Bible. "My souvenirs," she said, shaking her head. "All I have to show for my terrible mistake."

We sat in silence until the intercom buzzed from the security door downstairs. I got up to let Zhenya and a pizza deliveryman into the building. We shared pizza and salad. Zhenya looked at her wristwatch and changed the TV channel. It was time for the next installment of *Gypsy Passion*, her favorite show – Rosa's as well. We ate ice cream and watched the band of singing gypsies roll through modern Moscow in horse-drawn wagons, causing outbreaks of passionate singing and emotional mayhem everywhere they went. It was impossibly silly, but it made us laugh – even Rosa smiled.

The next morning, the courtyard between my building and the Jewish Institute swarmed with morning dog walkers. They nodded greetings to the three of us as we hurried to catch the No. 156 bus to meet with Ambassador Miller. We arrived at the Vysotka at the same time the American Embassy vans were unloading. I came up to John Miller and gave him a hug, startling his State Department minders.

"Hey! It's Mother Theresa." He hugged me back. "Good to see you."

"This is Zhenya and Rosa," I said. They shook hands. "They're joining us from the Survivors' Network."

Vlad and his brother Alexei, our bookkeeper, arrived with Oleg Kouzbit. We climbed the stone steps as a group. "This is quite a building," said John, gazing up at the Stalinist Gothic towers that soared skyward.

"Until the 1980s this was *the* apartment building for the Communist elites," said Oleg.

"There are underground tunnels connected to the Kremlin," I said. "It was part of a private railway system. There are even secret stairwells that the KGB used to 'disappear' people from their apartments in the middle of the night."

"That's a myth," snapped Vlad in Russian. "Where do you get this stuff?"

"The babushkas in the lobby," I answered. "Those grannies know things."

We entered through the heavy oak doors and the Americans gawked at the high stone arches, cathedral ceilings, mosaics, and frescoes. "This looks like a church," John exclaimed.

"It was meant to," said Oleg. "It's a temple to the atheist state. These elites considered themselves gods."

I pushed the elevator button and nodded to the grannies lined up on a bench. They watched us surreptitiously. I'd have to fill them in later. Our offices had been visited by Christopher Smith from the US Congress, Natan Sharansky from the Israeli Knesset, members of the Russian State Duma and Moscow City Duma, representatives of the Russian police and European Law Enforcement Liaisons, and a steady stream of journalists and celebrities. The babushkas kept track of them all.

After our presentations to Ambassador Miller and his many aides, he asked me to step out on the balcony. We were free of minders for less than a minute.

"Ambassador Vershbow is insisting that the State Department audit your program," he said. "They're sending a team from the General Accounting Office to Moscow. He wants you shut down."

"Why? Auditing us will cost the government ten times more than our total grant funds. Does that make sense?"

"It doesn't have to."

"Factor X." I grimaced. Before I could explain what that meant, the balcony door opened, and we were separated by anxious minders telling the ambassador that it was time for him to leave.

Rosa left us as well. She was ticketed on the express train to St. Petersburg for a stay in Natalia Khodyreva's safe house. She hugged me with powerful

Ambassador John Miller with the Angel Coalition, Moscow

arms. When she pulled away, there were tears on her cheeks. She handed me her Bible, which I took respectfully, holding it with both hands.

"Thank you, Rosa," I said, kissing her cheek. "We'll make the most of this, I promise."

I opened the Bible. Every free space and margin was artfully packed with an engineer's tiny Cyrillic text. This was a time capsule of her life as a slave, a piece of her soul that must be handled with great care. The entries were chronological, starting on the front inside cover. It would take a magnifying glass and many hours to read. Each page held gold – everything we'd need to open a case in the Netherlands.

"It's all in there," Rosa said. "Names, places, dates – I wrote it all down including the names of the women still in jail and their Russian contacts. When you speak to their families, don't tell them about the prostitution, please," she said.

"We won't, I promise."

I handed the Bible to Afsona. As the Angel Coalition attorney, she was always frustrated by the lack of evidence brought back by trafficking victims. The women were often confused about where they had been, their minds addled by trauma and drugs. They wanted to go home and forget, not remember.

Within days we brought back the rest of the women and contacted the Trafficking Task Force in Amsterdam to initiate a case against the Russian traffickers. Within a few weeks, the evidence recorded in the Bible was translated to English and sent to the General Prosecutor in The Hague, who opened the investigation against a particularly vicious international trafficking ring associated with gangsta' rap.

Before returning to join her daughters in Siberia, Rosa flew with me to Washington DC to testify before a congressional committee hearing chaired by Congressman Christopher Smith. I'd first met the congressman in 1999 in St. Petersburg when he was traveling with a delegation from the Organization for Security and Cooperation in Europe – OSCE. They had asked me to introduce them to representatives of Russian NGOs and trafficking survivors.

Rosa testifies before Congress, Washington D.C.

The following year Congressman Smith co-authored the American anti-trafficking law, the Trafficking Victims Protection Act (TVPA) making human trafficking a crime in the United States and enabling prosecution of international traffickers.

Chapter Twenty-six

ANGELS, COPS AND CARABINIERI

Nizhny Novgorod, Russia – 2004

In the spring of 2004, I flew through a snowstorm aboard an old Tupolov prop plane with wood paneling and ruffled pink window curtains. I was traveling to Chelyabinsk in the Ural Mountains with delegates from the Swedish organization Kvinnoforum and police officers from Malmo, Sweden to conduct a police training. Our objective was to convince Russian police at each safe house location in Russia that protecting the rights and dignity of trafficking victims would make them better witnesses and result in a higher rate of criminal prosecutions. The usual aggressive police techniques resulted in victims who were more afraid of the police than of traffickers – a situation hardly unique to Russia.

The turnout for the training was excellent – seventy-five uniformed Russian police officers. The Swedish policemen in their blue uniforms were a major draw. Our Angel in Chelyabinsk, Larisa Vasilieva, a petite piano teacher, sat beside me at the speakers' table. We faced a room full of tough Siberian cops – their scowling faces skeptical that a humane approach to police work would improve anything, ever.

During the two-day training, I discovered that Siberian police were willing to share their stories over a good lunch. Tough-as-nails cops spoke freely about their frustration with having to deal with violence and crime every day, and how they'd had to harden their hearts to the terrible suffering they saw. Burn-out and alcoholism were high, and a growing number of police were committing suicide. I recalled my first experience with Russian doctors whose brutality to their patients was so easily reversed. I floated the idea of a counseling program for police officers. We were already working with juvenile police in Moscow to prevent burn-out and help them deal with stress. But that was Moscow. This was Siberia.

I was the final speaker on the last day. Half the audience was dozing off, only staying because the next event was dinner. Instead of summarizing like I was supposed to, I decided to talk about the support programs we were conducting for police in Moscow. I had my flash drive with a PowerPoint presentation that we'd used for the Moscow City Government.

"To close my presentation," I said, "I'd like to share a video clip of our psychologist, Konstantin Kamarov, a police officer himself, doing stress reduction exercises with a group of officers. The program is now required for juvenile police by the Moscow Ministry of Interior – GUVD. Over 1500 officers participated last year ... "

The cops' faces remained unreadable, eyes riveted to the screen. Afterwards, no questions were asked, and they filed out of the room.

"What do you think?" I asked Larisa later at dinner.

"They listened," she said. "Time will tell if they heard anything."

I'd just returned to Moscow when Zhenya called. She and Nadezhda had identified a trafficking ring in Nizhny Novgorod disguised as an employment agency recruiting women over age fifty to work as nannies in Slovenia, then trafficking them by bus into Italy to supply boutique brothels in Tuscany for men who wanted sex with older women. They'd managed to get four of the women home but most were still in Italy.

Zhenya helped the women file a criminal complaint against the agency, but because the crime took place in Italy, the Russian police submitted the case to Interpol, and waited ... and waited. Nothing happened.

"We have to do something," she said. "Interpol takes so long that the brothels have moved by the time they act."

"Why don't the Nizhny police call the Italian police directly? The European countries all have trafficking task forces," I said. "They are very good."

"Our police insist on following some old protocols. They won't call Rome themselves, but we can, can't we?"

"I was just in Rome teaching a class to Catholic Bishops at the Gregorian University," I said. "They connected me with Caritas, the Catholic charity that works with the federal police – the *Caribinieri*. I'll start with them."

"I'm so frustrated," Zhenya broke down in tears. "We've got a dozen women trapped in Tuscany and that damn crooked agency down the street keeps sending more. I finally organized a protest in front of their offices with the victims' names and pictures. It was on the news."

A chill shot down my spine. "Be careful, Zhenya. Those people will hurt you."

"What else can I do? Everyone needs to know what they are up to."

"I'll contact Italy tomorrow. In the meantime, please don't risk your life."

"My life?" A long silence, then sobs. "I just told Gennady that I can't marry him because I'm not a woman anymore. I've been eaten inside by those rapists' diseases. I can never have children."

That explained her gauntness and pallor. I said, "Zhenya, you're an amazing young woman – and very much loved. Please, please be careful… " She hung up before I could say more.

The next morning, I called Caritas Internationalis in Rome and was referred to Major Giuseppe Battaglia, Head of the Organized Crime Division of the *Carabinieri*. He expressed his own frustration that the Russian police kept deferring to Interpol, then complaining about how slow the Italian police were to respond. "If they would talk to me directly, we could close down this whole operation in weeks," he said. "I can't seem to get that idea through to the Russians."

"I think I have a way to do that," I mused. "How would you like to come to our Nizhny Novgorod law enforcement training in February. You can speak with Russian police and prosecutors in person."

The major joined our training team in Moscow. We boarded a train to Nizhny Novgorod with Swedish police officer Thomas Ekman from the Anti-Trafficking Department of Gothenburg, Sweden, and Ingela Hesius, Senior District Prosecutor of Stockholm.

Following a speech by the deputy mayor of Nizhny Novgorod, our Angel partner Nadezhda Belik opened the conference by introducing two of the Tuscany trafficking survivors to a hall packed with Russian police investigators and federal prosecutors, Interpol, the FMS – Federal Migration Service, NGOs and media. The survivors' testimony implicated the local employment agency, the one Zhenya was picketing, as the guilty trafficker.

The chief prosecutor for Nizhny took the podium and launched into a rant on how difficult it was to work with the Italian authorities. "They don't care about Russian women. They refuse our invitation to work on prosecutions." He closed with the classic Russian lament, "*Shto delat*? – What's to be done?" A roster of local officials followed, repeating the same self-defeating fatalism.

Major Battaglia sat in the front row, his head tilted toward his translator. Finally, he'd had enough. He stood and addressed the startled crowd. "You call me disinterested? I've come all the way from Rome to beg you to call our task force directly whenever you have cases involving Italy. Now that I'm here, give me your cases, give me everything you've got. Let me interview the survivors and see your files. Together, we'll get these damn crooks before any other women are hurt."

Major Giuseppe Battaglia, Head of the Organized Crime Division of the Carabinieri. Nizhny Novgorod, Russia.

The room fell silent. I looked over a sea of stony Russian faces with eyes glued to the major. No one moved during the translation from English to Russian, but gears were creaking in Russian brains. The sudden shift was visceral. The Nizhny prosecutor jumped to his feet, extended his hand to the major, and said, "We'll give you everything and cooperate in every way we can." He thumped the major on the back – Russian code for "break out the vodka, it's time for a toast." The room broke into cheers and applause, everyone talking at once. There was vodka all around and toasts to Italy, Russia, Sweden and an end to human trafficking.

After the meeting, Zhenya took me to a hospital to meet two trafficking survivors who had been sent back with the help of Caritas. Local television filmed an interview with Zhenya and one woman, who was sitting up in bed. The other, Valentina, had been raped with a broken bottle. She'd had surgery in Rome but appeared close to death. The doctor signed to me that he could do nothing more.

Zhenya's compelling interview was picked up by national news. Her pale face and haunted blue eyes became the symbol of human trafficking from Russia. Within weeks, the brothels in Tuscany were shut down with much fanfare, and cases opened against the traffickers. Zhenya and the Angel Coalition were busy bringing women home.

The following month, she called to say that Valentina was better and wanted to talk to me. I agreed to come during the weekend. It was a heady time for the Angel Coalition. The help lines were deluged with calls following the launch of a new Russian mini-series on trafficking called *Matryoshka* (Nesting Dolls), which concluded each segment with our help line number. Our team was giving training to embassies from Europe, Middle East, Africa, and Asia, and I was leaving soon to speak in Helsinki, Brussels, Strasbourg, and Frankfurt.

I caught the Friday night Air Siberia flight to Nizhny Novgorod and stayed with my Korobeniki musician friends. We had a late dinner and a good laugh about the night I'd sung "Moscow Nights" for the Nizhny government. They showed me tapes of the concert recorded by local television. I'd never seen them. I looked like Little Orphan Annie in my baggy jeans, over-sized shoes, and windblown curls. "I'll never do that again," I said. "Pft, pft, pft."

Saturday morning, we drove to a health resort where the musicians were performing. The men went ice fishing on the Aka River, and I joined the women for a sulfurous, bubbling mud bath. On Sunday, I took a tram to the sanatorium where Valentina was recovering. She looked much better with her hair brushed and spots of color on her cheeks.

All four beds in the sunlit room were occupied by survivors from Tuscany. They gestured for me to sit in the only chair. Valentina began her story the way that women always did. She spoke about her life before being trafficked. She wanted me to know who she'd been before her dignity was ravaged and she'd become invisible.

Valentina was a middle school teacher of fifty-five when she answered an advertisement for attractive "mature" Russian women to work as nannies in Slovenia. It never occurred to her that she would fall prey to "white slavers" – she was too old. She and the other ladies went on to provide detailed information about the links between the Russian and Albanian mobs who had taken them by bus through the Alps and into Italy.

I asked if they had shared this information with the Russian police. "Good God, no," said Valentina. "I want you to send it to Major Battaglia, the Italian officer. He can decide what to give our police. Ask him not to say that it came from me."

A woman with gray hair said. "A lot of our policemen take blat – bribes. They're afraid of the traffickers, and for good reason. Those Albanians are killers."

Another woman said, "You'd better tell that young hot-head Zhenya to be careful. We saw the protest she made in front of the employment agency on TV. Her face was all over Russian news. They'll come after her for sure."

"Talk some sense into her," said Valentina. "She needs to understand what a dangerous bear she's poking."

I called Zhenya from the sanatorium. "How about meeting me for dinner before I fly back to Moscow?" I asked. "I'll take you to Aquarium – your favorite restaurant."

"I'd love to, but I can't," she said with a sigh. "I've got entrance exams for law school. I'm studying all night. If I do well, I might qualify for a scholarship to London or Paris."

"Good luck," I said. "I know you'll be brilliant."

"Pft, pft, pft ... " She spat.

During the spring, we weathered the scrutiny of twelve American embassy officials and a scowling team of prosecutors who had come all the way from Chicago to harass us. They were followed by three government auditors from Washington DC who, after a month of examining every accounting entry since our inception, finally found a $54 discrepancy – a bouquet of flowers purchased for a press conference in Petrozavodsk charged to the wrong account.

We were visited a few more times by the Russian tax police, who liked to linger and gossip over coffee. "We keep getting rat-line calls from your embassy," said the tall one. "You ought to have your office swept for bugs. They know too much stuff about you."

Vlad called his friend Vasily from a security firm. He walked through our office holding an electronic box the size of a cell phone. It chirped excitedly in every room. "Americans," he said. "I recognize their signals." He held up a different device that emitted higher-pitched squeaks. "You've got Russians too. It'll cost you about $1500 to do a deep sweep and remove all these bugs; but honestly, they'll just keep coming back like cockroaches. You'd have to sweep every week like the big companies do."

"What can we do?" I asked. "I can just imagine what the government auditors would say if we showed 'bug sweeping' as an expense, especially since it's the American Embassy doing it."

"I suggest that if you have something important to say, leave your cellphones in the office and take a walk where there's lots of traffic noise. Or go out on your balcony."

In the beginning of 2006, our relations with the US Embassy improved dramatically with the arrival of a new ambassador, William Burns, an elegant diplomat fluent in Russian. He made a point of recognizing our work with a personal visit to the Angel Coalition office. He came alone with no minders, or so I thought. Later, the babushkas regaled me with descriptions of all the Russian and American security agents who had inspected the building prior to his visit and then accompanied him, waiting inconspicuously on each floor.

We continued to have sticky relations with the International Narcotics and Law Enforcement (INL) division of the embassy, but as far as the diplomatic offices were concerned, we were treated with a respect that would continue through the next several years and the tenure of Ambassador John Beyrle, a seasoned diplomat whose father was a much-loved Russian hero – an American soldier who had escaped the Germans and fought courageously with the Red Army as they advanced on Berlin.

Chapter Twenty-seven

ANGELS IN TAJIKISTAN

Dushanbe, Tajikistan – Summer 2007

Our Swedish-funded police training program was much in demand throughout Siberia and was extended into Central Asia, beginning with Kazakhstan, Kyrgyz Republic and then Tajikistan, a mountainous, landlocked country bordered by Afghanistan, Uzbekistan, Kyrgyzstan, and the People's Republic of China and victimized by each of them.

Tajik traditions left the population uniquely vulnerable. If a man kidnapped and raped a Tajik woman, she was forced by her family to marry him. Afghan militants and Kyrgyz raiders carried off older Tajik women to work as domestic servants and sold Tajik girls into prostitution. Tajik boys were forced to fight with insurgents in Pakistan and Afghanistan. Tajikistan was also a source of trafficking for prostitution and labor in the United Arab Emirates (UAE), Turkey, Saudi Arabia, Kuwait, and Iran.

We decided to hold an international working conference in the Tajik capital, Dushanbe. We invited delegations from every one of the receiving countries including China, and, by the time I boarded Tajik Airways for the flight from Moscow, all had responded positively except China and Iran. American experts Dr. Laura Lederer, Dr. Donna M. Hughes, and Dr. Louise Shelly, Director of the Terrorism, Transnational Crime and Corruption Center at George Mason University, joined me from the US. Our Swedish partners flew directly from Stockholm. We met at the Hotel Mercury compound in the center of town.

The three-day conference was opened by the vice president of Tajikistan. On the last day, a sizable contingent of Afghans arrived in a convoy from Kabul. They provided important information about how women were trafficked through Afghanistan into the UAE and Iran. Although the UAE Criminal Investigations Division in Dubai had responded positively to our invitation, they'd failed to receive travel approval from their foreign ministry. Dubai was repeatedly iden-

Tajik Angels Gulchera Mirzoeva and Afsona Kadyrova.

tified as a major receiving country for victims from the former USSR, so I decided that it was time to go there for a personal visit. I asked Oleg to arrange it once we'd returned to the Moscow office.

At our closing banquet, I sat at a table with the Swedish delegates, the vice president of Tajikistan, and the deputy foreign minister. Dr. Hughes and Dr. Lederer had both become so ill after the first Tajik meal that they remained in bed at the hotel. I'd had to read their speeches at the conference and felt guilty about encouraging them to enjoy the delicious Tajik food.

Oleg Kouzbit, Director of the Angel Coalition, came up behind me and whispered, "Those Afghan diplomats want to talk to you." He nodded to the next table where a group of swarthy men smiled and blinked expectantly.

"Who are they, exactly?" I asked.

"The Afghan ambassador and their foreign minister to Tajikistan. The rest are probably ex-mujahideen. They will be armed," said Oleg.

"What should I do?"

"Wait here. I'll go speak with them first." Oleg had done military service in Afghanistan, though he never spoke about it. He added, "A woman shouldn't approach them alone."

The Afghan ambassador came back with Oleg and invited the two of us to join their table. He introduced me to the deputy foreign minister, the chief of police of Kabul, chairman of the Movement for Freedom and Democracy political party and the chief of border guards. After we were seated and mineral water poured, the deputy foreign minister began: "Trafficking is a terrible problem in Afghanistan. Our government has asked me to invite you to Kabul to set up a program for Afghan police and border guards. We are driving back tonight. Will you join us?"

"How far is Kabul?" I asked, awed by the proposal. I looked at Oleg, who rolled his eyes.

"It's only four hours," the deputy replied. "It's quite safe. We have excellent vehicles and bodyguards, of course."

I'd seen their dust-covered cars parked outside. They looked like old Russian Ladas. Bouncing down a rutted road through the Afghan frontier at night with an armed convoy of mujahideen seemed ill-advised on many levels.

"I would need a visa for Afghanistan, wouldn't I? I don't have one."

"No problem," said the chief of border guards. He moved his chair close to mine and pulled a stamp from his case, opened an ink pad, and said, "Give me your passport. I'll stamp it and we can leave."

"You are very kind," I laughed as if they were joking and patted the arm of the man holding the stamp, laying my hand on something hard under his shirt. He proceeded to pull a huge, shiny Glock 23 out of its holster and set it on the table.

I knew what it was because he said, "It's a Glock 23."

I tried to ignore it. "I would like to come to Kabul," I said, "but not tonight. Please have the Foreign Ministry invite me officially and I will fly there from Moscow. If you stay in touch with Oleg, he will arrange everything. I must have a proper escort from my own people."

I said good night with much hand kissing and returned to the Tajik officials who were signaling for me to join them in a van with the Swedes.

I left Oleg and the Afghans exchanging cards. They remained in discussions until January 2008, when an insurgent commando squad invaded the luxury Serena Hotel in downtown Kabul where we were schedule to stay, killing seven people, including Americans.

Chapter Twenty-eight

WHEN ANGELA CALLED

Dubai, United Arab Emirates – Spring 2007

In April 2007, I flew Air Emirates to Dubai for a meeting with our contact on the UAE Trafficking Task Force. I'd been officially invited through the Human Rights Care Department of the United Arab Emirates. After breakfast at the Hotel Monarch, I asked the concierge for the address of CID, the Criminal Investigations Department of the Dubai Police.

"Is there a problem?" he asked, looking concerned. "Do you have a complaint?"

"Not at all," I said. "I just need the address. I have an appointment."

"Are you going by taxi?"

"Of course."

"There is no need for an address. Every taxi driver knows the CID."

He was right. The turbaned cab driver knew where it was – and refused to go all the way. I walked the final two blocks and entered a chaotic scene that recalled Saturday nights as an intern in the Harborview County Hospital emergency room.

It must have been one hundred degrees in the crowded atrium that served as both bookings room and complaints department. The humid air was saturated with familiar smells of blood and vomit, with overtones of alcohol. I chose the Complaints Desk and approached a fierce, six-foot, five-inch Pakistani policeman with scars like a prize fighter. His nametag said, "Sergeant Khan."

"So, madam," he said, looking me over and scowling. "What's your complaint?"

"No complaint," I answered, forgetting the full name of my contact. "I'm here to see Captain Ahmad. Here is my card."

"We have a dozen Captain Ahmads. What department?"

"He's on the Trafficking Task Force. The Human Rights Care Department invited me." I fumbled in my purse. "Here's my letter of invitation. It's from Captain Ahmad Obaid Bin Hadibah."

"One moment," he said, snapping my picture with a digital camera. "Have a seat."

There was no place to sit. The few chairs were occupied by bloodied drunks. Everyone else squatted, sweating, against the walls or sprawled on the floor unconscious. I didn't have to wait long before Sergeant Khan beckoned. He unlocked a gate and let me through, saying, "Down the hall, around the corner, second door on the left. Enter where the sign says, 'Human Rights Care Department.'"

I made my way along the narrow corridor, passing more over-sized Pakistani policemen in khaki shorts. I rounded a corner and counted the doors. There were no signs of any kind. I looked at each door until I reached a squad room where men in long, white robes and headdresses worked at computers. I retraced my steps back to the front desk. "Excuse me," I said to Sergeant Khan. "There is no sign."

The sergeant frowned and made another phone call. He hung up and seemed to be listening for something. I thought I heard an electric drill. When it stopped, he said, "You are mistaken. Go back and look again." This time there was a sign. I knocked and it was opened by a woman wearing a burqa. A few minutes later, I was escorted to a meeting with the rest of the Trafficking Task Force. Their conference room had a large map on the wall, marking the routes of human trafficking into Dubai. It was my turn to take a digital photo.

"Right now, we have 96 Russian women in jail for prostitution," said Captain Ahmad. "If you can arrange for their papers and transportation back to Russia, we will release them."

"We've already made an agreement with the Russian Consulate in the UAE to process their citizens and send them home," I said. "What about the Tajik women?"

"A much bigger problem. Their families won't take them back. It's why our foreign ministry wouldn't let us come to Dushanbe. They are in dispute over this issue."

"The Tajik government is willing to help them return now. They have opened a safehouse outside of Dushanbe. The women will have to deal with their families with the help of counselors."

"Get us the papers and we'll let them go."

Over the next year, more than 900 Russian and Tajik trafficking victims – men, women, and children – were freed from UAE prisons and sent home. At the next meeting in Dushanbe one year later, the UAE was fully represented.

My voice for the voiceless was being heard. I was globe-trotting, flushed with success, proud of myself. I wished that Bella Abzug was alive to see how far I'd flown, what I'd achieved. I was proud of my family, too, and had all but forgotten my earlier concerns. My son was studying for a master's degree in education, my daughter an Olympian and an Ironman Marathon champion, studying law.

Back in Moscow, my kitchen table was much like Nadezhda Krupskaya's must have been during the Russian Revolution – a gathering place of activists, journalists, and human rights reformers. The lights were always on, the wi-fi running twenty-four hours a day.

The Angel Coalition help lines operated around the clock. The staff took turns carrying an emergency cell phone for nights and holidays. It was preferable to have native Russian speakers answering, but, when the rest of the staff was unavailable, I picked up the slack. It was close to midnight. I was nodding off, reading in bed when the ringtone startled me with a burst of Middle Eastern music.

"Angel Coalition," I answered in Russian. "I'm listening."

"Allo? Allo? Do you hear me?" It was a child's voice. The connection was poor.

"Can I help you?" I responded, putting the phone on speaker, cranking up the volume. "Allo?"

"Julietta? Oh, thank God. It's me – Angela." A bolt of electricity shot through me. Angela – on the international help line? Wasn't she in Uglich? "I'm in Cairo."

Everything that was safe in the world fell away. Adrenaline surged, my heart raced, my breath came in short gasps. I recalled the day I'd awakened to find my two-year old son missing, the front door open. I had called 911 and couldn't speak.

"Julietta?" her voice quavered. "Are you there?"

"I'm here." I barely controlled my speech. "Are you all right?"

"I think Tanya, Lara, and I may be in some trouble. Maybe not, but I thought I should call. Zhenya gave me the card with this number. She said to use it if I was worried … "

I switched into automatic pilot – not a second to lose: "Where in Cairo? Can you give me an address? I'll send someone to get you."

"I don't know. All I can see is a big cemetery across the street. People are living there in the tombs. It's creepy. We wanted to see the pyramids." I heard the other girls in the background. "And the Sphinx. Tatyana Safarovna never lets us go anywhere fun."

"Do you have your own cell phone?"

"I got this prepaid Beeline phone in Yaroslavl."

"We'll keep rubles in the account so you can call us. Here's my personal number – put it on your phone."

"I've got it."

"How did you get to Cairo?"

"We went to Yaroslavl to model our sewing at Young Pioneers. There was a travel agent. She offered us jobs in Hergada. That's in Egypt on the Red Sea Riviera. She gave us airline tickets and passports and everything."

"Now you're required to pay them back, right?" I tried to damp the anger from my voice. Hadn't she paid any attention in Zhenya's class?

"They said it would be easy because I'd make a lot of money as a hostess. Egyptian men think red hair is beautiful," said Angela. "They'll give me big tips if I let them touch it."

I shivered, sickened by her naive words. "I've always said that you're beautiful."

"I know. Now you're mad at me, but … I got worried when these Ukrainian guys took our passports away. They seemed kind of mean."

"Did they hurt you?"

"No, not really. They locked us in this little room. The window's so dirty I can barely see out. Besides, it's dark." Panic rose in her voice. "It's hot in here. I'm scared."

"Angela dear, it's okay. We will find you," I said with optimism I didn't dare feel. Cairo had an excellent trafficking task force, but it was a huge city. There was no GPS on cheap Russian phones. We needed more information.

"They're coming," said Angela. "I've got to go."

"Call me again tomorrow. Read me a street sign or the name of a shop… "

The phone was dead.

I alerted our Cairo trafficking liaison on his private cell phone. "We've got three Russian girls," I told him. "The oldest is fifteen, the other two are fourteen and thirteen. They are locked up across the street from a cemetery. All they could tell me is that people are living in the tombs."

"Cairo is an ancient city. There are hundreds of cemeteries. People live in all of them."

I gave him the girls' names. "I'll send you their photos and information in the morning. They're underage so the passports they have with them must be false."

"If the names or nationalities are forged, we have little chance of stopping them at the border."

"At least you'll have accurate data."

"We'll watch for your girls. I cannot promise more than that."

How many times had I heard that said? How seldom had it led to a rescue? We needed to tell the police exactly where to go and Angela was the only one who could tell us. Her fate and that of her friends was on her shoulders. I recalled the first time I'd seen her – a wailing newborn with a tuft of red hair and wide-open eyes. Was she spunky enough? Was she brave? Did she have any sense at all?

I tried calling Uglich Orphanage. No one answered. I didn't have Tatyana Safarovna's cell number. I'd have to get that from Vlad, and he wasn't answering. I could do nothing more until morning. I curled up on the couch, opening my laptop to the file of open cases. I studied the black-and-white passport photos of missing girls, my cheeks growing hot with anger. Tomorrow we'd add Angela's, Lara's and Tanya's faces.

They'd taken Zhenya's class and knew the risks but had gone with the trafficker anyway. I recalled an undercover videotape of traffickers at a party in Moscow City, laughing about how easy it was to deceive Russian girls, how stupid they were – and desperate, particularly orphans.

I opened a folder labeled "Cold Cases" – girls who'd been missing five years or more. There were over one hundred. An ache gripped my chest. Heaving sobs breached the dam of my resistance, plunging me into a well of grief. Too many lost faces – shattered dreams. No matter how much my work was praised, it wouldn't bring them back. I cried until there were no tears and I nodded off. In the early hours of dawn, fear moved in – a roiling, black cloud of voices shrieking: "You're too weak. You can't save them. You can't even save yourself."

I woke with a start to daylight and forced myself into motion. No one answered at Uglich Orphanage. I called Vlad. He gave me Tatyana Safarovna's cell number. She answered. "We're at the police station. We've got three girls missing." Her voice trembled. "They didn't come back from Young Pioneers. They've been gone all night. We've been looking for them everywhere."

"They're in Cairo," I said.

"What?" she shrieked. I heard anxious voices in the background. "They're in Egypt? All three of them?"

"I'm afraid so. They went with traffickers from Yaroslavl."

"Well, tell them to get back here now. They're in big trouble."

"I'm working on it," I said, my throat catching. I heard Anna weep, Dada Igor curse. *Action! Keep moving!* "I need you to fax me copies of the girls' documents." I forced a professional tone. "The police will contact Interpol from Uglich. We're already in touch with the Egyptian Trafficking Task Force."

"Those scamps are on kitchen duty from now until forever. God save me from red-heads."

I received the faxes within an hour and scanned them into electronic dossiers that I sent on to Cairo. Then I waited, a powerless shell. I insisted on carrying the phone for the next few days, resisting the urge to call the girls. I didn't tell Tatyana Safarovna that Angela had a cell phone. Keeping it secret was the girls' best hope. A week passed in slow motion.

On Saturday night, I had the phone on the pillow when Angela called. Relief battled fear as I asked, "Did they hurt you?"

"We're okay," she said. "There's nothing to worry about." She sounded excited. I was wary. "Guess where I am." I heard a mewling in the background, like cattle lowing. "That's a camel. We're walking across the desert in a caravan. We travel at night and sleep in a tent all day because it's so hot."

"Are the three of you still together?"

"Yes. It's dark now," she said. "We walk all night toward sunrise."

They were traveling east. They must be crossing the Sinai Desert with a Bedouin caravan destined for the border with Israel. Bedouins had traversed those sands for centuries, transporting all manner of goods, including human slaves. They relied on mobile phones, so the cellular reception was generally better than in Europe.

"Call me back when you reach a border crossing or as soon as you can identify a road. We'll come and get you."

"Maybe I don't want to go back to Uglich." She sounded dreamy, a child on a big adventure. "It's beautiful here – a million billion stars." I imagined those three small girls in Bedouin robes that slipped over their hands and trailed in the sand. I prayed that they could be rescued before their world was shattered. There wasn't much time.

"Tatyana Safarovna is in a terrible state." I played the guilt card. "You've broken her heart. She wants you girls to come back."

"Tell her I'm sorry, but I don't want to come back. She never lets us have any fun."

"Call me when you cross the border." I didn't want to let her go. "Promise me! Say it."

"I might," she said. "Or maybe I'll become a famous dancer, or a fashion model." The phone clicked off.

Once again, I'd have to wait. Informing Egyptian or Israeli border guards that a slave caravan was approaching could be more dangerous for the girls than allowing the Bedouins to smuggle them into Israel. If the Egyptian Army or the Israeli Defense Force approached, the smugglers would likely bury the girls under the sand with only a breathing tube. Many had been buried and never found, entombed and mummified in burning sand.

If Angela called from Haifa or Tel Aviv, we could set up a rescue within minutes. Jerusalem was more difficult. The internal politics in that city of contradictions were labyrinthine.

I was half asleep when a breaking news banner flashed across the laptop screen. A prominent lawyer had been murdered in the stairwell of her apartment building. The killers were identified as Chechen hit men. They had disabled the elevator, then waited for her to climb the stairs. Three shots – a chest shot, a head shot, and a kill shot. No name was mentioned, but she was likely to be someone I knew.

It was much too easy to kill in Moscow. There was only one way in and out of an apartment building. Hit men could be hired for $500. The real killers, the millionaires who ordered the crimes from the towers of Moscow City – the City of Gold – would never be brought to justice.

Chapter Twenty-nine

FINDING ANGELA

Moscow, Russia – Winter 2008

On Monday morning, I stepped out into a biting gale and crossed the icy courtyard to the bus stop. It was slow going against the wind and all I found was trampled snow – the bus had gone. I set off for the office, wary of cars driving on the sidewalk. Moscow pedestrians were fatally mowed down every day by cars jumping the curb to avoid traffic. The police didn't seem to care.

Last week, a huge black SUV barely missed me and a young mother pushing a pram. The grannies waiting at the bus stop were infuriated and blocked the sidewalk, looking like angry badgers in their fur hats and coats. The driver honked. The grannies pounded on the roof and hood with purses and umbrellas. The driver revved the engine, threatening mayhem while a cop directed traffic about twenty feet away, ignoring the ruckus. The driver pulled out an air gun, opened his window and started shooting the grannies. An even bigger crowd attacked the car, dragging the driver onto the sidewalk. They commandeered his air gun and shot him with it, multiple times while his passengers ran away. I left when the police started arresting people.

Today I had no time for bad drivers, traffic jams, or angry babushkas. Afsona had the Angel Coalition phone and all I cared about was being nearby when Angela called. I rounded the corner of the Union of Industrialists and into the food shop to buy some kefir for lunch and a bag of pistachios. Once through the heavy oak doors of the Vysotka, I shook snow from my coat and boots in the heated vestibule.

"*Dobroe utro* – good morning," I greeted the old ladies lined up on a bench. I breathed in the lobby smells of wet dog and boiled cabbage and gave them the pistachios.

"*Dobroe utro*," they replied. "The lifts are kaput again."

All four elevators to the tower were unresponsive to my button pushing. The only alternative was the single staircase to our tower. The other staircases, which were rumored to have once given the KGB access to every apartment, had been sealed off years ago, if they'd ever existed. I entered the dark stairwell and started up the eighteen flights to our office.

Snowfall dimmed the windows at each landing, casting the passage in yellow light. I had gone about five floors when I spotted a man on the landing above. He kept to the shadows, drawing on a cigarette. Men smoking in stairwells was not unusual, but after the murder of a colleague this weekend, I felt a stab of fear. I turned around and started down the stairs, but another man blocked my way. I froze, fumbling in my purse for a spray-can of mace. I heard footfalls. The second man descended the stairs – I was trapped between them. I found the can, flipped off the safety cap with my thumb and pointed it at his face.

"Whoa, Trigger," he said in English, raising his arms. "I'm on your side."

"Holy shit, Fritz! I nearly maced you," I exclaimed. "What are you doing hanging around in stairwells?" I turned to the man below me. He was smiling, too. "You scared the bejesus out of me, Franz."

The men were European Union law enforcement attachés. The Angels called them Fric and Frac because Fritz and Franz were difficult for the Russians to say. They were the only embassy attachés who seemed concerned for our safety, suggesting ways to upgrade our security. Unfortunately, the equipment they recommended was beyond our means. Instead of $3000 a week for bug removal and video surveillance, we paid 1000 rubles per month ($30) to the babushkas in the lobby – our traditional Russian alert system.

It had worked for us so far. The office phone would ring: "Bunch of bad guys on the way up," the grannies would say. "Don't open the door." If someone suspicious was hanging around, they would meet us on the stairs to open the massive padlock on the back door when we left to go home.

"You were spotted taking photos on Yaroslavl Road," said Franz, jabbing his cigarette at me for emphasis. "You're rattling the golden cages. The big money guys will swat you like a bug."

"At the very least, stay out of stairwells," said Fritz. He handed me a card, blank except for a phone number. "Program this into your phone, then shred the card. Any problems – anything at all – call that number."

"Why didn't you go up to the office instead of scaring me to death?" I asked, tucking the card into my purse.

"Elevators are broken, and eighteen stories is too much of a climb. We thought we'd wait and teach you a lesson." Franz coughed and lit another cigarette. "The Americans attachés will be visiting you today."

"They didn't tell me," I said. "How do you know?"

"We just came from the monthly law enforcement briefing at the US Embassy. We suggested to our American colleagues that they help beef up your security. They nixed the idea, but I think you should ask them again when they come to see you," said Fritz. "They really don't like you."

"I know." I shrugged.

Fritz and Franz had been at a meeting on trafficking legislation in the Russian State Duma when the US Embassy representative turned to a delegate from the State Department and said in a loud whisper, "Don't worry about that Angel Coalition. We'll shut them down before Christmas."

They'd also overheard the moderator, a Russian general, apologize to me for the rudeness of my own countrymen. "We have no control over those people," he'd said, kissing my hand. "They do not represent in any way the views or feelings of the Russian Federation." I didn't know how to reply so I said nothing.

More voices were coming upstairs. Olga and Oleg startled when they saw us. "It's okay," I said. "It's just me and our friends from the EU."

We talked about the assassination – a civil rights lawyer, one of the few who had been willing to take low-paying trafficking cases. Her death was a serious setback. We were bringing back more victims than the tiny safe houses could handle. The Angel Coalition had been contacted in the past week by young women stranded in Tel Aviv, New York, Miami, London, and Cairo. Each one needed legal representation and police protection, neither of which came easily.

The lawmen said good-bye. We tried the elevators again and found them operational. Marianna was already in the office when we got there. She'd been working day and night on the case of a girl from Ukraine who attempted to escape from a brothel in Cyprus by tying bed sheets together and climbing out a third story window. The sheets didn't hold, and she fell to her death.

Her father, a retired military policeman, had acted as the primary investigator in the search for his daughter – something Ukrainian police had been unwilling to do. We helped him raise money to follow the trail of Ukrainian and Romanian traffickers through Eastern Europe to Cyprus. Marianna was briefing the team on the girl's tragic death when Tatyana burst into the conference room.

"Come quick," she said. "Afsona has a girl on the phone. She says she knows Julietta."

"It's Angela," I exclaimed. "Where is she?"

"The call is routed through Ankara. She's somewhere in Turkey."

In the call room, Afsona was gesturing for Oleg to call Ankara police on the second line. While Oleg dialed the director of the Trafficking Task Force for Turkey, Afsona said, "Angela, I am the lawyer for the Angel Coalition. We have the police on our other phone. They're going to rescue you. Can you tell me what city you're in?"

"I don't know. We flew from Haifa and drove for hours in the back of a van. I can't read anything. I don't even know what country I'm in."

"You're in Turkey. We don't know what city yet. Are you near a busy road?"

"No. I'm hiding in an alley."

"Go to a road where you can see buses. I need you to tell me the number of a bus."

We waited until we heard the sound of street traffic. Angela said, "I see a number 32."

"Good. Now go to an intersection and give me the number of another bus."

"I see a number 256."

"That's very good, Angela. Now go to a porch where you can hide and give me the number that's over the door."

"I'm at No. 1855."

"Now stay there."

According to the Turkish police, Angela was in Istanbul. I bit my lip. The Turkish Task Force identified the cross streets and informed the Istanbul police. She was in the Old Quarter near the Hippodrome, a tourist area with deep entryways to hide in. Our job now was to keep her on the phone, making sure that she didn't panic and run when she saw the police.

"How are you going to find me?" Angela sobbed. "I'm so scared. Maybe it was a bad idea to call you."

"Stay calm. The police are sending two detectives to rescue you. They won't speak Russian. When they call you by name, you must get into their car and show them where the rest of the girls are. Can you do that, Angela? Can you help the other girls?"

"What if someone sees me? That guy will be back any minute. He'll kill me if he finds out I have a phone."

"You'll be fine. Can you show the police where the brothel is?"

"It's not far away, just down the alley. Maybe I should go back before they know I've gone."

"Stay in the doorway. Hide in the shadows. Help is coming."

We heard sirens in the background. They weren't for Angela but set our nerves on edge. Afsona signaled for me to get on the phone. "Julietta is here. She wants to talk to you." She handed me the phone and whispered, "Keep her there."

"Angela?" I said. "Are you all right?"

"No. I'm wearing horrible, hooker clothes that stink and high heels. They want me to be a prostitute. If I don't get out of here, I'll kill myself."

"You'll be out soon. Help is on the way"

"Where am I?"

"Istanbul – we can tell from the bus numbers. That was good work. We know exactly where you are. Are Lara and Tanya still with you?"

"They are back at the house." Her bravado crumbled. "I've been so stupid. I've made a mess of everything."

"We're going to rescue you in just a few minutes. Then we'll save your friends. You are going to be all right. All of you."

"Oh, no." She gasped. "I see a police car. What will happen if they catch me?"

"It's okay, Angela. They're going to help you. Stay where you are."

"They'll think I am a whore. They'll arrest me. I know what happens to girls in those prisons," she sobbed. "I'm not a whore."

"Don't be afraid – these are good policemen. They work with the Angel Coalition. We're bringing you home. Everything will be all right now."

"Angela?" It was a man's voice. My heart was in my throat, willing Angela not to run.

"They're here," she wailed. "What do I do?"

"Go with them. It's okay. I'll stay on the phone with you."

"I'm getting into their car. He's giving me a blanket."

"They won't hurt you. Now take them to the brothel, so they can help Lara and Tanya. Then you'll go to a safe house and the Russian Consulate will send you back to Russia."

"I don't know … Can they help all of us? There are lots of girls … " Her cell phone beeped three times, and died, the battery finished.

We stared at one another, hardly daring to breathe. We'd done everything we could from Moscow. Now, it was up to the Turkish police. Oleg called the safe house in Istanbul to inform them that Angela and her friends were coming. An hour later, the safe house director called back to say the girls had arrived – twelve Russian and six Moldovan girls, all underage. Police had raided the brothel before the pimps realized they'd been compromised.

I called Tatyana Safarovna and let her know that the girls were safe. "*Slava Bogu*," she said – thank God. "When are they coming home?"

"They've agreed to testify against the traffickers. They'll be sent home in a few weeks."

"Were they hurt? Did anyone lay a hand on those girls?"

"They say no, but a Turkish doctor will examine them tomorrow."

That evening, I stayed after the others had gone home. As predicted by Fritz and Franz, the Americans had showed up that afternoon. Their questions were always the same: Why were we still working in the Vysotka and when did I plan to go back to the US and get a real job?

By the time they left, I had a headache. My mind wouldn't focus. I was pumped with adrenaline after the rescue, my nerves raw from the embassy visit. I sat in my darkening office reliving Angela's rescue. I thought about her humiliation – skimpily dressed, sitting in the police car with two big Turkish detectives. At least they sounded kind.

I pulled on my coat and stepped onto the balcony to clear my mind. Far below, the grumble of snowplows and the jingle of electric buses were comforting street sounds. Wind gusted. Swirling snowflakes buried the Kremlin under a carpet of white.

Beyond the curve of the river, the high-rises of Moscow City sparkled. The City of Gold, the billionaires' island, was lit up 24/7. Criminal oligarchs planned thefts, fraud, and murders in the oddly shaped skyscrapers that rose from the ground like diamond-studded dragon's teeth.

"Fuck you." I shouted, giving them the finger. "We've just saved eighteen souls." The Vysotka spotlights switched on as if in reply, flooding the balcony with brilliance that bored through my skull. I went inside and lay down on my sofa.

I was startled awake by the screech of rusty hinges. Pots and pans hit the kitchen floor. I flew off the sofa and grabbed the heavy metal statue of Alexander Nevsky from my desk. I dashed down the dark hall to confront the intruder, negotiating the final corner in a slide.

"Hello, Angelova," said Ruslan.

My upstairs neighbor stood in the kitchen, holding a pot in each hand. The door to the KGB staircase was open.

Chapter Thirty

SECRET STAIRWELL

Moscow, Russia--2008

Ruslan extracted Alexander Nevsky from my grasp and set the statuette upright in the sink. "Is that any way to greet a visitor? I've come to invite you to dinner. My kitchen is this way." He was pointing to a staircase barely visible through a door that I had searched for and never found. During nights of terror and political purges, the KGB once used those stairs to enter apartments and arrest the occupants, bundling them down to an underground train that ran from the Vysotka to Lubyanka Prison, or so the grannies had said.

"Damn!" I exclaimed. "The babushkas were right. There is a secret door."

"Those old ladies are always right," he said. "You should listen to them."

"So it's true that you have a gold-plated Jacuzzi tub with diamond studded faucets?"

"What?" He looked surprised. "Where did you hear such nonsense?"

"Never mind," I said, rubbing my temples. "It's been a long day and I've got a headache."

"Sure you do. There were European spooks hanging out in the stairwell and I saw your Americans," he said. "I'm inviting you to relax and eat kartoshka. Can't you smell those potatoes?" I caught a whiff of frying onions and garlic. My stomach growled. "Come on, or are you afraid of me?" He grabbed my hand and pulled.

I resisted, sliding to the floor with my back against the wall. I'd had a day full of cops warning me to stay out of stairwells and here was Ruslan beckoning me into the worst of them – a secret well of crimes, a dungeon of long forgotten whispers and tears. "I think you should take your pans and go home," I said.

"These are your pans. They fell off. Who hangs a pan rack on a door?" said Ruslan, sliding down beside me.

"Besides," I struggled to formulate excuses, "the cops said, 'Avoid stairwells and strange men.'"

"I'm not a strange man. You hurt my feelings. I've had bad day, too."
His head was down. His shoulders shook. He seemed to be crying; then I
realized that he was laughing.

"What's so funny?" I snapped, punching his arm, resisting the urge to smile.

"Ow ... your face. You have funny face."

"You have a face like a pig's cookie," I said, mangling the Russian insult.
"Oh crap! I always get that wrong."

"Oink, oink," he snorted. "It's ass ... pig's ass." He jumped up, pulling
me to my feet. "Get your shoes. We're eating at my place."

I followed Ruslan through the steel door. He handed me his flashlight
while he locked the door behind us, using a key the size of my hand. The
mechanism slid home with a clunk, and all was still. What was I thinking?
I'd just been locked in a hidden staircase with an arms trafficker. I fingered
the cell phone in my pocket and thought about calling Fritz, but what
would I say? What could he do?

"How did you get that key?" I asked.

"I can't tell you."

"Spetznatz? FSB?"

"Just say that I have connections."

"Fine, but next time you plan to break in, call first. I might have beaned
you with Alexander Nevsky."

"You don't scare me. Let's go eat potatoes."

Ruslan didn't scare me either – I'd known him for years now as a fel-
low member of the Vysotka kolektiv – the apartment association. He used
to look much wilder when his teeth were capped in stainless steel, then
in gold. Now they were porcelain. His girlfriend, Eleanora, had cleaned
him up, dressing him in expensive European suits and sweaters. He wore
his hair short and, with his white smile and North Face outdoor gear, he
looked like a Wall Street banker – with a gold earring.

His footsteps scuffled up the stairs, but I didn't follow. I lingered, frozen in place, mesmerized by the cold staleness of the air. The Vysotka's
exterior spotlights shone through vertical metal bars on filthy windows,
illuminating long, silky cobwebs that shimmered in the disturbance of
our presence. The stone steps were thick with dust. The only indication of
life was Ruslan's footprints.

I peered over the railing, shining the flashlight into the core of the
stairwell, but saw nothing except lifeless reflections from a forest of cobwebs. I'd half expected to see ghosts. How many women screamed, children cried, men begged for mercy on these steps? There should have been

blood, broken toys, discarded clothing; but that grim procession had crumbled into dust decades ago. The only life here was my own. This is how death will be, I thought, closing my eyes. My breathing slowed. I listened to the thump-thump of my heart.

"*Radi boga* – for God's sake." Ruslan grabbed my hand, pulling me upstairs and through another open steel panel into his warm, clean kitchen.

I had been in Ruslan's apartment a few times since the slide show on Africa. He liked to show me expensive furniture and artwork that he'd picked up in Paris, New York, and Milan after selling blood diamonds or rare earth minerals.

A recent addition was spotlighted in his foyer – an ebony statue of a panther about three feet high, standing upright in high heels with enormous human breasts. The animal was posed like a petulant porn star looking into an open jewelry box that contained a huge pink diamond. The base of the statue was a globe. Diamonds, rubies, and sapphires studded a mosaic that depicted continents, oceans, and ice caps. Africa was blood red. "Eleanora had it made for me at Ananov in St. Petersburg. It's for luck," he'd said, paying homage to the continent that had made him rich.

I sat in his glass and marble kitchen, watching him cook the traditional Russian peasants' dinner of potatoes, onions and garlic in a blackened frying pan using a primus stove. He ignored the overhead rack of gleaming copper pots and professional gas range. "That pan looks like it's seen a lot of campfires," I said.

"It's my lucky pan. I've had it since the army." He paused to pour me a generous dollop of vodka in a dented tin cup. "Kristal Elite – one thousand US dollars a bottle, the most expensive vodka in the world. Look at this." He swirled the bottle in the light. The clear liquid sparkled. "Diamonds." He wiggled his eyebrows, upended the bottle and took a gulp. "You like the Beatles' White Album?"

"Sure," I said. "I was in college when it came out."

"You're a very old lady." He smirked. "Turn on the stereo, granny."

"You're no spring chicken yourself." I pushed the start button on his sound system. The Beatles sang "Blackbird," one of my favorites. I sang along with Ruslan as he danced around the kitchen, banging on copper pans and poking the potatoes with his spatula.

We ate the kartoshka, served up on Lomonosov gold-rimmed porcelain plates with slices of kolbasa sausage and pickles, and accompanied by more cups of vodka. I sat on a kitchen stool; Ruslan crouched on his haunches with his plate on the floor.

"Great potatoes," I said.

"Of course. This is what we eat every night in Africa. They have good onions, but we bring our own Russian potatoes." I looked behind him, through the expansive window. The snowstorm had abated, and Moscow City glittered in the distance.

"This must be one of the best views of Moscow," I said. The vodka had heated my veins until my words slurred. "You can really see that goddamn City of Gold."

"I'm moving there with Eleanora. She's decorating my penthouse."

"You own a penthouse?"

"I own the whole fucking building. It will be the tallest apartment in Moscow when it's finished." He opened another bottle of Krystal and filled our cups. "It was Lena's idea. She likes fancy things. I'm just a pilot. I'm only happy when I fly." He dished me more potatoes and asked, "What makes you happy, Angelova?"

"Hmmm." I forced myself to think, the gears in my brain were sluggish. "Saving three girls from Uglich today. That makes me happy."

"Let's drink to that." He raised his cup, "To Angelova, who likes to save the world!"

"It sounds silly when you say it like that. I sound like Don Quixote."

"Maybe you are," he said. "You save one girl and let one hundred others slip away."

"Who are you to talk?" I retorted, emboldened by alcohol. "At least I didn't sell my soul for blood money."

"You want to talk about me? Are you so much better than I am?"

"You're killing the world! The grannies say that you sell weapons to whoever can pay you. You've built your skyscraper on an ocean of blood."

"That's very dramatic, but I am just a businessman. I sell a product. I'm not responsible for what's done with it. If I sell a car, am I to blame for future accidents?"

"You're making my headache worse."

"Because I'm making sense." He grinned and held up the bottle. "Have some more Kristal and tell me, why do you stay in Russia? Who are these lost girls to you?"

"No child should be sexually exploited."

"Agreed, but that doesn't answer my question, does it?" He sounded sober. "Think about it. People will get killed because you care. Maybe the Americans are right in what they said today – it's time to go home."

"How do you know what they said? Did you bug my office, too? My phone? I am going home – to my apartment, now." I stood up unsteadily, reeling from the vodka. Ruslan caught my arm. I shook him off. He let go and I stumbled again. I'd never be able to walk home on the ice. I was furious.

He jangled his car keys. "Let's take my car. I have a new Hummer. Shall we give it a test drive?"

"You? Drive?"

"I drive better than you walk."

Ruslan drove like I imagined that he flew, unafraid of fighter planes or traffic lights, laughing at death, and at me as I searched for a seatbelt.

"I cut them off. I don't use the damn things when I fly ... you don't need one when I drive."

The next morning, I arrived at the office for the daily staff meeting with a hangover, wondering how many diamonds I'd swallowed in Ruslan's vodka the night before. Marianna handed me a cup of coffee and asked, "Why is Alexander Nevsky standing in the kitchen sink?"

"And why are there pots on the floor?" asked Elena.

"It's Ruslan's fault," I said, pointing to the ceiling. "He came through that secret KGB staircase and took me upstairs to dinner."

"And too much vodka?" Oleg smirked. "Your eyes are red."

"Secret staircase my ass. I call bullshit," said Vlad. "Show us your mysterious tunnel that doesn't exist."

We trooped into the kitchen to look for the hidden door. It had vanished. No one would have believed me, except that Ruslan's footprints emerged from the back wall, passed several times around the kitchen, then disappeared into the wall again.

"See?" I pointed at the proof. "It does exist. It's on the other side of this paneling."

"Shit," said Vlad, examining the seamless wall panel.

"We can get Ruslan to open it again, if you want to see it." I paused. No one was smiling.

"My grandparents were killed that way," said Oleg, "taken in the night and shot."

"My family was seized and exiled to Turkmenistan. Most died before they got there," said Alex.

"Everyone lost loved ones," said Marianna. "And it wasn't very long ago – in our parents' time. I don't want to think about it."

Now I understood why my Russian colleagues didn't want the secret staircase to be real. For me, it had no special meaning but for them the memories of Soviet terror were less than a generation away.

I said, "Let's forget it and get back to work."

Chapter Thirty-one

LOSING ELENA

Moscow, Russia – 2008

A few weeks later, Tatyana Safarovna called. "Julietta?" I could hear anxiety in her voice above the static between Uglich and Moscow. "Angela and the girls are being deported from Turkey tonight. I must meet them in Moscow, but no one can tell me what flight they're on. Can you make some calls?"

"I'll call you back when I know something." I said and hung up. They had confiscated Angela's phone at the safe house. Had they returned it? I dialed – no response.

I hurried into Oleg's office, calling for Marianna and Afsona to join us. "We've got another deportation problem with Turkey. Angela's coming, but we don't know when or on what airline."

"Why do the traffickers always seem to know but we don't?" asked Afsona. "We lost a group of girls last week. Women traffickers were waiting in the arrivals hall with Angel Coalition signs. The girls thought they are from us and went with them. They didn't fool the airport police, though, and were detained until we got there – thank God."

"Flights from Turkey land at four Moscow airports. Call the safe house. At least they can tell us what city the flight originates from," said Oleg. "We can figure it out from there."

At midnight, I waited at the international arrivals gate of Domodedovo Airport with one arm around Tatyana Safarovna and the other around Anna the teacher. Anna was the first to spot the girls exiting Customs. She hooted and waved. The girls Tanya and Lara ran into Tatyana Safarovna's open arms, then Anna's and mine.

Angela stood apart, staring at the ground. She'd cut off her hair and looked like a boy of ten – or a novitiate. I approached her, touching her shoulder. Every ounce of me wanted to pull her close, kiss her stubbly head and thank God that she was okay. But some dark power emanated from her that kept me back.

"I repulse you, don't I?" she said. I knew when she said it that Angela had been raped. The Turkish doctor hadn't said anything, but I knew it in my woman's soul.

"My precious child," I hugged her. "You are so beautiful." She didn't hug me back. She barely looked at me or Tatyana Safarovna as we walked to the orphanage van, nor did she greet Dada Igor, who was driving.

The girls climbed inside with Anna. Tatyana Safarovna took me aside, shaking with rage. "They got her, didn't they? Those monsters." She wiped away tears. Her hands trembled. "I don't know what to do. I'm afraid I'll say the wrong thing. You've got to come with us."

I hadn't planned on going to Uglich until the weekend, but that was before I knew the truth. "Is there room for me?" I asked.

"We'll make room," said Anna.

The younger girls slept, safe in Anna's arms. Angela sat staring at her hands, pressed between me and Tatyana Savarovna, who pleaded with her eyes, asking me silently: "Is she gone? Is she coming back?" I didn't have an answer. I saw no sign of the red-headed scamp who played tricks on visitors and taught the little kids shrooming.

Until that moment, I thought that I knew how to treat a victim of sex trafficking. I'd written a course syllabus on how to interview trafficked children and handle physical and psychological traumas. I'd taught police how to treat them with kindness to make them better witnesses. But Angela was my *zolotaya* – my golden girl – so everything was different.

I knew from experience that younger girls had the worst prognosis for recovery. Children from orphanages, particularly those abandoned by their parents, were the least able to differentiate the violence inflicted on their bodies from the person inside of them. What was going on in Angela's mind? Her stony affect frightened me.

Four hours later, we arrived at the sleeping orphanage. The younger girls were put to bed. Angela and I sat on the front stoop, watching sunrise. Angela lit a cigarette. I waited for her to speak.

"Egypt was wonderful and terrible," she said, blowing smoke. "People in robes, camels everywhere. The air smelled like spices. And then the caravan – I saw shooting stars. The sky was filled with them. You never see the stars like that from Uglich. In Haifa, they sold us at an auction. They charged extra for my red hair." She paused and asked. "Lara and Tanya are okay. No one touched them."

"They'll be fine," I said. "You will, too. You did the right thing to call. And you were very brave."

"Brave or stupid – what's the difference? You think I'll settle down now and marry some poor alcoholic peasant who beats me? That I'll be happy in a Russian village pissing in a hole in the ground until I'm an old baba and my teeth fall out at forty?"

She looked at me and I winced at her anguish. "I've seen Cairo. I've seen Istanbul. The world is a big place. There must be somewhere in it for me. I don't belong in Uglich."

"You must be patient," I heard myself say, knowing the futility of the words. Angela was fifteen – a child in an adult body, a girl forced into womanhood too soon. "I've got a scholarship lined up for you. You can attend an institute in St. Petersburg. If you do well, you can go to university."

"You always say I'm smart." She shook her head. "I'm not. I'm terrible at math. I hate science. I hate school."

"Education is your best tool." Did I sound as desperate as I felt? "Be patient, learn a job skill. Once you're grown up, you have choices … "

"I am grown up." She stubbed out her smoke and went inside, leaving me bereft.

I spent most of the day commuting back to Moscow on a crowded, dirty train that stopped in every village. I'd just unlocked my apartment when Afsona called: "I'm at Sheremetyevo, waiting for another victim from Istanbul," she said. "Our safe-house flat in Yugo-Zapadnaya is full. Can I bring her to you? It's just for tonight. She'll take the train to Saratov tomorrow."

I groaned. We'd taken the second apartment to handle the excessive volume at my place. I was looking forward to a night alone. I'd been helping Zhenya write a grant proposal to expand the Trafficking Survivor Network and we planned to add Angela as a case study of teenaged victims. Zhenya and I were working by Skype.

"I can't take her." I told Afsona. "Zhenya's grant is due Monday. We're re-writing it to include younger victims." I told her about Angela.

"Is she all right?" asked Afsona.

"No and I don't know what to do."

"You'll figure it out," she said. "Tonight, we have to help the girl from Istanbul. Her name is Elena. She's a lawyer. I'm sure she's very quiet."

"What about drugs?" Girls returning from Turkey were often addicted.

"They said 'no drugs.' Gotta go – I see her at the gate. She doesn't even have a coat. We'll have to find her some winter clothes."

"Okay, bring her by. I'll have dinner ready," I said.

Dusk gathered quickly. It had started to snow when Afsona rang my doorbell. "Did you know that the security door downstairs is broken again?" she remarked, leading a rail-thin young woman who shivered in shorts and sandals into my apartment. "This is Elena."

"Let's warm you up," I said, wrapping my thick bathrobe around her and handing her sweatpants and shearling slippers.

"Thank you," she replied, her teeth chattering.

"Come into the kitchen. It's the warmest room in the flat. I've got my famous chicken chili borscht on the stove."

Afsona excused herself, saying to Elena, "I'll bring some warm clothes for you in the morning. We've got spare coats at the other apartment."

Elena sat at the table, tying the robe. "Afsona is very nice," she said, "and smart."

"Yes, she is." I dished a bowl of steaming chili. "I've known her since she was a law student. Now she's the lawyer for the Angel Coalition."

"I'm an attorney, too." Elena stared into her bowl, her green eyes unnaturally bright.

"Have some dinner," I said, pouring tea. "Then we'll call your family."

"Oh no," she gasped. "They mustn't know anything bad happened to me. I'll go home and tell them I was on vacation for six months." She tossed her wavy mane and a glamorous woman lit up her face for a few seconds, then faded. "What's that?" she jumped at the bark of a dog in the hallway and the elevator door slamming.

"It's only my neighbors walking their poodle, Marpha," I said, buttering a slice of bread and spreading it with honey. I gave it to Elena who took a tiny nibble. "The police called your family from Turkey. They already know what happened to you. Your parents are meeting your train in Saratov."

"You must hate me," she said tearfully. "I'm not a whore, and I'm not a drug addict. I told the police that I am not a drug addict."

"I'm a doctor, Elena. I can see that you're in withdrawal. What drugs did they give you? It's usually crystal meth."

"Yes, meth. Kemal promised it would take away my hunger. He was right. I didn't need to eat or sleep. Nothing hurt me."

"How are you feeling now?" I asked.

"Everything hurts," she sobbed and chattered. "I'm so cold! I forgot how cold it is in Russia." She was sweating and shivering violently. "It's all my fault for being stupid. I went to Turkey for a summer job. Kemal took me and the other girls from Bodrum Airport and drove us to the Bristol Bar. He made us live in the basement.

"There were other women's clothes and personal things everywhere – even purses. 'Those last five girls didn't work out,' he said, and pointed to

231

the wall. It was sprayed with rust. I thought it was rust, but it was blood. We found the bullet holes. It was horrible."

"Please drink your tea. You need to hydrate yourself. Flush out the drugs."

"I must go to church and light candles. It was an offense against God to kill those girls. Kemal made me wear their clothes. I'm a terrible sinner."

"First you need to wash the drugs out of your system. Please eat something."

"No." She pushed the food away, spilling her tea in my lap. "I'm sorry, so sorry," she wept, trying to mop up the mess.

"It's okay," I said. "I'll pour you another cup."

"Later – I'm so tired. I want to sleep now."

I gave her a flannel nightie and tucked her into bed. She rolled herself into a cocoon of blankets. I sat at the kitchen table with my laptop, trying to concentrate on the grant while keeping an eye on her. Around midnight, Elena was up, shouting, "Where's the goddamn telephone? I have to call God." I settled her back into bed and returned to the kitchen, working until I dozed off with my face on my arm.

"You old cow! You aren't God!" Elena stood in the living room, shouting into my telephone. "I have to find Him." I pried the receiver out of her hands and apologized to the woman who'd answered the call. I thought Elena was going to hit me, but her resolve collapsed into tears. I led her back to bed, sobbing. "I must see God. Take me to church now."

"It's the middle of the night. We'll go to church in the morning."

My personal cell phone erupted with Handel's Messiah. It was Carol Hiltner saying she'd be in Moscow the next morning. Could she stay at my flat? "Of course," I said.

Elena settled and I dozed again. I woke to a crash. Elena was pulling everything out of my medicine cabinet, opening bottles, and dumping pills on the floor. Then she was in the kitchen, pulling glass jars from the shelves. "Come back to bed." I coaxed her with words I'd heard Russian mothers say to their children. It was 3 A.M. and I could barely keep my eyes open.

There were two ways out of the apartment – the balcony and the front door. The balcony, nine stories above a courtyard, was the most dangerous. I pushed an old green sofa in front of it and lay down. She would have to move me and the sofa to get to the balcony. I woke up to find water pooling around my feet. The taps in the bathroom were running. Elena had thrown her blankets, sheets, and clothes into the overflowing bathtub.

"I'm dirty, dirty, dirty," she howled.

I pulled the mess out of the tub and mopped up the flood. When I looked up again, she had moved the sofa, and was standing naked on the balcony, shouting at the top of her lungs. "Come and get me. Aren't I pretty?"

So much for living in anonymity – Elena was doing a pole dance using the supporting struts of my satellite dish, wiggling her bare bottom toward the street. I heard a few drunken hoots from below. Someone honked a horn. "I like it when you fuck me, fuck me, fuck me, fuck me … " She was chanting some kind of gangsta' rap.

I pulled her inside, gave her a dry nightie to put on and covered her with the blankets from my bed. I returned to my post on the green sofa. My eyelids were heavy, my body aching for sleep. "Just for a moment," I said to myself, "I'll close my eyes for a moment."

The cold wind roused me. The front door stood open. Elena was gone. She had taken my long fur coat and suede boots with her. I locked the door and went back to sleep.

Dawn had infused the kitchen with anemic light by the time Carol rang the doorbell.

"You look dreadful," she said. "Sit down. I'll make coffee." She fried eggs and sliced black bread while I called the chief of the Trafficking Task Force of the Moscow Police. I knew what he would tell me.

"We have no right to hold her," he said. "If she wants to go looking for sex or God or drugs, that's her business. If she's committed a crime, we can arrest her. Did she steal anything?"

I thought about my irreplaceable fur coat. Reporting it could land her in a Russian prison. "No," I said. "Please keep an eye out for her. I'll send you a copy of her documents by fax." I didn't hold much hope that Elena would be found, but I was wrong. On Sunday evening the officer called me back.

"We found your girl," he said, and gave me the name of the *zholti dom* – yellow house or mental hospital – where Elena had been admitted. "She was picked up at *Partisanskaya* Metro wearing a fur coat with nothing underneath. She said the coat was yours. You can go get it tomorrow morning."

"Can I see Elena?"

"She's gone. Her parents came for her. They seemed like nice folks. Imagine, you put your daughter through law school, and she turns into a drug addicted whore in Turkey."

"It wasn't her fault," I said. "She was tricked."

"Yeah, yeah – so you say," he said. "Anyway, they were concerned that you get your coat and boots back."

The next morning, I bundled up in Carol's quilted parka and snow boots for the ten-minute trek to the Metro in the −30° weather. I was shivering by the time I entered Taganskaya Station, but once inside the system of heated trains and underground passages, I was warm enough.

I showed my identification card at the *zholti dom* and was admitted into the locked facility. The stench of urine and chatter of schizophrenics interspersed with wailing made me want to turn back. I didn't have to wait long before an attendant brought my coat and boots. Four 500-ruble notes were tucked in the pocket – a reimbursement from Elena's parents, a customary gesture from a respectable Russian family.

Elena was treated at an asylum in Samara for drug psychosis. The next time she came to Moscow, she was herself again – a strong, sensible, and intelligent young woman who barely remembered her night at my flat. Elena became part of the network of trafficking survivor advocates who worked with the Angel Coalition and the Ministry of Internal Affairs to develop policies protecting the rights and dignity of repatriated survivors. Later that year, she accompanied me to Washington DC to testify before Congress.

Carol left for Seattle on Monday morning and I left for work. After our staff meeting, I handed the help line cellphone back to Afsona. Next, I called the Kremlin Medical Center to ask for something to help me sleep.

"I've barely slept for a week. When I get this tired, I won't be able to sleep."

"I'll give you the Russian favorite," said Dr. Kriminskaya. "It's guaranteed to put you out *kak ubit* – like death – in thirty minutes. I can have it delivered to your office this morning."

"Yes, please do that." I hung up, wondering what she would prescribe. I was so tired that I barely cared. I left work in the late afternoon and walked to the Physical Health Center. If anyone could pound the tension out of me, it was Borat the Siberian masseur with hands the size of catchers' mitts.

By 10 p.m., I was home relaxing. I had been massaged, pounded, and stretched into rubber, enjoyed a long, hot shower that used up every drop of hot water, and dined on a veggie pizza from Jack's – my favorite home delivery. I brewed a pot of blue herbal tea from the wildflowers Camille had sent me from Azerbaijan and sat in the kitchen savoring its aroma.

While the tea cooled, I opened the white pharmacy bag to see what the Russian doctor had provided. I was surprised to find Phenobarbitol, a powerful barbiturate once used to treat epilepsy and now to anesthetize farm animals. This was not something I would ordinarily take. The effects could last for days.

I stared at the box of tablets and rationalized: What harm could it do? I was tucked in for the night – safe, warm, and alone in my apartment. The security door had been repaired and I wasn't on call for the help line. Outside, it was thirty below zero. A gusting wind blew snow against the windows, but I didn't care. I was snug in my nest. I popped out a tablet, bit it in half and swallowed one piece – one quarter the recommended dose.

A flash of light. The windows exploded with a BOOM, showering me with slivers of glass. Freezing winds howled through the apartment, pummeling me with ice and snow. The lights went out. I heard screams and car alarms outside – then sirens. A bomb had exploded, breaking every window in the huge apartment building. The blast had come from the courtyard we shared with the Jewish Institute. The kitchen where I sat was the safest place to be in case of a second blast, but I was in my pajamas and needed warm clothes. They were in the front rooms.

I only had about thirty minutes before the Phenobarbital took hold. If I fell asleep in the subzero cold, I would die of hypothermia. I had to move my body, keep my brain working, and figure out what to do.

I felt my way to the coat rack in the dark hall and pulled on all the warm clothes I could find. I located the flashlight by the front door and surveyed the damage. Glass shards covered everything. I wanted to peer out the window to see if the explosion had come from the Jewish Institute, but what if there was another bomb? It often happened that way. The courtyard between our building and the institute was a popular place for my neighbors to walk their dogs. What if someone was hurt? I should go down and see if someone needed a doctor.

On the way downstairs, I called the landlord on my cell phone. I had to try several times before he picked up. "Allo?" I heard his sleepy voice.

"Alexander Sergeivich – it's Julietta. There has been a bomb, an explosion, the windows blew up, there's glass everywhere."

"Okay, I'll come by in the morning to look at the windows."

"Alexander Sergeivich, there are no windows – boom, gone. There is snow falling on the floors, everything is ruined. I don't know what to do. It was a bomb."

I could hear Alexander Sergeivich relaying my words to his wife, Irina Borisovna. She grabbed the phone.

"We'll be right there," she said. They had a car and lived out of town in the village of Pushkin. Once they were on the road, she called me back. "We've heard about the bomb on the radio. Are you all right?"

"I'm fine. I was in the kitchen – the best place to be."

"We've made some calls. Buran will come to fix the windows." Buran was the Tajik building engineer who lived with the maintenance crew in a barracks under the building. "We will be there in about thirty minutes."

My neighbors were gathering on the landings of each floor, talking excitedly about the Jewish Institute. I hurried past them, climbing down nine flights of stairs and through the security door. Walking to the front of the building meant passing through a tall archway just wide enough for a car. I emerged under a waterfall of glass. Fortunately, I had a thick fur hat on and had the good sense not to look up. Ambulances were treating people who had been injured.

I joined my friends from the institute who were standing amidst police cars. They told me that the bomb had been placed in the outside stairwell of the abandoned building next door to them. No one had been killed and the institute was untouched. The bomb had exploded in my direction.

The Fire Department switched on spotlights and surveyed the damage done to my building. The windows on the block-long structure had been blown out. Shattered glass slid down the facade with a roar like rushing water. My balcony was tilted toward the river – its underside blasted away.

The police told us to go back into our apartments and wait for the bomb squad. We weren't allowed to go through the tunnel again because of the glass, so I joined the ranks of the tenants walking two blocks around to the back of the building. I climbed up the nine flights of darkened stairs to find two detectives at my door, accompanied by uniformed police with German shepherds. After they inspected my apartment, one of the policemen said, "I'd stay off that balcony if I were you."

My landlords, Alexander Sergeivich and Irina Borisovna, arrived with Buran and a crew of Kyrgyz workers wearing leather harnesses and carrying ropes. They set up a glass-cutting shop on my big kitchen table and went to work replacing all of the missing windows with temporary glass.

Once my landlords took charge, I surrendered to the barbiturate – I really had no choice. Wrapping myself in a quilt, I crawled under the kitchen table – the one place that wasn't littered with glass.

The last thing that I remember before sleep was Irina Borisovna saying to Alexander Sergeivich, "Those Americans sure can sleep through anything."

Chapter Thirty-two

THE BROTHELS ON YAROSLAVL ROAD

Moscow, Russia – Fall 2009

On a Saturday afternoon in September 2009, Zhenya and I climbed into the back of an old Gazel van. Gunther, a German reporter who had been pestering me for a story, was at the wheel, wearing a road workers jacket and fur cap. He was taking us to photograph the mamochkas (madams) who fronted for mobile brothels that sold children along a notorious stretch of highway between Moscow and Yaroslavl called Yaroslavl Road.

From there it was a short drive to Sheremetyevo Airport. Zhenya was ticketed for the night flight to Paris. She had been awarded a fellowship from the European Commission to study human rights law.

Gunther assisted Zhenya with her suitcase. "Congratulations on your scholarship. You will be a fine lawyer."

"And she'll be safe," I added.

He started the van and spoke over his shoulder, "I've brought my cameras. They're under the tarp. And there are coveralls for you, like you asked."

I lifted the canvas. "That's an impressive collection of lenses."

"It will be dark and snowing – we'll use that Nikon with the big lens for low light."

"We'd better keep it covered until the last minute," I said. "They shoot reporters."

"Do they?" Gunther looked worried – just the way that I wanted him.

"Of course," said Zhenya. "This is big business for the Ukrainians, Albanians, and Romanians. If you think the Russian mafia is brutal, the Macedonians are ten times worse."

"We'll be fine," I interrupted before Zhenya scared him too much. "You help us get the photograph that will bring Yaroslavl Road to the attention of the Moscow government and we'll give you your story."

"Okay," he said. "If you're sure it's safe."

"Of course." I patted his arm. "Let's go. We'll change clothes on the way."

We moved into traffic and headed north. Zhenya and I slipped on the canvas coveralls, then crouched on the cold floor. "Ouch!" she exclaimed when we hit a pothole.

"Wouldn't you be more comfortable up here with me?" asked Gunther.

"Undoubtedly," I answered. "But we need to stay out of sight."

"Then, if you don't mind, I'll start my recorder." He pressed record and a red light came on. "Please explain what we're going to see tonight."

I held the tiny machine and said, "The *tochkas* are mobile brothels run by different ethnic mafias – Russian, Ukrainian, Moldovan, Albanian, and Serbian. At night, caravans full of children roll into Moscow from different regions of Russia and the former USSR. They park off the road behind the trees and station a madam or *mamochka* on the street. She has a radio connected to the gangsters, who stay out of sight. When a car stops with a prospective client, she chats them up while the gangsters listen in. If they signal that the customer is legit, she gets into the car and directs it to where the caravans are parked."

"Question, please," said Gunther. "If this practice is so widely known to law enforcement, why don't the police raid the brothels and rescue the children?"

"The tochkas work together to make it difficult for the police to catch them. If a mamochka even suspects an undercover cop, she broadcasts a code. Dozens of caravans start their engines and drive away. The Moscow police won't follow them once they cross the city limits, which are just a few blocks from here. That's why we need city approval to get the federal police involved. So far, the city government denies that children are trafficked in Moscow."

"How can they?" asked Gunther. "Don't they care?"

"It's simple," said Zhenya. "If they acknowledge that a crime occurs in their city, they have to do something about it."

"The federal police report that 50,000 kids are trapped in those brothels," I said. "Still, they do nothing."

"They're just a bunch of lazy Russian *muzhiks,*" said Zhenya. "They're scared of the mafias. Afraid they'll get shot."

"Their fears are legitimate," I added.

"How many of these tochkas, these caravans, are there?"

"Who knows?" I shrugged. "Dozens? Hundreds? It's a long, lonely stretch of highway."

"We've arrived," said Zhenya. "Looks like there's a mamochka every fifty feet."

"It's Saturday night," I added. "Busiest night for sex tourism."

"Look," Gunther slowed down and pointed. "There's one talking to a Mercedes."

I pulled down his arm. "Don't point at her. Look away."

"Too late," said Zhenya. "She's spotted us. Keep driving."

"I see something better anyway," I said. "Pull into that car park and turn around."

Gunther drove into an empty lot and parked facing the road. "You're right," he said. "That next madam is standing under an Angel Coalition billboard."

"Now we wait for a car to stop and you'll have your prize-winning shot," I said.

"Let's finish the interview," said Gunther, clearing his throat. "How do these foreign men find their way here to this particular stretch of highway? Are they tourists? Pedophiles?"

"They make their contacts through the big hotels. Each tochka sponsors concierges and drivers. They bankroll those expensive cars and pay bonuses for client referrals."

"I still don't understand why the Moscow police don't shut these brothels down. Sexual exploitation of children is a felony in Russia."

"As long as the city refuses to call child trafficking a crime, the Moscow police can't act, nor can the federal detectives. Meanwhile, the local cops are well paid to provide protection against journalists and people like us. They'll show up in a few minutes and you'll see for yourself. Hopefully, we get our pictures before they chase us off."

"Is it really so lucrative – this sex trade in children?"

"Profitable beyond imagining," said Zhenya. "It's part of a global network of organized crime – guns, drugs, and human trafficking. The mafias are so filthy rich they can buy politicians and cops, and terrorize the ones they can't buy. International banks make obscene profits laundering trillions of dollars in blood money. Bankers don't care where it comes from. They believe that they're untouchable … "

"Oh no, she's coming," Gunther coughed. "That mamochka is headed our way."

Zhenya and I pressed into shadow. The madam gave our van a good look-over while speaking into her handset. Gunther opened his lunch pail and unwrapped a sandwich. He poured tea from his thermos and dialed the car radio to Russian pop. An old van with a workman eating supper was of no interest to the madam. She returned to her post and ignored us.

Gunther had his camera ready when a silver SUV stopped curbside, drawing her attention. He used his night lens to photograph the transaction between a man in the passenger's seat and the madam. In less than a minute, she was in the SUV, which disappeared down a side road and into the forest. Lights appeared behind the trees.

"I got the perfect picture," Gunther exclaimed, checking his camera's digital monitor. "The madam is under the Angel Coalition billboard talking to the client. It's all in focus."

"They're driving to the tochka. We've got to leave," I said.

"Follow them," Zhenya insisted. "Get close enough to photograph the girls. We'll put their faces in all the papers. Gunther will be a hero."

"Good idea," said Gunther, starting the engine and driving onto the Shosse. "I want a picture of the little girls."

"No!" I exclaimed. "Terrible idea; you'll get us all killed."

"Stop being a coward," Zhenya hissed at me, her eyes slits. "Follow that SUV."

Gunther was ready to turn off the highway when a police car pulled behind us with blue lights flashing.

"There's no siren," I said. "Keep driving. He's warning us off. If you try to get near that tochka, we'll be the ones in jail."

"Damn cops," said Zhenya.

"Better a night in jail than dead," I said. "We've got our photos. It's what we came for."

"That's nothing!" She grabbed my arm, tears on her cheeks. "There are hundreds of scared little kids behind those trees. How many of them will be hurt while we do nothing but take a few pictures? How is that going to fix anything?"

"You know we can't get to them. We'll use this picture to help convince the city government that child trafficking is a heinous crime that occurs under their jurisdiction. When they understand how these tochkas work, they'll call in the federal detectives because the feds are the only ones who can shut them down. That's how this will change."

"That's just lame and you know it. What are you calling your conference? Oh yeah, 'Children Brought to Moscow by People Other Than Their Parents for Purposes of Exploitation.' That's a real snoozer."

"I agree with Zhenya," said Gunther. "It's not a catchy title. Why don't you call it 'Children Raped on Moscow Highway,' or just 'Yaroslavl Road – Moscow's Highway of Pedophilia.'"

"Because we're not writing for the tabloids, like you are. This is a conference for the Moscow government. We have to use their own words against them in the title."

"What will that accomplish?"

"We want to make them care enough that they decide to fix this."

"Words are weak," said Zhenya.

"Words are our only weapons and words are powerful. If we start with insults, we'll get nowhere."

"Only actions count," she pouted.

"What's weak is you doing crazy stupid things that'll get you killed. How's that going to help anybody?"

Zhenya turned on me: "You are such a hypocrite! You couldn't be satisfied with being a rich doctor in America so you're here in this crazy country, sticking your nose into criminal business that will get *you* killed? Everyone knows my reasons. It's personal for me. What are yours? Why do you care about trafficked girls so much anyway?"

"I've wondered that myself," said Gunther, sniffing a story. "Your involvement does seem very personal."

"Turn off that damn recorder," I snapped. "And drive to Sheremetyevo. Zhenya has a plane to catch."

At the airport, Zhenya pushed me away when I tried to hug her. She stalked off to join the crowd at Passport Control without turning back.

"She's a brave young woman," said Gunther as we walked back to the van. "And an angry one."

"She's a hot-headed young fool," I said. "At least she'll be safe in Paris."

We drove back to Moscow and, like a good reporter, Gunther kept probing at me. "I'd still like to know your real reasons for becoming such a crusader – especially here. I've read about your Russian grandmother, but that couldn't be it. What was your family like? Where did you grow up? Can you tell me about your childhood?"

"I don't remember it," I snapped, wishing I'd said nothing. It was the truth, but it wouldn't satisfy a journalist. Gunther was a pro.

"How can that be? Something must have happened to you. Was it terrible? Your childhood? And your children – what do they think about your dangerous work?"

"Look, this story isn't about me, or my children. Take me home. The interview is over."

We rode in silence past Red Square and along the Moscow River.

"Are you angry with me?" he asked.

"Not really. I just don't appreciate being psychoanalyzed by a bloody journalist."

"I promise that you shall remain a woman of mystery to my readers." He laughed. "This is your building, if I am not mistaken."

It was well past midnight when I crawled under my covers. Sleep eluded me. Zhenya's accusations and Gunther's questions turned over in my mind, went unanswered, rewound, and played again. The results were always the same.

Somewhere in the unfathomable murk of my childhood, powerful drivers had propelled me to strike out on my own at seventeen, put myself through university and medical school, achieve professional success, and then to give it up to come to this strange, sad country that felt like home. I'd worked with psychiatrists and psychologists on memory recovery, but the past remained inaccessible. My childhood was a black hole.

I brewed some tea and sipped it at the kitchen table, watching the news on my laptop. The late edition led with the arrest of a Moscow man who confessed to chopping up his friend in a drunken argument over pickles. Gunther e-mailed me the perfect photo for the conference – the mamochka, the silver SUV, and our billboard. I sent the image to our graphic designer, Dima Shinkarev, to put on materials for the upcoming conference.

My cell phone rang. "She's gone!" Tatyana Safarovna shrieked. "Angela left for school, but never got there. The other kids saw her get into a car. Tanya and Lara said it was that travel agent from Yaroslavl, the one who trafficked them before."

"Have you reported this to the police?"

"I'm at the police station now." There was a pause as hopelessness set in. "Let me know the moment she calls you."

"Of course," I said, knowing that she wouldn't.

Chapter Thirty-three

EIGHTY YEARS OF CHILDREN'S PRISONS

Moscow, Russia – Fall 2009

"Gunther took a great photo," said Marianna at our next staff meeting. "And right under our sign. Everyone will know that this is Yaroslavl Road."

We were looking at the mock-ups of the conference program. I had to focus on the task at hand, though I kept glancing at the emergency phone, willing it to ring.

Vlad frowned. "This is a terrible title: 'Children Brought to Moscow by People Other Than Their Parents for Purposes of Exploitation.' Can't we just call it 'Child Trafficking in Moscow'?"

"No, we cannot," I said. "In fact, each time we bring up trafficking in our presentations we must say, 'Children Brought to Moscow by People Other Than Their Parents for Purposes of Exploitation.' We will keep repeating those cumbersome official words until government officials get tired of them and start saying, 'child trafficking in Moscow.' They must be the ones to put the term into common usage, not us. Once they take ownership of the language, they will start to care about the issue. It's psychology."

"So, by saying it, they admit that it's happening," said Oleg.

"Precisely," I said. "The next logical step will be to call in the federal police and shut down the tochkas – the child brothels."

"Our contacts at the Federal Bureau of Detectives said they'll raid as soon as the city asks for assistance," said Vlad.

"Is anyone concerned that the assassination last week might discourage attendance at our conference? That lawyer was running for the State Duma." Marianna asked. "Should we delay?"

"If it's not assassinations, it's wars or terrorist attacks. I say we go ahead as planned," said Oleg. "And who knows what this killing will mean to those government people? We might get an even bigger turnout."

The staff set to work. I was busy with e-mail, hoping to find something in my inbox from Zhenya. I'd heard nothing from her since she'd left for

Paris a month ago. Tatyana came into my office to remind me about an event at Altufevo Prison for Children. "The car is waiting downstairs," she said.

I had forgotten all about it. "Do you really need me?" I asked. I wanted to go home early. I was exhausted from worrying about Angela.

"It's important for you to be there. The Ministry of Internal Affairs will be giving awards to teachers who are working in our programs. If we're going to continue reforming child prisons, Altufevo is the biggest and most important."

At the prison, we were escorted through a steel gate by armed guards and into the great hall that had once been Altufevo Cathedral. The hall was packed to capacity with uniformed officials and still they pressed in. Medals decorated every breast. Bigwigs from the Ministries of Justice and Internal Affairs were clapping one another on the back. A banner proclaiming, "Celebration of 80 years of Children's Prisons" hung above the flower-bedecked stage where the Moscow Militia Balalaika Band played rousing folksongs. There wasn't a child to be seen.

We were greeted by the teachers and shown to our seats. The air was stiflingly hot, but I shivered. What was there to celebrate about children's prisons?

The lights dimmed. The program began with a specially produced film on the history of the facility. Grainy archival footage showed Altufevo Monastery when it was a thriving religious center at the turn of the twentieth century. In 1928 during the Stalin purges, Altufevo became a prison for children whose parents were executed by the KGB. Smiling teachers, doctors, and psychologists were shown posing with terrified children who had been stripped of their clothes and possessions, and their heads shaved until it was no longer possible to tell girls from boys.

The work of molding Soviet citizens was documented through the war years with the advancement of psychological conditioning in the postwar '50s and '60s, and finally with the construction of the modern Altufevo facility in the 1970s. Until the 1990s the incarcerated children had been political orphans. Today, they were mostly victims of trafficking – lost kids, unprotected, with nowhere else to go.

At the end of the film, I felt nauseous. I would have left if I weren't completely hemmed in by broad-shouldered police officials who were applauding robustly. How could these people look so happy? Everyone in that room knew how badly the system was broken, and yet they were celebrating it, not fixing it. I'd had a similar reaction when I attended a dinner put on by the Vatican at the Hotel Ritz in Rome. We were served an extravagant seven-course dinner to celebrate the church's fight against poverty and hunger. I couldn't eat a bite. They'd spent enough on that one banquet to run our program for months.

The Moscow Militia Balalaika Band began to play as my immune system crashed. I needed to go outside and fill my lungs with clean air but couldn't. I had no choice but to sit and watch the Deputy Mayor of Moscow hand awards and gifts to Altufevo staff, commending their good works. No argument there. The teachers and staff were fine people, genuinely kind and concerned about the children. The juvenile police officers who came to our trainings cared deeply about the lives of the kids they met on the streets. They were open to changes, improvements. Maybe it was too painful to acknowledge the harm because they, too, were trapped in the system.

Celebrating 80 years of children's prisons.

When the event finished with a choral tribute from the Bolshoi Theater Choir, the applause was deafening. The lights came up. The audience rose and pushed noisily toward the doors. Many people were carrying bouquets or gifts of small appliances. I had been given a book, a DVD of the film, and a pin that said, "80 Years of Children's Prisons."

Tamara Serafimova, the director of Altufevo, appeared at my side. "What did you think of the program?" she asked, nodding to colleagues and well-wishers while pushing me through the crowd.

"You've done remarkable work here," I said, meaning every word. Tamara had worked tirelessly to convert the sterile prison into a more home-like environment. She had supported our remodeling of the interview room and the child-friendly training of police sponsored by the World Childhood Foundation. "I find it difficult to celebrate the imprisonment of children. How could anyone be happy about it?"

"Because things *are* changing. Those eighty terrible years are behind us and we foresee a different future – a better one," she said. "You're coming to our party, aren't you?" Without waiting for an answer, Tamara signaled for a prison guard to take me by the arm. "Put Julietta on the bus," she commanded. "I have to change."

Four buses waited beyond the gates. The guard handed me up to the driver of the lead bus, who indicated that I should sit on the first seat. Afsona and Tatyana squeezed onto the seat beside me and the buses filled with police, guards, and officials. Spirits were high as the doors closed and we prepared to edge out into gridlocked rush-hour traffic. It didn't look to me like we were going anywhere, until I noticed patrol cars blocking off intersections along the way. We sped across town in a fast-moving convoy. Police cars raced alongside with sirens blaring and blue lights flashing – ignoring the angry motorists forced to wait.

"What the hell is happening?" I whispered to Afsona.

"We're going to the annual Ministry of Internal Affairs staff party. It was on the invitation."

"I should have read it," I admitted. "Do we have to do this?"

"Unless you want to jump off the bus." Tatyana laughed. "Besides, it will be fun, and we're honored guests."

Within minutes we had reached the banquet hall. Lights shone from tall windows and a band played rock music. We were escorted to our places at a long table in a hall set for a sit-down banquet for 500 people. We were seated at a table labeled Honored Guests. Soon the places around us were packed with bull-necked law enforcement officers in crewcuts, intent on toasting themselves into oblivion. We stayed until the drinking and dancing degenerated into fighting. When someone was tossed through a window into a tree, the three of us slipped away.

I rode the underground Metro train home to Taganskaya. The clacking of the wheels reminded me of my night in the platzkart from Perm to Moscow and the soldiers, poet, priests, singers, and scientists who had formed our kolektiv. We had sung the passionate Russian laments of persecution and exile, the sad ballads of people who had suffered tragically at the hands of men like the ones I'd just left – men who were granted the authority to burst into any apartment, shake the unlucky occupants from sleep, and spirit them into oblivion.

A few days later, our conference on Child Trafficking, co-sponsored by the Moscow government, was packed. The pivotal adjustment in language came in the afternoon of the first day when the government participants finally lost patience with saying, "children brought to Moscow by people other than their parents for purposes of exploitation" and brought the term "trafficked children" into common usage.

The true paradigm shift occurred the next morning. In the middle of a presentation by the federal prosecutor, the Angel Coalition emergency cellphone rang. Afsona answered it. Three teenaged girls were calling from a shop near Red Square. They'd been trafficked to Moscow from Kyrgyz Republic, had escaped from their captors and were requesting our help.

Afsona gave the phone to the prosecutor at the podium who followed protocol by handing it to the chief of the Trafficking Task Force of the Moscow Militia, instructing him to investigate. Two detectives got up and left the room at his command, returning about thirty minutes later with the young women. They were startled to see the group, but eager to share their stories.

We could not have designed a more effective team-building exercise and, significantly, the trafficking survivors were treated as part of the team – an encouraging development for future survivors.

At the end of the conference, the senior member of the trafficking team from the Federal Bureau of Detectives gave me a nod. There would be action on Yaroslavl Road very soon. Within days, dozens of children were rescued from the tochkas.

There was a downside. A police lieutenant was shot during the first raid and fought for his life in hospital.

Chapter Thirty-four

THE DEAD SEASON

Moscow, Russia – January 2010

I am jolted into the present when I hear the announcement: "*Ostorozh-no, dveri zakryvayutsa – sleduyuschaya stantsiya, Taganskaya* – Danger, the doors are closing – next station, Taganskaya." The Ring Line train accelerates out of Kursk Station on its way to Taganskaya again. That's my stop.

I've been riding under Moscow for hours, round the great circle – through the thickening mass of commuters at rush hour that thinned to almost nothing after dinner. Now the crowds are back. I check my watch – it's nearly ten o'clock. Muscovites are returning with their families to celebrate New Year's Eve on Red Square.

This morning seems an age ago, my conversation with the Colonel a ghost from the past. I see the manila envelope in his hands, the 8 x 10 photograph that he holds – the jumble of heads and feet in Zhenya's trunk. "It's time for you to go home." he said. What was familiar and comforting a few hours ago, has become foreign. Part of me is already gone.

I am standing, pressed against the rear window. The air in the car is insufficient, saturated with wet fur, moth balls, and beer. The past, present, and future whip around me, tangling behind my third eye. My head aches. I seek a way back into my reverie, to lose myself in my Russian story but cannot. The train lurches. I'm thrown forward into the crowd and back against the window.

We plunge into a dark stretch of tunnel, screeching into a long, slow turn that crushes me in the press of bodies. Anyone in this car could be my killer. I see my death in every pale, somber face. How easy it would be to stab or shoot me in the dark. I wouldn't even fall. I can't stay on this train any longer. I will suffocate. I'm tired, hungry, and scared.

I hum "Amazing Grace" and slow my breath to conquer panic. I tell myself to stay centered, to think clearly – that nothing has changed since this morning, except that it has. I've seen the photo of Zhenya, *Zhenya!* My pulse speeds. I breathe in short gulps. I want to vomit.

"*Stantsiya Taganskaya* – Taganskaya Station," says the mechanical voice. This is where I get off. This is where everyone gets off. It's the closest Metro station to Red Square. It's nearly time for the fireworks.

The snow has ceased. The night is clear and still. I realize that I'm famished and join the line at the Kartoshka, Kartoshka kiosk for a baked potato smothered in onions and cheese. I eat while I walk down the hill toward my apartment. The Colonel's black Mercedes is parked in the drive. Ivan Ivanovich waits near my door. If I go home, he will take me to the airport. I decide to go to the office instead. The staff will be there to watch the fireworks. I'll join them for one last party.

I switch off my cell phones and pull out the batteries so that Ivan can't track me. I am anonymous in my black furs amidst the revelers walking to Red Square. Once I reach the embankment, the road is barricaded to traffic. For tonight, it belongs to pedestrians. I keep pace along the frozen river, balancing on the ice with short, flat-footed steps like a Muscovite.

Plumes of steam from the MosEnergo Heating Plant across the river rise and freeze in the air. Music pulses from Red Square. The onion domes of St. Basil's are brightly lit. Multicolored lasers project shimmering geometric shapes into the sky. Roman candles explode around my feet. Children laugh and shriek, waving sparklers. Cannons shoot colorful pyrotechnics along the length of the river. Bottles of beer and vodka are passed through the crowd. The big fireworks haven't even started.

I am suddenly flanked by two tall men. Each takes one of my arms and they march me forward. I struggle until I realize that it's Vlad and Alex having a good laugh. They're on their way to our party. I'm not walking fast enough for them, so they slide me along on the ice while the crowd cheers each new explosion. More vodka goes around.

A babushka unlocks the front door, waving us into the Vysotka. Vlad and Alex give the grannies a bottle of cognac and we wish each other a Happy New Year. We are the last to arrive at the office. The rest are on the balcony listening to the Red Army Chorus sing the Russian National Anthem, ending with cannon fire, lasers and pyrotechnics.

President Medvedev takes the podium and wishes everyone a Happy New Year. The Kremlin clock chimes midnight. The crowd shouts "Urrah, Urrah, Urrah." It's 2010. The fireworks begin over the square and along the length of the Moscow River. Explosions echo, pinging off the granite buildings. We are high enough that the bursts of color and fire seem close enough to touch. We are pelted with bits of charred paper after each explosion. My ears ring.

In the distance, the City of Gold is alight with fireworks of its own. Ruslan lives there now with Eleanora. They invited me to their party, but I declined. I didn't know that within a year, Ruslan and his eight Ukrainians would be dead – killed when their Ilyushin cargo jet exploded over Pakistan. In the last seconds before impact, their flaming behemoth veered just enough to miss a crowded population center in Karachi, plowing instead into an empty construction site. I'd like to think it was an act of atonement for the shattered lives they'd left behind in Africa.

I start to cry, but no one notices. They're leaning over the stone balustrade, cheering. I slip through the door into my office. It's dark except for my desk lamp. My computer is still on. My briefcase is open the way I left it this morning. I sit at my desk, accepting that this is the last time. I decide to take the statue of Alexander Nevsky with me to America. The rest will stay behind.

I put the batteries back in my phones. The Colonel's burner phone blinks, vibrates and plays "Come Home, Bill Bailey." I pick it up and say, "Three days. I need three days. Then I'll go if I can get a ticket."

"Your ticket will be at Aeroflot," he says and rings off.

"Come on, Julietta," Marianna says from the door. "Let's eat."

The conference table is set with a feast of Tajik dumplings, New Year's praenik – honey cake, and champagne. There are plates of smoked herring, bread, cheese, and pickles. Olga adds a platter of hot piroshky and Tatyana, a plate of blini with honey.

I eat a few bites but can't stop the tears. I take my plate to my desk and close the door. I say nothing about Zhenya or that I'm leaving for the United States. I see no way to exit tonight with any grace. I still clutch at the secret wish that I'll wake up tomorrow and none of this will be true. I'll discover that the meeting with the Colonel never happened, our work will continue uninterrupted with Zhenya safe in Paris. And Angela will call.

When I wake up at my apartment the next morning, Moscow is a ghost town. Streets are abandoned to the husks of burnt fireworks. Cars are at home locked in tin garages. The shops are closed, stripped bare. Shortages of toilet paper, bread, cheese, and meat will soon churn up bad memories of Soviet times when shoppers formed lines at one store, then another, in hopes of buying anything at all. The dead season has begun.

My neighbor Lyudmila stops by to let me know that a kiosk up the street is selling toilet paper – I should get some while I can. "I hate these holidays," she says, shaking her head. "What is it with this country and toilet paper?"

I turn on the television. The illusion of falling back to Soviet times is reinforced. News programs play recaps of old stories. ORT and NTV re-broadcast champagne gala concerts from the '60s and '70s by beloved Soviet-era performers. The concerts are interspersed with old war movies. I imagine Russians reliving World War II, The Great Patriotic War, from their stuffy living rooms while they drink vodka and eat sprots-on-toast.

I watch TV and sort through my belongings, fighting back grief. I am packing up a lifetime and can only take a few treasures. That means hauling most of my possessions down to the dumpster to be picked over by my neighbors. I look up when I hear the familiar, gravelly voice of Vladimir Vysotsky singing a sad ballad about lost youth and failèd promise. The black-and-white image of his performance from 1975 flips back and forth between a blurry close-up of the singer's face and an audience whose Slavic cheek bones are streaked with tears.

The elevator isn't working, so I drag my Hefty bags down nine flights of stairs to the icy parking lot. The temperature is 20 below zero. I stack virtually all of my clothes and shoes by the dumpster. By the time I carry down my household items, a swarm of people is going through my things. I see my coats, hats, and sweaters on the Kyrgyz workers who live under the building. I invite Buran and his men up to the apartment to take whatever furniture they want – my yellow leather couch, my antique glass hutch. My neighbors call the police when they see Buran carrying away my TV. The officers arrive, hung over and annoyed by having to climb nine flights of stairs. I give them my toaster and blender.

I'm leaving behind my Lomonosov tea seat, a gift from the mayor of St. Petersburg and my set of hand-painted Turkish plates, a souvenir from Anatolia. I roll up my best Turkmen carpets and stuff them into suitcases, but my Tunisian and Egyptian rugs are too heavy. I carefully pry the canvases of my favorite paintings from their frames – the Goddess Nut carrying the sun across the ocean, a troika racing through Nizhny Novgorod, villagers driving a tractor through a field of wheat, children building a snowman. I roll them around Alexander Nevsky's figure and wrap the package in a black Hefty bag.

No matter how energetically I work on packing, I move in slow motion. A tidal wave is breaking over me. I need to run, but my legs have filled with sand. The bite of fear hovers nearby like a sharp-eared black dog in league with the demon Chort. Now that there is no work to distract me, I am afraid. The rooms are shorn of the precious mementos that marked the milestones of my life. My apartment is fading to white and I am sinking into despair, blending with the ice and snow that blows in horizontal streaks past my windows. With only six hours of daylight, winter is sealing me in. The glacial cracking of ice on the roof is pervasive. Blocks the size of Volkswagens split apart overhead and slide off the edge of the building. They soar past my windows and crash into the courtyard nine stories down. Long icicles dangle from ledges and balconies until they snap and fall like daggers.

On my last night, I stand on my balcony in head-to-toe furs. It is one of 72 identical balconies in nine horizontal rows, unique only in that it tilts toward the river since the bomb blast. I take in the panorama that sweeps down the Moscow River from the Kremlin and St. Basil's to the glass-domed Philharmonic. I hear voices from other balconies, the everyday chatter of souls and a waft of cigarette smoke. Siberian winds howl down the frozen river, driving ice crystals into my face.

I close my eyes. My lashes freeze and stick. The air has dropped to 40 below zero, too cold for more than a few minutes outside. I breathe the night air, longing to take in and hold the memory of being alive in Moscow. I press my coat sleeve to my nose. Winter smells like wet fur.

Dawn breaks. I sit in the kitchen and scan the remaining case files and photographs onto my flash drive. These are the cold cases – the 1,234 girls we've never found. I search each young face one last time before I shred the paper files. I haven't cried for these girls since the night Angela first called from Cairo. By tricks of my imagination I've kept them alive – young, beautiful, full of promise. I've moved them around on my mental grid like fireflies, holding onto the belief that one day they will call on the helpline and we will bring them home like Angela and her friends.

It's been four years since Angela disappeared. Lara and Tanya have finished high school and are studying dental hygiene in St. Petersburg. They refuse to talk about Egypt or Turkey or Angela. They have moved on. I haven't. I scan Angela's file, but cannot shred it – holding onto the hope that I'll see her again.

If only I could hope the same for Zhenya. I stare stupidly at the folder that summarizes her short life. What shall I do with her file? It's thicker than all the others. I summon the courage to open it and leaf through newspaper articles and grant reports, press photographs of Zhenya doing interviews and leading protests in front of dodgy businesses she knows are trafficking. She was reckless and brave – and was swallowed alive. I am bereft. I'd like someone to grieve with. I telephone Nadezhda Belik in

Nizhny Novgorod. There is no answer. I didn't expect one. She visits her daughter in Kaliningrad every holiday.

Ice groans and cracks overhead, sending another block off the roof. I stuff Zhenya's file into my last suitcase. It's time to leave for the airport but I am afraid to go outside – afraid of being shot, afraid of the arctic cold, falling icicles, SUVs speeding down sidewalks – afraid of walking alone. The risks that have thrilled me in this strange country now frighten me. A van comes to drive me to the airport. My luggage has grown to five over-stuffed suitcases and the long package of rolled up paintings wrapped in black plastic that looks like an assault rifle.

I arrive early at Sheremetyevo Airport, braced for arguments with everyone from security guards and Customs agents to Aeroflot officials about my pile of overweight bags. I step through the door and am waved on. Instead of berating me for my three extra suitcases and charging me exorbitant overweight fees, Aeroflot takes my luggage without a word. My strange carry-on is x-rayed once, but never examined. I am hurried through the airport and directed to the gate.

I see familiar faces in the crowd – the plain-clothes detectives who are always present at the airport. I have been here often enough picking up trafficking victims in Immigration Control to know their faces. Our eyes meet and some of them give me the Russian blink and nod that in this case means good-bye.

When Aeroflot starts boarding, I join the long line of passengers inching toward the gate. My purse buzzes to "Come Home, Bill Bailey." I dig out the Colonel's phone.

"Allo? Kolonel?"

"Julietta? Is that you?"

"Angela?" I freeze in place – stunned at the sound of her voice. I am jostled from behind and step out of line. "How did you get this number?"

"I got a text. It said to call immediately. How did you get *my* number?"

"That's a story for another day." I silently thank the Colonel for his parting gift. "I'm so happy to hear from you. Are you all right?"

"Of course." Her voice has a rasp to it that I don't like. She coughs as if she's been smoking. "I have a great life. I'm in love with Demitrios. He bought me at an auction in Cyprus. He's crazy about my red hair. Men pay extra to touch it – all over my body."

"Where are you?"

"I work at his club in Cyprus. He treats me like a princess," she gushes and coughs. "He buys me clothes and jewelry. I sit at his table while he smokes cigars with the big guys, the Albanians – real gangsters. I keep their cigars lit. That's my job. Then I go upstairs with his special friends. I'm helping him with his business. It is very important work."

"What's the name of the club?" I fumble in my purse for a pen and notebook. "What road is it on? I can send someone to get you."

"How stupid you are. I'm in love. I'll never go back to Uglich. My life is here. Besides, I'm pregnant."

I don't know how to answer. The line inches forward. There are only a few of us left. "I'm getting on a plane, Angela. I will call you from America."

"Don't," she says. "I won't pick up."

"Angela, wait. You're a sex slave. You deserve better."

"This *is* better. Anything is better than Uglich." She clicks off.

I stare at the phone wondering if she's right. It rings again. "Angela?"

The Colonel asks, "Do you see the Aeroflot agent holding open a Chanel bag?"

"She's standing in front of me."

"Drop the phone in the bag before you board."

"I don't want to go." My voice cracks. "I'm not done yet."

"You'll come back."

"When will that be?" I'm desperate to keep him on the phone. My life in Russia hangs by our fragile connection.

"When you're ready. Go home to America and discover who you really are."

"I don't know where to start."

"Start with your uncle – the one I knew at Bletchley Park. Now get on the plane and be safe."

"*Do svidaniya,*" I say. "Until we meet again."

MEDIA SUMMARY FOR
DR. JULIETTE ENGEL

ENGLISH LANGUAGE PRINT MEDIA SUMMARY

Dr. Juliette Engel has been featured in *Money Magazine, Hemispheres, Horizons, Seattle Times, Washington Times, Coast Magazine, Evolution Magazine, Moscow Times, Minnesota Weekly, Eastern European Quarterly, Aljazeera, Deutsche Welle, NewsNet14, Russian Journal, Johnson's Russia List News, Johns Hopkins University Journal, Give and Take* (ISAR) *Journal, Congressional Journal* (Committee on International Relations), *Reuters, Associated Press, Giraffe News, Global Game, UNJobs* (Lebanon), *Journal of Russian and Asian Studies, AllGov* (Germany), *By-George!* (George Washington University), *American Spectator, National Review Online, AngloFritz* (Germany), *St. Petersburg Times, East-West Report, Spiked Online, Antara News, Soroptimist International, The Exile, US Embassy Mission in Turkmenistan, SAGE Journal* and others.

FOREIGN LANGUAGE PRINT MEDIA

Dr. Engel has been featured in news articles in Russia including *Ria-Novosti, ITAR TASS*, and regional newspapers and magazines in 55 Russian regions, Turkmenistan, Tajikistan and Uzbekistan. She has also featured in news media from Norway, Sweden, Denmark, Finland, Baltic Countries, Germany, France, Spain, Belgium, Italy, Turkey, Israel, UAE and to most Arab countries via Aljazeera and Al-Aqsa news services.

BROADCAST MEDIA – RADIO

Dr. Engel appeared as a guest expert on numerous Russian language radio programs throughout the former Soviet Union including *Ekho Moskvy, Radio Russia* and regional broadcasts.

TELEVISION – ENGLISH LANGUAGE

Dr. Engel has done multiple interviews for CNN including a feature stories with Jill Dougherty and Siobhan Darrow, a feature with Bryan Gumbol on HBO Real Sports on trafficking in Germany at the World Cup, interviews on MTV, Sky News, Russia Today, Aljazeera, Press TV, C-SPAN, EuroNews, regional news programs throughout the US, Scandinavia and Europe.

TELEVISION – RUSSIAN LANGUAGE

Dr. Engel has appeared on national Russian television, featured in "Person Behind the Mask" with Vladimir Pozner, News Magazine on ORT, news features on ORT, NTV, REN TV and CTC TV and regional programs in Moscow, St. Petersburg and 55 Russian regions and former Soviet Republics.

MAJOR PUBLIC SPEAKING APPEARANCES ON CHILD TRAFFICKING

1997 – American Association of University Women, Moscow: "Women's Health and Human Trafficking as an Economic Issue."

1997-9 – More than 200 Town Meetings in Murmansk, Petrozavodsk, Yaroslavl, St. Petersburg, Veliki Novgorod, Nizhny Novgorod, Uglich and Moscow regions, Russia: "Human Trafficking as a Threat to the Russian Population." Covered by local/regional television, radio and newsprint.

1999 – Organization for Security and Cooperation in Europe, Review Conference in Vienna: "Stop Selling Your Children – Preliminary Report on Human Trafficking in Eastern Europe and Eurasia." Sept 1999. https://www.osce.org/files/f/documents/3/b/16709.html

1999 – CSCE/Helsinki Commission - US Congressional Delegation to Russia, St. Petersburg: "Human Trafficking as a Global Criminal Business." Covered in local, national and international media.

1999 – Russian State Duma, Legislative Committee on Organized Crime and Corruption, Moscow: "Human Trafficking and Organized Crime in the Russian Federation." Covered in internal newsletters of the Ministry of Internal Affairs.

1999 – XVI Soroptimist International Convention, Helsinki, Finland: "Threat of Human Trafficking to the World's Women and Girls." Covered in local and international media, publications of organization. http://www.viaf.org/viaf/154844208

1999 – Ukrainian Parliament, Kiev: "Human Trafficking for Prostitution and Slavery – Linkages to Russian and Ukrainian Organized Crime." Covered on local/regional television, radio and newspapers.

2000 – Moscow City Duma, Moscow: "Human Trafficking – Russia as a Sending, Receiving and Transit Country for Trafficked Children." Covered on national and international television, radio and newspapers.

2000 – International Women's Forum, Irkutsk, Siberia: "Human Trafficking." Covered in local/regional television, radio and newspapers.

2000-1 12 Town Meetings in Rostov-On-Don, Voronesh, Novocherkask, Nalchik, Kaminsk, Taganrog, Russia: "Human Trafficking as a Threat to the Russian Population." Sponsored by regional Ministries of Education. Covered on local/regional television, radio and newspapers.

2001 – Launch of MiraMed Public Information Campaign with speeches by Dr. Engel in Moscow, St. Petersburg, Veliki Novgorod, Petrozavodsk, Nizhny Novgorod and Yaroslavl: "Don't Get Hooked by False Promises – Get the Facts!" Sponsored by Angel Coalition and local partners. Covered by national and international television, radio and newsprint.

2001 – Anniversary of Founding of Nizhny Novgorod, Russia: "Human Trafficking as a Crime Against Russia's Children." Sponsored by Governor of Nizhny Novgorod. Covered in local/regional television, radio and newspapers.

2002 – 27th Special Session of the General Assembly, Special Session on Children, United Nations, New York: "Child Sexual Exploitation and Trafficking in Russia." Covered in UN publications and radio interviews.

2002 – Opening of the MiraMed "Moms and Babies" Center in Moscow, Speech to City Government, Moscow: "Protecting Vulnerable Populations from Exploitation in Moscow." Covered by local/regional television, radio and newspapers.

2002 – Trans-Balkan International Anti-Trafficking Conference, Greece: "Effective Public Information Campaigns Against Human Trafficking." Covered by local/regional media.

2002 – Vatican Conference on International Human Trafficking, Vatican City: "Human Trafficking as a Health and Security as well as a Human Rights Issue." Covered in Vatican publications and international wire services.

2002 – Gregorian University Guest Lecture to Bishops, Rome: "Protection of Vulnerable Populations Through Acts of Charity and Hospitality." Covered by University publications.

2002 – Dominican Sisters, Motherhouse, Detroit: "Exploitation of Vulnerable Children by Criminal Traffickers – A Role of Prevention for the Catholic Church." Dominican newsletter.

2002 – Ablate House, Washington DC: "Exploitation of Vulnerable Children by Criminal Traffickers – A Role of Prevention for the Catholic Church."

2003 - Pathbreaking Strategies in the Global Fight Against Sex Trafficking sponsored by the U.S. State Department Office to Monitor and Combat Human Trafficking, Washington DC: "Human Trafficking Contributing to the Global Spread of AIDS and other STDs." Covered by national and international media.

2003 – United Nations Commission on the Status of Women, New York: "Trafficking of Women and Girls from Eastern Europe and Russia for Purposes of Prostitution." Covered by Voice of America and Radio Liberty.

2004 – High Level Government/Russian Law Enforcement Trainings in St. Petersburg, Moscow, Petrozavodsk, Yaroslavl and Nizhny Novgorod, Russia: "Implementing UN Protocol and Plan of Action to Counter Human Trafficking in the Russian Federation."

2004 – US Embassy in Ashgabat, Turkmenistan Human Rights Guest Lecturer, Ashgabat: "Human Trafficking from Central Asia."

2004 – International Organization of Migration, Ashgabat, Turkmenistan: "Illegal Migration Resulting in Human Trafficking."

2004 – University of Turkmenistan, Ashgabat: "Human Rights, Women's Rights and Protecting Vulnerable Populations."

2005 – European Commission, Strasbourg, France: "Human Trafficking from Russia to Europe."

2005 – XV International HIV/AIDS Conference, Bangkok, Thailand: "HIV/AIDS as a Global Threat to Women's Health." Local and international news, conference newsletters.

2005 – Project Launch – Safe Return and Recovery, Stockholm: "Trafficking from Russia to Sweden for Labor and Prostitution." Sponsored by Kvinnoforum. Covered by Swedish media.

2005 – City Administration of Oslo, Norway: "Relationship of Human Trafficking and Legalization of Prostitution." Covered by Norwegian media.

2005 – State Department of the United States, Washington DC: "Lessons Learned from The Russian Project on Human Trafficking." Voice of America Radio.

2006 – United Nations Commission on the Status of Women, New York: "Counter Trafficking & Victim Assistance in Russia." UN Radio.

2006 – Preventing and Combating Human Trafficking – Exchange of Experience, Development of Strategic Approaches and Strengthening of Cooperation, Sponsored by President's Administration of Tajikistan, Dushanbe: "Human Trafficking and the Threat to the Health of Tajikistan's Population." National and international television, radio and newspapers.

2006 – US Congress, House International Relations Committee, Washington DC: "Trafficking of Russian Women and Girls to Germany for Prostitution." Covered globally by television, radio and newspapers.

2006 – US Congress, House International Relations Committee, Washington DC: "Helping Russian Trafficking Victims Share Their Stories." National/international coverage on television, radio and newspapers.

2006 – Russian Law Enforcement Training in Nizhny Novgorod, Irkutsk and Chelyabinsk, Russia: "Developing Successful Prosecutions: Trafficking Survivors as Witnesses, NGOs as Partners." Covered by local/regional radio and newspapers, some television.

2006 – World Childhood Foundation, Royal Palace, Stockholm, Sweden: "Ending Child Trafficking as a Global Priority." Covered in Swedish media.

2007 – Criminal Investigation Department, Emirati Federal Police, Dubai: "Human Trafficking from Central Asia to the United Arab Emirates."

2007 – Croatian Counter-trafficking Task Force Meeting, Dubrovnik: "Human Trafficking and the Spread of AIDS." Croatian and regional Balkan media.

2007 – Moscow City Government, Moscow: "Recognizing the Crime of Child Trafficking in Moscow."

2008 – National Webcast for Health and Human Services Campaign to Rescue and Restore Victims of Human Trafficking, Washington DC: "Trafficking from Russia to the United States."

2008 – George Washington University Elliot School of International Affairs, Washington DC: "Developing Counter-trafficking Programs in Russia and Central Asia." *ByGeorge! https://www2.gwu.edu > may08 > trafficking*

2008 – US State Department, "Protecting Women and Children from Human Trafficking." Presentation with Undersecretary of State Paula Dobriansky. May 3, 2008.

2008 – US – Russian Business Council, Washington DC: "Human Trafficking and Human Rights in Russia."

2008 – Women's Human Rights Speaker Series. Sex Trafficking and Human Rights in Minnesota, Minneapolis: "Trafficking in Women from Russia to the United States for Prostitution." Covered by local media.

2008 – Project Kesher, Chicago: "Human Trafficking is a Crime Against Women and Girls."

2008 – 2nd International HIV/AIDS Conference sponsored by the Mayor of Moscow, Moscow: "Direct Relationship Between Human Trafficking and the Spread of HIV/AIDS." Covered by Moscow and Russian national television and newspapers.

2009 – Southern California Task Force on Trafficking, San Diego: "Human Trafficking of Eastern European Women Through Mexico."

2009 – Voice of the Child Conference, Russian Ombudsman for Child Rights, Moscow: "Child Trafficking in Moscow." Covered by Moscow television, radio and newspapers.

2009 – Global Centurions, Washington DC: "Counter-trafficking Work of MiraMed and the Angel Coalition in Russia."

2009 – Department of Homeland Security and International Customs Enforcement Training for Agents and Embassy Attaches, Casablanca, Morocco: "Fighting Human Trafficking in Russia and Central Asia since 1998." Covered in embassy publications and internal newsletters.

2009 – George Washington University, "Trafficking in the 21st Century". Graduate students in School of International Studies, Washington DC. Internal newsletters.

2009 – Project Kesher, "Trafficking in the 21st Century", a lecture for 30 women attorneys and community leaders, Chicago IL, Newsletter.

2009 – Harvard University, "Trafficking in the 21st Century", Kennedy School for International Studies, 45 graduate students and faculty, Cambridge MA.

2009 – Multiple Presentations in Seattle - Seattle Against Slavery (SAS), International Justice Mission, Stop Child Trafficking Now Walk; Western Washington Coalition Against Human Trafficking; Youth With A Mission; Tierra Nueva; The Abolition and Freedom Initiative, Task Force at University Presbyterian Church; Love 146, Operation Nightwatch, World Concern, World Vision; Women with a Purpose at Overlake Church; Buying Sex is Not a Sport; (campaign in Vancouver BC); International Christian Alliance on Prostitution (ICAP), "Child Trafficking in the 21st Century, lectures for human rights groups in Seattle, Seattle WA, multiple newsletters.

2010 – Voice of America – Report from the Field – "Human Trafficking in Russia – Is it Decreasing?" January 10, 2010, Moscow.

2010 – Center for Missing and Exploited Children – "Child Trafficking and Pornography in Russia," January 27, 2010, Alexandria VA.

2010 – National Security Council, Presidential Commission US – Russian Working Group on Civil Society, Corruption, Child Pornography and Child Trafficking, "Status Report on Child Trafficking in the Russian Federation," January 27, 2010, US Department of State, Washington DC.

2010 – Soroptimist International, President's Convention – "Trafficking of Children from Russia to Netherlands." August 17, 2010, Amsterdam, Netherlands.

2010 – Purpose Prize Presentation Conference – "Building an Encore Career in Human Rights." November 2010, Philadelphia, PA. https://encore.org > Purpose Prizes

2011 – Capital Speakers Club of Washington, D.C. -- "Angel Coalition. A Successful Model of an Underground Railroad in the Former USSR." February 21, 2011. Chevy Chase Country Club, Chevy Chase, MD.

2011 – Society for Prevention of Cruelty to Children – "Combating Child Trafficking in Moscow." March 15, 2011, Moscow, Russia (videoconferenced).

2011 – Bilateral Safety Corridor Coalition – "Trafficking Children from Mexico to San Diego through Imperial Beach, California." May 16, 2011, San Diego, California.

2011 – Glasgow Police Department – "Trafficking in Children from Russia to Glasgow's Calton District." July 12, 2011, The Police Museum, Glasgow, Scotland

2011 – Council on Foreign Relations – "Dignity and Human Rights – Russian Model," November 19, 2011, CFR, Washington DC.

201 – United Nations General Assembly – "Why Millenium Development Goals Do Not Adequately Address Trafficking in Children." December 7, 8 2011, New York, New York.

2013 – Council on Foreign Relations – "Human Trafficking and Globalization Relative to Millenium Development Goal Number Eight," September 23, 2013, CFR, Washington DC.

2013 - University of Washington School of Medicine – "Physicians as First Line Defenders Against Human Trafficking." June 2, 2013, Seattle, WA.

Podcasts and Online Interviews

May 31, 2013 – Alumni Humanitarian Award, University of Washington School of Medicine. https://vimeo.com/67433359

April 10, 2020 – Charles Moscowitz Live, Sex Magick Cult Run by the CIA. https://podbay.fm/p/charles-moscowitz/e/1586549070

October 27, 2020 – RedPill78 – Friday Night Live Stream with Dr. Juliette Engel. https://redpill78news.com/tag/juliette-engel/

December 22, 2020 – Trine Daily – Mind Control in Very High Places. https://trinedaily.com/2020/12/22/the-journey-podcast-21-dr-juliette engel-mind

April 30, 2021 – Sparky: Surviving Sex Magick. The Opperman Report. https://www.spreaker.com/user/oppermanreport/sparky-surviving-sex-magick

Feature Articles About Author

July 28, 1991 – *Seattle Times,* "Doctor Plans Moscow Birth Center"

September 15, 1991 – *Ukrainian Weekly*, "Birthing Center in Kiev Opened"

January 21, 1992 – *Seattle Times,* "Effort to Help Russia Tackle Prenatal Woes Gains Federal Attention" http://community.seattletimes.nwsource.com/archive/?date=19920121&slug=1471349

October 1, 1993 – *CNN, Money Magazine* http://money.cnn.com/magazines/moneymag/moneymag_archive/1993/10/01/88327/index.htm

April 3, 1996 – *Seattle Times,* "Cruise Russia – for the Kids – Caring tourists Help Orphans Get a New Start"

October 15, 1996 – *The Seattle Post-Intelligencer*, "Doctor Felt Russia Needed Her More" P. C1

November, 1996 – *Hemispheres* (United Airlines Magazine), "Practicing Peaceful Medicine"

March 2, 1997 – *Chicago Tribune,* "X-Ray Vision: Radiologist Sells Her Thriving Practice to Take Medical Supplies and Expertise to Russia."

June 1999 – "Who Is Trafficking CIS Women? Preliminary Survey Report on Sexual Trafficking in the CIS." MiraMed Institute.

February 20, 1999 – *Johnson's Russia List*, no. 3063, item 3

September 1999 – "Trafficking in Human Beings: Implications for the OSCE" (cited), http://www.iom.pl/res/files/traffickstop/lf_osce_1trafficking.pdf

May 9, 2000 – *The Congressional Record*, Trafficking Victims Protection Act of 2000

June 12, 2000 – Humanite (France), "Russie. La Prostitution a l'heure." http://www.humanite.fr/popup_imprimer.html?id_article=226846

May 17, 2001 – *The Russia Journal*, "Campaign against Sex Slavery Launched."

May 17, 2001 – *LaRedo Morning Times*, "Russian Women's Groups Launch Anti-Slavery Campaign." http://airwolf.lmtonline.com/news/archive/051701/pagea12.pdf

May 19, 2001 – *BBC News*, "Russia Fights Sex Slavery." http://news.bbc.co.uk/2/low/europe/1339246.stm

November 21, 2002 – *National Review*, "Prostitution in Russia," by Donna M. Hughes

December 27, 2002 – Mondiaal Nieuws (Netherlands), "Russische Regering Erkent Probleem van de Mensenhandel." http://www.mo.be/index.php?id=63&tx_uwnews_pi2[art_id]=10699&cHash=5d3e3bbb97

May 9, 2003 – *The Times Higher Education*, "Prostitution Myth Has Strong Pull" http://www.timeshighereducation.co.uk/story.asp?storyCode=176609&sectioncode=26

October 15, 2004 – Voice of America, "Sex Trafficking." http://www.voanews.com/english/archive/2004-10/2004-10-19-voa66.cfm?moddate=2004-10-15

February 16, 2005 – "Slave Trade in White Russian Girls Grows in US." http://www.newsnet14.com/2005/02/slave-trade-in-white-russian-girls-grows-in-us/

February 15, 2005 – UNICEF's *Child Trafficking*, "Human Trafficking in US Gets Tackled."

May 4, 2006 – House International Relations Committee Hearing Transcript. http://www.internationalrelations.house.gov/archives/109/27330.PDF

May 4, 2006 – *Associated Press*, "Anti-Trafficking Advocates Spar with Germany over Prostitution during World Cup." Available:http://football2006.bluehyppo.com/fullnews.asp?newsid=200605042013205600000201.xml

May 5, 2006 – *Deutsche-Welle*, "US, Rights Groups Blast Germany over 'World Cup Brothels.'" http://www.dw-world.de/dw/article/0,,1993872,00.html

May 6, 2006 – *Frankfurter Allgemeine*, "Deutschlands WM-Bordelle," http://www.faz.net/s/Rub47986C2FBFBD461B8A2C1EC681AD639D/

Doc~EC192EF79A0E44177BE1D6E078BF698CD~ATpl~Ecom-
mon~Scontent.html

May 9, 2006 – *The Global Game*, "Soccerheads? | Bush says, 'We're beginning
to understand.'" http://www.theglobalgame.com/blog/2006/05/soccer-
heads-bush-says-were-beginning-to-understand/

June 14, 2006 – Committee on International Relations, U.S. House of Representatives, "Modern-Day Slavery: Spotlight on the 2006 'Trafficking in Persons Report,' Forced Labor, and Sex Trafficking at the World Cup" Briefing and Hearing.
http://www.internationalrelations.house.gov/archives/109/28104.PDF

July 7, 2006 – *National Post*, "Lessons from a German Brothel," by John Tur-
ley-Ewart. http://www.peers.bc.ca/inthenews.html

October 23, 2006 – *School of Russian and Asian Studies Magazine*, "Normaliza-
tion of Prostitution in Post-Soviet Russia." http://www.sras.org/normaliza-
tion_of_prostitution_in_post-soviet_russia

September 19, 2008 – *Moscow News*, Early Intervention Conference in Moscow.

December 11, 2008 – *Moscow News*, Fighting Back against the AIDS Epidemic.
http://www.mnweekly.ru/local/20081211/55360668.html

November 9, 2009 – *Moscow News*. Thinking Small to Help Those in Need.

Mention of Author in Other Books

Barany, Zoltan. *The East European Gypsies: Regime Change, Marginality, and Eth-
nopolitics*. Austin, TX: University of Austin Press, 2001, p. 275.

Pesman, Dale. *Russia and Soul: An Exploration*. Ithaca, NY: Cornell University
Press, 2000, p. 327.

Spady, Richard J. and Richard S. Kirby. *The Leadership of Civilization Building:
Administrative and Civilization Theory, Symbolic Dialogue, and Citizen Skills for the
21st Century*. Seattle: Forum Foundation, 2002.

Television Appearances

Multiple interviews for CNN including feature stories with Jill Dougherty
and Siobhan Darrow, a feature with Bryan Gumbel on HBO Real Sports
on trafficking in Germany at the World Cup in 2006, interviews on MTV, Sky
News, Russia Today, Aljazeera, Press TV, C-SPAN, EuroNews, regional news
programs throughout the US, Scandinavia and Europe.

Document Archives

PDF files of MiraMed Institute and Angel Coalition reports can be download-
ed via the author's website: www.JulietteEngel.com.

265